INCLUSIVE FINANCE IN NORTH-EAST INDIA

About the Editors

Vanlalchhawna is a Professor, Department of Economics, Mizoram University. His specialization includes economics of education and fiscal economics. He has to his credit a number of research papers published in national and international journals.

Lalhriatpuii is an Assistant Professor, Department of Economics, Mizoram University. Her specialization includes gender economics and regional economics. She has participated and presented a number of research papers in national level seminars.

INCLUSIVE FINANCE IN NORTH-EAST INDIA
Challenges and Prospects

Edited by
Vanlalchhawna
Lalhriatpuii

CONCEPT PUBLISHING COMPANY PVT. LTD.
NEW DELHI-110059

ISBN-13 : 978-93-5125-209-2

First Published 2016

Published and Printed by

Concept
Since 1974

Concept Publishing Company Pvt. Ltd.
A/15-16, Commercial Block, Mohan Garden
New Delhi-110059 (India)
T : 25351460, 25351794, *F* : 091-11-25357109
E: publishing@conceptpub.com, W: www.conceptpub.com
Editorial Office: H-13, Bali Nagar, New Delhi-110 015, India.

Cataloging in Publication Data—*Courtesy:* D.K. Agencies (P) Ltd. <docinfo@dkagencies.com>

North Eastern Economic Association (India). Annual Conference-cum-National Seminar (2013 : Department of Economics, Mizoram University)
Inclusive finance in North-East India : challenges and prospects / edited by Vanlalchhawna, Lalhriatpuii.
pages cm
Papers presented in Annual Conference-cum-National Seminar of the North Eastern Economic Association held on November 14-16, 2013 at Aizawl, hosted by Department of Economics, Mizoram University.
Includes bibliographical references.
ISBN 9789351252092

1. Financial services industry--India, Northeastern--Congresses. 2. Poor--Government policy--India, Northeastern--Congresses. 3. Economic development--India, Northeastern--Congresses. I. Vanlalchhawna, 1961- editor. II. Lalhriatpuii, editor. III. Mizoram University. Department of Economics, host institution. IV. Title.

HG187.I4A56 2013 DDC 332.10954162 23

PREFACE

Inclusive growth has been one of the top agenda of national planning in India especially since the Eleventh Five Year Plan. Since then, financial inclusivesness has become one of the main strategies for inclusive growth and development. Under this context, financial inclusion, especially access to financial services by the poor and marginalized people, assumes a significant strategic development issue in the country as these groups formed a large proportion of the population. The diversification and strengthening of financial sector play a crucial part in delivering financial services and products at the doorsteps of the poor. In these regards, Central Government and financial institutions including Reserve Bank of India took several initiatives across the country.

To examine various facets of financial inclusion and its links with economic development and empowerment of the poor in the North-Eastern Region of India, the North-Eastern Economic Association selected financial sector development as the theme of its Annual Conference-*cum*-National Seminar held on November 14-16, 2013 at Aizawl, hosted by Department of Economics, Mizoram University. The present volume is the outcome of the papers presented in the Conference. These papers examine the link between economic development and financial sector development in India's North-East and throw light on various aspects of financial inclusion strategy pursued so far in a regional context. Specifically, the following issues have been addressed: (i) Growth and diversification of financial institutions, markets and services in the North-East; (ii) Concept and relevance of financial inclusion in the context of India; (iii) Instruments and technological option; (iv) Achievement of financial inclusion made by different financial sectors so far; (v) Performance of micro-credits, insurance sector and workings of informal financial markets in the North-East; and (vi) Other related development challenges like food security, social sectors development, and international trade relevant for the North-East.

We deeply appreciate the contribution made by all the participants in the Conference. We hope that the present volume will enrich and enlighten policy-makers and all the stakeholders in understanding issues relating to financial inclusion in the North-East.

AIZAWL
10.11.2015

Vanlalchhawna
Lalhriatpuii

CONTENTS

LIST OF TABLES

LIST OF FIGURES

LIST OF CONTRIBUTORS

A.K. Agarwal, Professor, Department of Economics, Mizoram University, Aizawl (Mizoram).

Angshuman Sarma, M.Phil. Student, Sikkim University, Gangtok (Sikkim).

Arambam Sophia, Department of Economics, Assam University, Silchar (Assam).

A. Sundaram, Associate Professor, Department of Economics, Government Saiha College, Saiha, Mizoram.

C. Vanlalkulhpuia, Research Scholar, Department of Management, Mizoram University, Aizawl (Mizoram).

Daniel Lalawmpuia, Research Scholar, Department of Economics, Mizoram University, Aizawl (Mizoram).

Elangbam Nixon Singh, Professor, Department of Management, Mizoram University, Aizawl (Mizoram).

Gopal Kumar Sarma, Assistant Professor, Department of Economics, B.B.K. College, Nagaon (Barpeta), (Assam)

Jyoti Bikash Chakma, Ph.D. Scholar, Department of Commerce, Mizoram University, Aizawl (Mizoram).

Laishram Gyanendra Singh, Associate Professor, Department of Commerce, Government Aizawl College, Aizawl (Mizoram).

Lalhriatpuii, Assistant Professor, Department of Economics, Mizoram University, Aizawl (Mizoram).

Lalhunthara, Assistant Professor, Department of Commerce, Pachhunga University College, Aizawl (Mizoram).

Mayanglambam Sarda Devi, Senior Lecturer, Kakching Khunou College (Manipur).

N.V.R. Jyoti Kumar, Professor, Department of Commerce, Mizoram University, Aizawl (Mizoram).

N. Rokendro Singh, Associate Professor, Department of Commerce, Mizoram University, Aizawl (Mizoram).

Navin Kumar Rajpal, Research Scholar, Department of Economics, Mizoram University.

P.K. Chaubey, Professor, Indian Institute of Public Administration, I.P. Estate (New Delhi).

Rajashree Dutta Purkayastha, Guest Lecturer, Department of Business Administration, Assam University, Silchar (Assam).

1

INCLUSIVE FINANCE FOR FINANCIAL INCLUSION

P.K. Chaubey

Micro-finance sector in India has witnessed tremendous growth in the last three decades, but perhaps little development as there was huge demand for micro-credit, partly promoted by revamped subsidized rural development programmes run by the Central Government and State Governments. There has been a huge unmet demand from formal institutional sources also as non-so-recent data sources show a decline in the proportion of institutional credit. Some malpractices have also been reported about micro-finance institutions in recent years in India — particularly in Andhra Pradesh in March 2006 — the year Muhammad Yunus gets Nobel Prize for Peace along with Grameen Bank which he created in 1983 in Bangladesh, after running pilot project for about seven years, for the very activity of micro-credit.

It is right time to deliberate upon the growth and development of micro-finance, need for support and prop from the government and perils in the absence *versus* presence of the government in overseeing the operations of the micro-finance institutions. There is a strong reason to suggest that there has to be a sound yet not stifling regulatory mechanism for this proliferating business. Whether it is Andhra story of micro-credit mismanagement or financial meltdown at global level, opaque financial operations can cause havoc not only in the body financial, but also in the body economic and the body politic. Former Governor of RBI, Y.V. Reddy (2011) points out that overfinancialization, as unconnected with real sector, is not good as financial sector enables, but does not lead economic development.

In this chapter, I wish to lay emphasis on inclusive finance as distinct from financial inclusion and the role of micro-finance in ensuring inclusive finance. It may be noted that in financial inclusion the focus is more on some connection of an individual with formal financial system like opening a savings bank account with a commercial bank or getting some other financial service like transfer of money from a formal channel other than money order[1] whereas inclusive finance connotes promotion of credit, savings and insurance in that order to the poor and vulnerable sections, with emphasis on availability of financial credit services to the real sectors of production involving micro-enterprises. Financial inclusion includes activity of inclusive finance, but is not co-extensive with it. In other words, micro-credit is a part of micro-finance, and micro-finance is a part of financial inclusion.[2] What we propose here is that there has to be an active interface between micro of MSME and micro of financial system.

I

Under ordinary course of operation of positive economic forces, other things remaining the same, in most economies of current dispensations, certain sections of a society, certain regions of a country and certain sectors of a production system are likely to get excluded or at least continue to remain excluded. That all constituents do not get well included in any growth process is an empirical fact because neither all constituents are equally endowed nor are services of all of them demanded with equal intensity. In such circumstances, not only these sectors, sections and regions just lag behind but at times they remain stagnant while others march fast.

In India, in the last couple of decades while we have had a slew of multi-billionaires, the level of poverty has not diminished as fast as it was expected due to acceleration in growth rate since early 1980s aided by direct poverty alleviation programmes. Level of inequality has risen vertically among persons and horizontally across sections and regions. In fact, growth process generally engenders these inequalities. For example, weaker sections are generally employed in sectors which have low demand elasticity and/or they are employed on discriminatory institutional basis as low-paid informal workers. Low demand elasticity sectors, usually primary sectors, are generally dominant producers in backward regions. Except oil producing countries in the middle-east since 1970s, all primary producing countries, in Asia and Africa, have been poor and so is the case with States and regions in a country.

However, for a sustainable society, a certain level of inclusion is desired. Some deliberate policy interventions are attempted by the State.

State is created in a differentiated society with a high level of productivity so that employees of the state organs, engaged in 'non-productive' activities could be maintained. All such States are class States. Yet they normally try and are expected to create institutional distributive mechanism in the realm of positive forces so that peace, tranquility, if not harmony, is maintained.

It is important to note that movements towards micro-finance and decentralized governance also gained momentum around the time of so-called liberalization of restrictions on economic life took place in new forms, a little before or a little after. Earlier, the same objectives were the guiding forces in the early fifties behind cooperative movement as far as financing was concerned and similar principles were behind the panchayats' refurbishment in the late fifties. In between a number of redistributive programmes involving heavy dose of subsidies were launched. In the wake of economic reforms, subsidy withdrawal from a number of sectors was proposed though finally not fully carried out. It was echoed at that time that the job of government is to enable financial services, not to provide them. Micro-finance, like cooperative finance was seen as the answer, which meant integrating the financial needs of poor people into a country's mainstream financial system.

II

Inclusive growth process, with certain reservations on the phrase as T.N. Srinivasan (2011) for instance has, is an attempt to modify current intervention policy matrix in the light of increasing relative exclusion of certain sectors like agriculture, certain regions like Orissa and within Orissa KBK (and much of the North-East), and certain sections like scheduled castes/tribes and backward sections among the religious minorities in the development drama of the country. People are worried with the fact that while growth rates got accelerated, certain sections, sectors and regions remained largely excluded. The strategy was changed, therefore, from trickle down growth to shared growth to pro-poor growth to inclusive growth. And all strategies involved some kind of programmes enhancing employment and income or improving consumption — including consumption of food, education and healthcare.

Exclusion may well be a perception but there is hardly ever a smoke without fire. I do believe that generally speaking the poor have not grown poorer but the rich have definitely grown richer and indefinitely richer. And the poor stay side by side with the rich, not in seclusion. Exclusion without seclusion has its own perils. Monarchs and feudal lords could save themselves in feudatory dispensation but not even superbly rich in a democracy could save themselves without facing troubles.

Immediately after Independence, many institutional reforms were carried out and thereby forces of growth were unleashed. As a result, growth rate had a quantum jump from less than one per cent per annum in the first half of the twentieth century to over three and a half per cent per annum in the fifties with around two per cent growth in population. In the sixties, the tempo was maintained despite severe dislocations caused by two wars, severe droughts, and forced devaluation of currency and consequently abandonment of the Fourth Plan (1966-1971) — drafted and launched. Growth rate was nevertheless a bit higher close to four per cent per annum while population growth rate also rose by quarter a per cent. It may be noted that it was not so much because of high saving rates but because of low capital output ratio which was slowly rising. Low capital output ratios are likely to be associated with high labour output ratios which improves employment but not necessarily incomes of the poor. Poverty so far was understood to be reduced by rise in growth and lowering of inequality, but some direct poverty programmes were also ushered in.

Poverty removal and self-reliance were the twin objectives of the Fifth Plan. There was a poverty line during 1960s and 1970s but there were no official poverty estimates till 1979 though a few scholarly estimates on poverty had become available. It was the time World Bank also focused on poverty alleviation. A lot of political upheaval in the country and two oil crises dampened the growth rate below the mark of three per cent per annum. Population growth did not slow down as mortality conditions improved. In this backdrop, Raj Krishna asserted that the Hindu (constant, non-accelerating) rate of growth that was witnessed in the quarter of a century after Independence was not high enough to trickle down to make a dent on the poverty level. Keeping technicalities aside, it was widely accepted that a non-accelerating growth rate at 3.5 per cent per annum would not help in reduction in poverty percentage. Direct poverty alleviation programmes were seen as doing some good to the poor. The programmes were both on production side like self-employment and wage employment ones as well as on consumption side like public distribution of essential commodities. Yet there was not much dent on the poverty ratio and the absolute size of the poor remained static, conclusively till 1993-94.

Yet it needs to be added that the period from 1969 to 1980 was the period of financial inclusion in more than one ways. Many banks were nationalized and priority sector lending was imposed. Rural Regional Banks were opened in 1975. A refinance development institution NABARD was created in 1982 to cater to the needs of rural development and agriculture. A little later, SIDBI was created as "the principal financial institution for the promotion, financing and development of industry in the small-scale sector and to coordinate the functions of the institutions engaged in the promotion and financing or developing industry in the small-scale sector and for matters connected therewith or incidental thereto." This small-scale sector is now better known as micro, small and medium enterprises. Banks were involved in loaning to the vulnerable sections in several government schemes. Besides, there was general penetration of banks and banking services.

Limited and cautious liberalization in government intervention in the Eighties showed acceleration in growth rate, but it was more from the debt incurred from foreign commercial sources. It was a sort of borrowed growth. With acceleration in growth rate, poverty ratio came down quite a bit. But debt created an unprecedented crisis of default on servicing the loan for paucity of foreign exchange. Gulf crisis engulfed the Indian economy as it did not have enough foreign reserves to pay for imports even for a month and our imports, having oil as a major item, were critical and crucial. The crisis forced a sudden change in our economic policy matrix in terms of short-term stabilization and long-term structural adjustment. A new policy regime liberalizing restrictions on industry, restructuring public sector enterprises and inviting foreign investment was put in place. In terms of growth rate, the nineties were no different than the eighties, but otherwise there was a sea change in the composition of growth in the decade before 1991 and the decades after 1991.

It should be added that whole growth in the nineties was in terms of service sector growth. Growth rate in agriculture shrank a bit and that in manufacturing also slowed down and these are the two sectors which have a lot of informal components and weaker sections get chance to participate in. In service sector, besides trade and transport, there is little chance for the poor of the present profile to participate. Now, these traditional sectors have been dented a bit. Thus, this kind of growth is not very inclusive, as it is not pro-poor.

Growth rates accelerated on long-term basis since 2002-03 till 2008-09. In the context of explaining inflation, it is often being pointed out that per capita income of the country has doubled in the last eight years. Poverty did decline, numbers apart, between years 1993-94 and 2009-10. What led to that reduction howsoever low it is? Is it working of direct poverty alleviation of programmes or is it because of growth process? Was growth process inclusive enough or is there a scope for making it more inclusive? Should we be happy with a shared growth strategy or should we attempt to have an inclusive growth strategy.

Once upon a time proponents of growth had argued that higher the growth rate more are the resources at the hands of the government and, therefore, more it can spend on poverty alleviating programmes and more on poverty alleviating sectors such as education and healthcare. This is known as shared growth today and perhaps growth with social justice or growth with redistribution earlier. This is how development had come to be defined in early seventies, putting behind Clark-Fisher structural shift conception. But growth could cause poverty under circumstances was not duly recognized, except in international context by likes of Gunder Frank and Samir Amin. Simon Kuznets did point out that inequality is likely to increase with growth in the initial stages of development but he did not examine whether it could lead to increase in poverty or stagnation in poverty as poverty was not the business of research in his times. In absolute numbers, poverty did stay put for a pretty long period. Modern analysts suggest that poverty may worsen because of economic relationship in goods, credit and labour markets.

It is in this backdrop that a new policy framework of inclusive growth process was proposed at the beginning of the Eleventh Plan and is being pushed further in the Twelfth Plan. It was always proposed by our planners that growth process has to be engendered with inclusiveness through participation though their phrasing might have differed with time. A high pace with only certain patterns makes the growth inclusive. It is now being reiterated and hopefully acted upon.

Crucial parameters for economic participation of the people are access to four kinds of market: labour market (employment), to education and skill formation market (employability), to credit market (production) and to goods market (sale). I shall, however, confine myself in this chapter to narrowly defined financial inclusion, which is inclusive finance or access to credit, which will only be complementary to other inclusions. If sections and regions are denied these accesses, they would remain excluded. It is through the production sectors that are inclusive by participation like agriculture and industry and through entitlement like education; skill formation and health that we hope to achieve inclusive growth.

III

Financial inclusion has been variously defined. One is general enough to suggest dispersal of financial institutions and penetration of financial services. The other has a specific context in which problems faced by the poorer sections of the society are addressed. The short point is about the availability of and access to various financial services including savings, credit, insurance, remittance facilities and pension, etc. specifically to the vulnerable section — slow income groups — at affordable cost and in a fair, safe, and transparent manner by mainstream financial institutions like banks and insurance companies. The sections that are often identified by official circles in India as financially excluded are: marginal farmers, landless labourers, oral lessees, self-employed, urban slum dwellers, migrants, socially excluded groups, ethnic minorities, senior citizens, women and informal sector enterprises.

There are so many conditions in such definitions and it is difficult to reconcile them all fully. Why should mainstream financial institutions come to 'aid' vulnerable sections? Why should they reach far-flung areas? Why should they encourage small savers while transaction cost of resource mobilization and operation is practically the same for servicing large savers and small savers, large borrowers and small borrowers? Why should they loan to people whose ventures are supposed to be riskier as they are not well linked with the market? Financial institutions have, therefore, been by bypassing them. Where they have come in, they devised mechanisms to reduce transaction cost and reduce level of risk and yet charged higher rates of interest. They are micro-financial institutions. However, many mainstream financial institutions of late have also realized that the area they would enter is a sound business proposition as they found group risk is much smaller, recovery rate is far better and rates of interest are lucrative.

Despite the facts that only 50,000 villages have a bank branch and average branch services over 16,000 persons, the majority of farmers in Central, Eastern and North-Eastern regions are totally financially excluded and they are all poor and marginal. Only 10 per cent population is exposed to insurance cover. However, quite a few financial institutions especially in micro-finance products have come into being and doing good business while helping the poor with savings/credit facilities. It is being realized at various levels that micro-finance business is neither a charity nor a social service, but a sound proposition and that is one reason that profit-oriented banks are associating themselves with micro-finance institutions through refinance. It is a win-win strategy. And more than that, there is a great potential. The statistics given in the beginning of the paragraph show a dismal picture of the current affairs but they also provide an idea of the vast potential lying ahead. Formal financial institutions underwent a kind of training through learning by doing and are approaching through a second layer of intermediation.

It was an initiative of NABARD that a pilot project of micro-finance was launched in 1992 — after almost 10 years later than establishment of Grameen Bank, in which self-help groups were promoted to inculcate habit of thrift, savings, banking culture with a view to prospering through collective wisdom in financial matters and economic activities. It was a way forward of mobilization of small savings that was carried out in several ways earlier. An attempt was thus made to evolve a prudent mix of strengths of informal credit system and formal financial institutions. The MoRD also gave fillip to this experiment by shifting the basis of assistance loan/subsidy to BPL households which form a society registered as a cooperative, a partnership firm or choose to remain an informal group. NGOs did a yeoman service by stepping as a go between or as a catalyst to help people in the group formation and approach financial institutions.

Further, if one looks at the composition of rural GDP one finds tremendous change in the recent years. Of the total national industrial production, the contribution of rural area has risen from 35 per cent in 1971 to 45 per cent in 2005 and that of the services from 20 to 33 per cent during the same period. If one looks at just rural GDP during the same period, one finds that the contribution of industry has risen from 10-12 to 22-24 per cent and that of the services from 8-10 to around 40 per cent. Generally speaking, the credit need of the rural economy should have risen on economic side.

It is in this context that micro-finance institutions could make some ways because of low transaction cost. These institutions are in someway between formal and non-formal sectors. If they continue on their own or as an extended arm of the banks in accepting small amounts, provide doorstep services, make available funds for all purposes, ensure ease of operations, their future is bright as is that of the people — the poor, the marginal in the rural and the urban areas. NSS survey do reveal that lower the asset holding of a household, lower is the institutional share in the credit. Rural and urban areas differ in details. Poor in the urban areas have worse access than their counterpart in rural areas and better off in the urban areas have better access than their counterparts in rural areas.

IV

Many scholars study financial inclusion in terms of regional financial depth which they usually measure in terms of bank accounts per adult population or by regression analysis of number of bank accounts against per capita income in PPP. According to a World Bank study, India is not found under-banked for its per capita income. In terms of savings bank accounts also, there were around 82 accounts for each 100 adult population in 2007. If one thinks that households below poverty line or at least those who do not save at all can be excluded from calculations, then the ratio well exceeds over 100. We may note that commercial banks, including regional rural banks, account for only 50 per cent of these accounts and the rest are with other financial institutions which serve rural areas in particular like post offices and primary agricultural cooperative credit societies. There are around 20 crore credit accounts by now. We may gleefully note that there are more than 60 crore savings accounts — of 10 per cent are with post offices, rural regional banks and urban cooperative bank each, 20 per cent with primary agricultural credit societies and fair share of 50 per cent with commercial banks. Undoubtedly, there are multiple accounts in higher income individuals and a few in the name of minors. Each household holds more than two accounts on an average whereas there are those who do not hold any account at all. Even then, the fact does not change in qualitative terms.

We all know that banks' operations increased multifold, after bank nationalization in 1969 and 1976, particularly in 1970s and 1980s. While the fifties and the sixties it was cooperative movement, in the seventies it was metamorphosis of commercial banks to provide loans to rural population. Cooperative did maintain some tempo during the seventies, it were mainly the commercial banks to improve its share from bare 2.2 per cent to impressive 28.0 per cent. During eighties, the trend was reversed: Cooperatives lost share while commercial banks improved theirs. During the nineties, while cooperatives picked up, commercial banks lost considerable ground.

It is pointed out that the slowdown in the tempo of commercial banks during the 1990s was due to imposition of enhanced prudential norms and stricter supervision to check what came to be known as non-performing assets. Cleaning up of balance sheets by the banks led to slow down in credit expansion to small-scale sector and agriculture. Further, financial reform measures during this period allowed public sector banks to be listed at stock exchanges and their focus shifted to investment side. The consequence was slippage in the coverage of the less well-off, particularly in the rural areas. Loss in share of commercial banks was not well made good by cooperative societies (*See* Table 1.1).

Table 1.1: Outstanding Debt of Rural Households by Source

Source of Credit	*1951*	*1961*	*1971*	*1981*	*1991*	*2002*
Institutional Credit	7.2	14.8	29.2	61.3	64.0	57.1
Government	3.7	5.3	6.7	4.0	6.1	2.3
Cooperative Societies	3.5	9.1	20.1	28.6	21.6	27.3
Commercial Banks	—	0.4	2.2	28.0	33.7	24.5
Non-institutional Credit	92.8	85.2	70.8	38.7	36.0	42.9
Landlords	3.5	0.9	8.6	4.0	4.0	1.0
Agricultural Moneylenders	25.2	45.9	23.1	8.6	7.1	19.6
Professional Moneylenders	46.2	14.9	13.8	8.3	10.5	—
Non-moneylenders non-institutional lenders	24.9	25.3	42.5	25.8	19.0	8.7

Source: Rakesh Mohan (2011).

According to All India Debt and Investment Surveys[3], which is carried out every tenth year, last survey was carried out in 2002, percentage of indebted households in rural areas came down from 63 per cent in 1961 to only 20 per cent in 1981 but it rose to 23 per cent in 1991 and to 27 per cent in 2002. The share of non-institutional credit came down from 93 per cent in 1951 to 36 per cent in 1991, with the share of moneylenders from 70 to 17 per cent. But between 1991 and 2002, the share of moneylenders had risen from 17 to 35 per cent while that of all non-institutional sources, from 36 to 43 per cent (*See* Table 1.1). But should the composition change so drastically over time as is revealed here?

It is true that the poor do need money for consumption needs, medical and other emergencies and for education of their children, if they see a ray of hope for change in fortune. According to one analyst, needs of the poor could be categorized in four groups: (a) Lifecycle Needs (weddings, funerals, childbirths, education, house-building, widowhood, old age, etc.), (b) Personal Emergencies (sickness, injury, unemployment, theft, harassment, death, etc.), (c) Disasters (fires, floods, cyclones, wars, etc.), and (d) Investment Opportunities (expanding business, buying land/equipment, securing job through bribe, etc.). According to one survey conducted in 2007 in India, of all the earners who take loan, 27 per cent took loan for financial emergency and 16 per cent for medical emergency whereas only 10 per cent sought it for business purpose. Non-institutional sources do come forward in cases of (a), (b) and (c) categories whereas the formal sector prefers to avoid them and chooses to finance only cases under (d) category. It is revealed by various studies. Any scheme of micro-finance must be useful to poor households: helping them raise income, build up assets and/or cushion themselves against external shocks.

A question has been raised by Rakesh Mohan as whether it is an indication of failure of financial system or a failure of public services and of the welfare system to meet the needs under (a), (b) and (c) categories. Should then donors come to help in a big way? It has been argued by an international committee supported by G8 that (international) donors should complement private capital, not compete with it; they should instead focus on capacity building. Micro-finance should and can pay for itself. As subsidies from donors and government are scarce and uncertain, and cannot be a permanent solution, micro-finance must pay for itself so as to reach large numbers of poor people.

V

It would be useful to see at this stage how most ubiquitous institution of our formal financial system is spread across the country, which help us gauge its efforts in helping people engage in economic activities — consumption, savings and investment. There are two kinds of regional distributions, one is often called spatial and the other we may call zonal. Spatial distribution is often given in terms of (i) rural, (ii) semi-urban, (iii) urban, and (iv) metropolitan and zonal in terms of (a) eastern, (b) western, (c) northern, (d) southern, and (e) central and north-eastern. It is to be noted that metropolitan areas had 18 per cent share of bank branches in 1969, the year of bank nationalization, which declined to 12 per cent by 1996, but it started rising thereafter and is again back to 18 per cent in 2009. Rural branches were only 22 per cent of all branches in 1969 and gradually rose to 51 per cent by 1996, but their share started declining thereafter and has come down to 38 per cent in 2009. Consequently, it is only the share of metropolitan cities in both deposits and credit that had been continuously rising from 1996 onward, thanks to new private banks and foreign banks (*See* Table 1.2).

If one looks at zonal distribution of bank branches one finds that southern and northern zones are best served, population served per bank branch being about 11,000 as against all-India average of around 15,000 while western zone is closely ahead with 14,000. Bank branches in the other zones are serving 19,000-20,000 persons per branch though situation improved quite fast in last few years. Difficult terrains require lower norms. Real issue, however, is about mobilization of the deposits (savings) and credit disbursement.

Table 1.2: Spatial Distribution of Banking Services

	Offices				*Deposits*				*Credit*			
	1969	*1996*	*2005*	*2009*	*1969*	*1996*	*2005*	*2009*	*1969*	*1996*	*2005*	*2009*
Rural	22.2	51.2	45.7	38.6	6.4	14.4	12.2	9.3	3.3	11.4	9.5	7.3
Semi-Urban	40.4	21.3	22.3	23.3	21.8	19.5	16.9	13.5	13.1	13.1	11.3	9.3
Urban	19.2	15.2	17.6	20.1	26.5	22.4	21.5	21.0	21.8	17.7	16.4	16.1
Metropolitan	18.2	12.3	14.4	18.0	45.3	43.7	49.4	56.2	61.8	57.8	62.7	67.3

Source: Rakesh Mohan (2011).

Table 1.3 points out that in recent years pace of financial inclusion has been pretty fast. Southern rural areas are best placed followed by northern, central and north-east. The worst is the eastern zone and western zone is a shred better. As far as the north-east is concerned, in terms of number of accounts rural habitations are better placed. By contrast, urban areas are far ahead except in the north-east. With average of 80 accounts per 100 persons, western zone leads with 133 (which has suddenly risen in recent past) closely followed by northern zone with 129 and southern zone with distant 104. This simply shows there are quite a few multiple accounts in these zones. Eastern and central zones have only around 50 and 51 accounts per 100 persons while the north-east finishes with 30 accounts only.

Table 1.3: Zone-wise Savings Accounts in Scheduled Commercial Banks per 100 Persons

	Total			*Rural*			*Urban*		
	1991	*2005*	*2008*	*1991*	*2005*	*2008*	*1991*	*2005*	*2008*
Northern	40.0	38.3	65.7	30.1	29.7	41.5	62.6	55.4	128.7
North-East	17.8	17.6	31.8	16.1	16.4	32.4	28.4	24.2	30.3
Eastern	21.8	20.5	36.2	17.7	16.9	30.9	40.0	36.1	50.0
Central	23.8	24.5	39.4	21.0	22.1	35.0	34.7	32.9	50.8
Western	35.5	32.5	59.8	24.7	23.8	31.4	53.8	45.2	133.3
Southern	37.0	37.6	67.6	34.6	35.5	53.8	42.7	41.8	103.6
All-India	29.9	29.2	50.8	24.5	24.4	38.3	45.6	41.6	83.3

Source: Rakesh Mohan (2011).

Compared to savings/deposit accounts, credit accounts are far fewer, which is understandable as practically everybody saves in small amounts which s/he can only deposit in a bank or post-office provided it is located nearby. But one seeks credit normally for business proposition or at times for home, education, or consumer durables. If very poor, one may have occasion for meeting emergencies (*See* Table 1.4).

Table 1.4: Zone-wise Credit Accounts in Scheduled Commercial Banks per 100 Persons

	Total			*Rural*			*Urban*		
	1991	*2005*	*2008*	*1991*	*2005*	*2008*	*1991*	*2005*	*2008*
Northern	6.4	5.7	7.1	6.6	5.1	5.1	5.9	6.7	12.2
North-East	4.4	3.3	4.7	4.4	3.2	5.1	4.4	3.9	3.4
Eastern	6.6	4.2	4.7	4.4	3.2	5.1	4.4	3.9	3.4
Central	5.5	4.3	4.6	5.8	4.2	4.9	4.4	4.5	3.8
Western	5.7	7.5	17.5	6.2	4.2	4.1	4.8	12.2	52.3
Southern	11.8	14.2	16.5	13.6	12.7	14.4	7.6	17.4	22.2
All-India	7.3	7.0	9.3	7.9	6.0	6.8	5.5	9.8	15.8

Source: Rakesh Mohan (2011).

Table 1.4 shows that credit accounts are also on rise during 2005-2008, credit accounts in urban areas rose from 10 to 15 per 100 persons. Year 1991 springs a surprise that rural credit accounts per 100 population were higher than their urban counterparts in all zones but the north-east where they were equal. But the situation has now reversed in half of the zones. The western zone urban areas have 52 accounts as compared to All-India average of 16 accounts, to southern average of 22 accounts, and to its own rural counterpart with 4 accounts (*See* Table 1.4). What is intriguing is that the number of urban credit accounts have come down in central, eastern and north-east zones during 1991 through 2008 as far as this three-point data show.

VI

The world of poverty has not changed a great deal though micro-financial institutions are thriving. Business of micro-finance is lucrative as anything else because rate of interest in micro-world continues to be high in contradiction to priority lending rates charged by commercial banks under advice by the RBI. One could argue that interest rates of micro-finance institutions ought to be high as there is one more layer of intermediary. They borrow themselves from other financial institutions like commercial banks. It is important to note that risks of lending to these small borrowers remain comparatively low because of the practice of solidarity lending or choice for women entrepreneurs. There exists peer pressure in the group where groups are loaned. Women are traditionally less risky.

However, micro-credit has to be more inclusive in terms of cost too as Rangarajan Committee points out. It means that organizational basis of micro-financial institutions has to be such as reduces transaction cost. An alternative of Business Correspondent model has been proposed by this committee to reduce the transaction cost as it is realized that it is very costly for banking system to reach to every village. Borrower/creditor has a smart card, BC holds a hand-held device and branch has a CPU. Information technology could be a great support in this attempt. But this has spread as much as was expected.

It is important to remember that the poor are likely to save, if they are assured of credit, to run their enterprises. In fact, most businesses start from their own savings and sustain on their own savings but there has to be minimum scale of operation before the enterprise turn into a profitable proposition. Policy makers would do well if they incentivize setting up such institutions as have low transaction cost and help the micro-entrepreneurs to flourish. Some studies show that most micro-entrepreneurs meet their fund requirement to the extent of 60-70 per cent.

Though I have taken a slant towards micro-credit — which is about inclusive finance rather than financial inclusion, specialists in the area prefer to broaden the micro-finance to include micro-savings, money transfers and at times insurance. It is to be noted that, in the UK, a Task for Micro-finance was set up in 2005, following a G8 supported committee which suggested that poor people need not just loans but also savings, insurance and money transfer services.

However, presently micro-finance institutions are normally functioning as loan-funding institutions. Three major allegations are made against the micro-finance institutions. One, they charge exorbitant rates of interest. In addition, they practice service charges. Further, they apply flat rate method whereby the interest is also charged on the principal refunded. That further exacerbates the cost of borrowing. Further, many micro-finance institutions lack transparency with regard to their interest rate practices, which is helping them to transfer various costs on to gullible borrowers. Mohd. Yunus is reported to suggest that micro-credit interest rate should not be more than 15 per cent over and above the cost of institution's long-term borrowing cost, which itself is huge. It is, however, pointed out that ceilings on interest rate may hurt poor people by preventing micro-finance institutions from recovering their costs, which may choke off the supply of credit.

The micro-finance institutions are also found to resorting to unethical ways of recovering loans by confiscating title deeds, using intimidation and abusive language, and combining multiple products like savings, insurance and loan to ensure prompt recovery. They are also alleged to aggressively poaching their borrowers from government and banks. They are luring the members of government supported SHGs by liberally financing them, leading to multiple financing. Micro-finance institutions should, therefore, be asked to measure and disclose their performance — both financially and socially.

The picture painted above reminds one of usurious moneylenders whom institutional finance was supposed to replace. However, that did not happen for variety of reasons. Nationalization did do a good job yet we fell short of the need. Are moneylenders returning? They are returning, but the shape is much different. Mostly they come in organized form. Some are local, small dealers, but others are corporate size though using local channels.

Malegam Committee has noted all this. It suggested that micro-finance institutions have to be regulated as a special variety of NBFC. A company which provides financial services predominantly to low-income borrowers, with loans of small amounts for short-terms, on unsecured basis, mainly for income-generating activities, with repayment schedules which are more frequent than those normally stipulated by commercial banks should be treated as a NBFC-MFI. In concrete terms, a NBFC has 90 per cent of its assets in the form of qualifying assets and has not to engage in other kind of services. It has further suggested a cap of 24 per cent on interest rate and within that cap has provided for a margin cap of 10 or 12 per cent depending upon whether the MFI has a loan portfolio of more than ₹ 100 crore or less, there has to be a cap, in its view, on the amount that an individual (₹ 25,000) or SHG (₹ 50,000) can be lent. Further, it has suggested that not less than 75 per cent of loan has to be in the form of income-generating activities. In order to ensure transparency in transaction, an MFI could not charge anything else except processing and insurance fees besides interest. It has attempted to check phenomena of multiple borrowing, ghost borrowing, coercive recovery, etc. through its recommendations. No two MFIs to lend to same to individual borrower and no individual to be a member of two SHG or JLG, and a time gap between disbursal and recovery.

VII

Finance is the link between the primary savers and the final investors. Primary savers are those who save positively a portion of their incomes after meeting their current consumption or save actively to meet or supplement their future consumption where 'their future' may denote their future generations. Final investors are those who invest capital funds in those activities which produce real goods and services for consumption of people and/or goods which build up physical capacity of the system to produce. The latter part is often known as capital formation. Generally speaking, it is in the physical form, but the new trend is to include human form and no-so-hard physical form like R&D activities in this fold and at times environmental form.

The link between primary savers and final investors is now-a-days provided by a series of intermediaries or companies or institutions. There might have been a time when saving in physical or financial form was directly available to the final investors. And there was a time, few analysts like Kurien noted, saving was a positive function of business opportunities. That is still true. Availability of credit is found supplemented by own resources to a great extent. Rutherford distinguishes between saving up, saving down and saving through. He thinks that loans may help poor to save to repay them. There are thirty three ways whereby poor make savings!

In most of the economies there are a host of intermediaries to act as go-betweens the primary savers and final investors. Financial intermediaries are often classified as banks and non-banking financial institutions. Non-banking financial institutions include financial corporations in the business of loans and advances, purchase and sale of shares, chit funds, etc., but also insurance companies. Then there are stock exchanges, in which investors keep exchanging their investment portfolio. Micro-finance institutions are a new breed, which come in different forms.

Each of them is in the business of accepting deposits (banks) or engaging in borrowings on the one hand and lending and investing in financial assets on the other. Banks, especially commercial banks are in the business of lending the deposits they receive from their constituents or account holders, keeping a fair share under rules for depositors should they make demand anytime. The difference between interest rates on deposits and lending is their wherewithal, called operating income, out of which go the salaries and wages to the employees and profits to the shareholders who own the financial institutions, besides taxes to the government. In essence, there is little difference between banking and non-banking institutions. For example, insurance companies accept premiums and loan out (or invest) their surplus over maturity claims to final investors. In this case, premiums are the savings of the policy holders. Micro-finance institutions belong to non-banking financial institutions as they are not allowed to accept/seek deposit from general public and provide banking services like remittances or transfer of money through instruments like demand draft.

Financial institutions, particularly banks, can help stimulate or inculcate saving habits in small income earners who, as an individual, are hardly material for any real investor who may not find it convenient to contract hundreds or thousands of small savers. Banks do business with others' money and allow savings not to remain idle. In fact, they help small income earners — for example salaried and the wage earners — to save and earn interest on the saving. They help thousands of savers on the one hand and dozens of investors on the others or, say, lakhs of savers and hundreds of investors. In modern times, they can transfer savings of Mumbaikars to Mizo investors or *vice versa*. Among the non-banking instruments for small savings were various national savings schemes and units floated by the UTI as well as ULIP which had an element of insurance. Now, there are several mutual funds serving the same purpose. Practically, all financial institutions have floated mutual fund subsidiaries. By and large these mutual fund instruments served the middle class very well as they were also income tax avoiding instruments.

By stimulating saving habits on small income earners they help raised the savings rate of the country and thereby growth rate of the economy. Growth through this kind of development is, therefore, inclusive to the extent small savers also get a share in this growth. However, usually these institutions did not encourage small savers to open accounts with them for the transaction cost of operating a small account is not far lower than managing a big account. That is why new private banks open their branches in urban areas and ask for high minimum balance in savings account. Recently, some new private banks are going rural as growth in urban areas is plateauing. Yet, no bank would love to write a cheque for ₹ 1! There was some reluctance on the part of the banks when accounts had to be opened for MNREGA card holders. But it is an important component of micro-finance which should not be lost sight of.

VIII

But what can be said about those who have technical skills as well as entrepreneurial skills but no savings of their own? What about those whose own savings are too small to establish an enterprise which can utilize their skills — technical and/or entrepreneurial. There are also just those who need margin money but have no collaterals to offer. They are micro-entrepreneurs running micro-enterprises. Howsoever, micro an enterprise, it requires a level of scale to be an economically viable proposition for which even sum total of individual savings of the group may fall short. Therefore, access to credit is an important element in successful running of one's enterprise.

To be fair, savings of all investors are too small to run the business of their choice. True, nobody does a big business with his/her own money. But for big business, there is little hurdle as there are people who have to lend/invest their savings and so have the financial intermediaries their deposits. There is cross institutional finance also available to them. A financial institution has only to assess the creditworthiness of the company and soundness of the project in terms of risk so that money is recovered.

Who can come forward to help these small entrepreneurs who can hardly establish their creditworthiness? Their relations too are poor and without any savings and, therefore, cannot help much. More importantly, they often compete in all kind of conditions rather than complement. Moneylenders were their traditional source. Their rates of interest were always usurious and they often took away the collateral property of the poor. They have been known as sharks to ruin their small borrowers with 24-36 per cent per annum and at times some of them collusively charged even 10 to 100 per cent per month. In their favour, however, there were the factors of convenience and speed with which money was lent. Unfortunately, they often did business with ulterior motives to usurp the assets of the poor as anecdotal stories would narrate.

Why should any profit-making business invest in too risky ventures? Cooperatives were an answer in small places where mutual help principle could work. However, if they are too poor even to start an enterprise on mutual help basis is difficult. There could come in some institution to lend help from outside, realizing that group-risk is far smaller than the sum total of individual risks. It took such a huge time to realize this possibility. However, the efforts of national planners and experts to develop financial services for most of these people have often failed in many developing countries.

That was the basis of micro-finance, strictly speaking micro-credit, started by Grameen Bank floated by Mohd. Yunus in Bangladesh just after its liberation in early 1970s. It was a sound business proposition for the Grameen Bank and decent livelihood option for poor entrepreneurs. These could use not just brawn, (could there be a wage employment programme like MNREGA), but also brain. They could utilize their spare time to think about new designs, new patterns, new products, new markets, new local resources, etc. — all that Schumpeter said about innovation and innovators. Finding that this micro-credit to groups with majority female members is far less risky than big ticket credit, many institutions have come in the business of micro-credit and micro-finance. Commercial banks have also shown interest and in most cases they have a micro-finance wing as well, like personal banking. Banks which earlier argued that the cost of administration of small accounts are high, are now arguing that their recovery rates are high! Their break-even point argument has now broken.

IX

Despite all refinancing attempts made at the behest of the Government and Central Banks for rural, agricultural, artisan and other small borrowers, attempts to micro-finance failed until it was shown by a private initiative on the part of Mohd. Yunus. Yunus asked the poor to form small groups with women members to start business. Women are usually good savers and there is mutual support as well as peer pressure to repay the loan. As business succeeds, loans are repaid and loans are taken for expansion of business. The lender, in this case Grameen Bank, was too happy to lend further. Observing that the arrangement is working fine, refinancing institutions also come forward.

Self-help groups, as they are known, have been formed in our country with membership generally of the people below poverty line. They pool in their own savings as kind of shares and borrow money from micro-finance institutions. As cooperatives differ from joint stock companies so do self-help groups from cooperatives. Principles of cooperative mutual help, peer support and pressure, group dynamics, solidarity lending and scale of operation come in their favour. Government of India also changed its strategy of rural self-employment programme from individual basis to group basis. To do business with them have emerged micro-finance institutions everywhere, particularly after the year 2005 was declared by the UN as the International Year of Micro-Credit. Among closed to 1,000 now, there are quite a few big micro-financing institutions like SKS (a listed company), Spandana, Bandhan, Microfin, Ashmita Microfin, BASIX, SHARE, Ujjivan, Micro-finance Foundation of India, etc. A few have been floated on cooperative and non-profit basis. They are also private or non-government in structure.

They are supported by commercial banks, including rural regional banks, and cooperative banks. Seeing possibility of high rate of interest and low recovery risk, even few private banks have come forward to support micro-finance institutions. There exists a national level association of MFIs in the country with the name Sa-Dhan.

This boost could be possible, it should be noted, by various rural development programmes supported by Central and State Governments which shifted the basis of subsidy from individual to self-help groups (SHGs) and enacted some support systems. NABARD finances more than 500 banks that on-lend funds to SHGs. SIDBI is also a partner in financing micro-finance institutions (MFIs). Banks in turn lend to MFIs as well as directly to SHGs. By 2009-10, annual bank loans to MFIs/ SHGs reached over ₹ 25,000 crore while outstanding loans were over ₹ 40,000 crore. Significant to note is that banks are finding it prudent to approach SHGs through MFI rather than directly. As a result, MFIs' share in banks' credit in the pool of micro-credit is rising.

SHGs generally comprise twenty or fewer members, of whom the majority members are women from the poorest castes and tribes. Members save small amounts of money, as little as a few rupees a month in a group fund. Members may borrow from the group fund for a variety of purposes ranging from household emergencies to school fees but also for commercial activity. As SHGs prove capable of managing their funds well, they may well borrow from a local bank to invest in small business or farm activities. There is a variant of SHG, called JLG — joint liability group — with a membership varying between 5 and 15. They are an informal group offering joint undertaking to a bank for availing loan to an individual member. Banks typically loan up to four times the size of the group fund. Groups generally pay interest rates that range from 12 to 24 per cent a year, based on the flat calculation method. Nearly 1.5 million SHGs comprising approximately 20 million women now borrow from banks, which make the Indian SHG-Bank Linkage model the largest micro-finance programme in the world.

Micro-finance goes a little beyond micro-savings (thrift) and micro-credit which we have discussed above. It includes micro-insurance and pension products as well as other banking services like money transfer/ remittance. Though micro-part of insurance has yet to establish in terms of risk, coverage, cap, etc. insurance products in the area of crop, health, disability, property are being devised. However, some analysts are pointing out that ill-designed products can do more harm than good.

X

Micro-finance Institutions are often alleged to use coercive methods to recollect dues and also charge usurious interest rates. Irked as the Government of Andhra Pradesh was, it brought out an Ordinance in 2006, proscribing MFIs using coercive recollection practices and charging usurious interest rates. It is well known that some of the micro-finance giants in India had earned net interest margin around 20 per cent. The Ordinance required MFIs to register with the State Government and gave the State Government the power, *suo motu*, to shut down MFI activity. A number of MFIs and other NBFCs were affected by the Ordinance, including sector heavyweight SKS Micro-finance. It is said that the AP Ordinance crippled the functioning of micro-finance institutions in the State. As a result, it was advised that there should be a Central legislation to regulate the micro-finance industry, which should supersede the AP Ordinance. A regulation Bill, Micro-Financial Sector (Development and Regulation) Bill, making NABARD the regulator, was introduced in the 14th Lok Sabha in March 2007, which lapsed with the expiry of the term of the Lok Sabha in 2009. It was found wanting on many counts. Meanwhile, the Andhra Pradesh Legislative Assembly passed The Andhra Pradesh Micro-finance Institutions (Regulation of Moneylending) Act, in 2010. There was a significant drop in micro-finance activity in the most vibrant state in the activity, Andhra Pradesh, once the State government sought, through legislation of Andhra Pradesh Micro-finance Institutions (Regulation of Moneylending) Act, 2010, registration of micro-finance institutions with the government. While the Act might have controlled the MFIs, it has also hit the small borrowers who may have to turn to moneylenders, the phenomenon which is on increase. Many micro-finance institutions questioned the wisdom of the AP legislation as they were already registered as non-banking institutions with the RBI. Some analysts also pointed out that moneylending is in the State list, not in the Concurrent List, of legislative domain delineated under Article 246 of the Constitution.

In July 2011, again a draft Bill Micro-Financial Sector (Development and Regulation) Bill, 2011 was circulated for public comments with the intension that it would be passed in the winter session of 2011, but it could not even be introduced. Meanwhile officials of the Government of Andhra Pradesh, the architects of the AP Act, called the Bill anti-poor as it will favour MFIs and will hurt the small borrowers. It may be pointed out while banking, central banking and savings banking are the items in the Union List, moneylending and moneylenders are in the State List for legislation and there is no item in the Concurrent List mandating such a legislation. In addition, it was argued that State machinery has better information about people and institutions. On the other hand, MFIs and its associational body MFIN (MFI Network formed in December, 2009) welcomed the Central legislation and hoped to recover their dues which they could not do due to AP Act. A new version of the Bill (62 of 2012) with statement of objects and reasons that the MFIs "lack a formal statutory framework for providing such micro-finance services, it is expedient to provide a statutory framework for the promotion, development, regulation and orderly growth for such MFIs and thereby facilitate financial inclusion", was introduced in Lok Sabha by Pranab Mukherji in May 2012. It now lies with the Parliamentary Standing Committee for Finance with Yashwant Sinha as chairperson. Meanwhile RBI has announced another Committee to look into the affairs of the sector.

The Bill proposes among other things registration of each micro-finance institution with Reserve Bank of India, irrespective of its colour — (i) ownership being private, cooperative, non-government, or (ii) orientation being profit-oriented and non-profit — provided its net own fund exceeds ₹ 5 lakh. It implies that the MFI activities are treated at par with banking activity. The Bill provides for a Fund and a Council at the national level with membership from NABARD, NHB, SIDBI, RBI and the MoF and MoRD, besides a Council at State level. A micro-finance institution would face danger of de-registration under the Bill's clause dealing with "desist and cease" provisions. The RBI may pass an order directing a micro-finance institution to cease and desist from carrying out micro-finance activities if it is found acting in a manner prejudicial to the interest of its clients or depositors. More importantly, the Bill proposes micro-finance institutions as an extended arm of banking and financial institutions.

The plateau has not yet come for micro-financing if it goes for financial inclusion of those who are potential micro-entrepreneurs. Let us hope present attempts do not fail as well-meaning Comilla experiment of 1950s in erstwhile East Pakistan did and does not face the impediments that cooperative societies usually face by the government machinery. There is some attempt to miff rather than regulate the micro-finance institutions on the pretext that they are indulging in various malpractices.

However, inclusion of the weaker, the meeker and the vulnerable would not depend just on their financial inclusion, but also on the better provision of health and educational services on subsidized basis for quite some time to come, if not for ever or for everybody — as is the case in some developed countries. Financial inclusion may help low income households to employ themselves better and be more productive.

NOTES

1. Financial inclusion in many foreign countries has often meant some kind of a deposit account with some basic services. Belgium mandates banks to open call deposit accounts with minimum facilities of money transfer, deposits and withdrawals and bank statements. In Germany banks are committed for an 'everyman' current account with basic banking services without overdraft facility. Canada requires all banks to provide accounts without minimum balances, regardless of employment or credit history — with minimum identification requirements. We also talk of no-frills accounts where minimum restrictions are placed.
2. Reddy (2011) thinks that financial inclusion is closely associated with economic inclusion whereas my contention is that inclusive finance is better associated with economic inclusion.
3. The very first survey was known as All India Rural Credit Survey 1951-52 as the survey confined only to rural areas.
4. In parallel, significant interest was expressed by the RBI in regard to extending micro-finance activity, essentially as extended arms of the individual branches of banks and not as parallel financial intermediaries. The concept of banking correspondents was also developed in this context. During this period, most of the MFIS were not for profit, while there were some, particularly NBFCs, other than those under Section 25, which were for profit. There was substantial micro-finance activity in the southern states, and in particular, in Andhra Pradesh. Most of the activity was driven by self-help groups.

REFERENCES

Arunachalam, Ramesh S. (2011). *The Journey of Indian Micro-Finance: Lessons for the Future*, Chennai: Aapti Publications.

Mohan, Rakesh (2011). *Growth with Financial Stability: Central Banking in an Emerging Market*, New Delhi: Oxford University Press.

Nair, Tara S. (2012). "Financing of Indian Microfinance", *Economic and Political Weekly*, Vol. XLVII, No. 25.

Rath, Neelkantha (2007). "On Microfinance Regulation Bill, 2007", *Economic and Political Weekly*, Vol. XLII.

Reddy, Y.V. (2011). "Microfinance Industry in India: Some Thoughts", *Economic and Political Weekly*, Vol. XLVI, No. 41.

Rutherford, Stuart (2009). *The Poor and Their Money: Microfinance from a Twenty-First Century Consumer's Perspective*, Practical Action Publishing (with Sukhwinder Arora).

Rutherford, Stuart (1999). *The Poor and Their Money: An Essay about Financial Services*, Institute of Development Policy and Management, Manchester, Internet.

Shylendra, H.S. (2006). "Microfinance Institutions in Andhra Pradesh: Crisis and Diagnosis", *Economic and Political Weekly*, May 20.

Srinivasan, T.N. (2011). *Growth, Sustainability, and India's Economic Reforms*, New Delhi: Oxford University Press.

Micro-finance Focus, RBI releases Malegam Committee Report on Micro-finance, internet download.

Bandhan, Micro-credit Foundation of India, Saadhana Microfin Society, Grameen Koota, Sharada's Women's Association for Weaker Section, SKS Microfinance Private Ltd., Asmitha Microfin Ltd. (29th).

2

MICRO-FINANCE MARKET AND FINANCIAL INCLUSION

Gopal Kumar Sarma

Introduction

The problem of shortage of capital and lack of finance, especially financial infrastructure for economic growth in developing and less developed nations are not new. Financial intermediation in general and credit and savings in particular, play an important role in economic development. Credit, savings and insurance can directly handle with risky economic environment in one hand and on the other; credit and savings enhance an economy's investment efficiency (Besley, 1995). It thus implies that credit, savings and investment can play an indispensable role in protecting the families of the poor against hardship and to overcome poverty. Since, poor people lack in asset and income, as such a bundle of financial services in small amount could make changes in their economic condition, and similarly, it can create an inclusive financial development of the economy.

But contrary to the theoretical expectation, the reality portrays a grim picture of the poor, which is evinced by the global poverty data (World Bank, 2013). The problem is rooted in their vulnerable livelihood condition, where lack of asset and income irregularities exerts as strong negative and chronic factors. Moreover, the poor are excluded from the formal financial market due to risk and cost components (Kritikos and Vigenina, 2005).

In Indian context the extent of financial exclusion is vast. Despite the vast network of rural branches, only 27 per cent of the total farm households are indebted to formal sources; of them, one-third also borrow from informal sources. There are parts of the country where more than

95 per cent of the farm households do not get any credit from institutional or non-institutional sources. Apart from the fact that exclusion itself is large, it also varies widely across regions, social groups and assets holdings. The poorer the group, the greater is the exclusion. There is evidence that farm debt is increasing much faster than farm incomes and the larger issue of the overhanging debt stock, as distinct from credit flow, has not even been on the agenda except of a few State governments (Planning Commission of India, 2006). According to NSSO data in the situation assessment survey on "Indebtedness of Farmer Households" (2003), 45.9 million farmer households in the country (51.4%), out of a total of 89.3 million households do not access credit, either from institutional or non-institutional sources. Further, only 27 per cent of total farm households are indebted to formal sources (RBI, 2009).

Besides, some studies also indicate the severity of financial exclusion. The studies reveal not only the magnitude of exclusion but also a wide variation across regions, social groups and asset holdings. The poorer the group, the greater is the exclusion (Rangarajan, 2007). Similarly, the results of the All-India Debt and Investment Survey of 2002, also indicate that the share of the non-institutional sources, in the total credit of the cultivator households, had increased from 30.6 per cent in 1991 to 38.9 per cent in 2002 (Karmakar, 2002).

Thus, it is clear from the previous studies and reports that despite vast network of financial institutions, financial institution in India is deficient by its target of financial inclusion. Moreover, the governments in some of the developing countries like India also has adopted the policy of financial inclusion, where it targets to cover all poor families with the facility of formal financial provisions.

Micro-finance, which was formally emerged in late 1970s in Bangladesh, envisaged in bridging the gap of access to credit facilities for the excluded sections of people. Although there is much expectation about micro-finance as a strategy of poverty reduction and financial inclusion, within a relatively short time, micro-finance has failed to keep the promise. Indeed, it is now described as "a poster child of exploitation of the vulnerable" (Priyadarshee and Ghalib, 2011).

With this backdrop, the chapter overviews micro-finance market potentialities in North-East India, especially Assam and examine the issues of micro-finance as a strategy of financial inclusion. The region for considering North-East India lies on the fact that both micro-finance market extent and financial inclusion is comparatively in the slower side in this region. Due to unavailability of data on MFI on the rest of North-

Eastern states of India, except Assam, therefore, the present study specially refer Assam in case of micro-finance market analysis. The chapter is organized in five sections. Apart from the introduction in Section I, Section II describes the concept of micro-finance and financial inclusion. Section III delves into the estimation of micro-finance demand supply condition in North-East India in general and Assam in particular, which is followed by the current scenario of financial inclusion in North-East India in Section IV. Finally, Section V sheds light on some of the issues pertaining to micro-finance as a strategy of financial inclusion and concludes.

The study is based on secondary sources of data. Data published by various institutions such as Government of India, World Bank, MiX Market, Reserve Bank of India (RBI), National Bank for Agriculture and Rural Development (NABARD), State Level Banker's Committee (SLBC), NSSO, etc. are used for the purpose of the present chapter.

II

Micro-Finance and Financial Inclusion: A Conceptual Review

Since formal credit institutions rarely lend to the poor, special institutional arrangements become necessary to extend credit to those who have no collateral to offer. Micro-finance, by providing small loans and savings facilities to those who have been excluded from commercial financial services, has been promoted as a key strategy for reducing poverty in all its forms by agencies all-over the world. The concept of micro-finance has undergone a tremendous change since inception and in recent times it includes broad ranges of financial services such as, deposits, loans, payment services, money transfers and insurance to poor and low-income households and their micro-enterprises. As noted by Robinson (2005) micro-finance is "a small-scale financial service for both credits and deposits that are provided to people who farm or fish or herd; operate small or micro-enterprises where goods are produced, recycled, repaired, or traded; provide services, in both rural and urban areas." In addition, MFIs also provide a wide range of services other than financial services, such as, education, awareness, monitoring of investment projects, consultation, etc. Among the three major types of micro-finance sources[1], MFIs are one of the prominent sources of micro-finance services in the recent times.

The mushrooming growth of micro-finance institutions (MFIs) across the world is due to its in-built features of lending mechanism such as peer monitoring, intra-group insurance, peer screening reduction of adverse selection and moral hazard (Besley and Coate, 1995; Ghatak, 1999; Ghatak and Guinnane, 1999; Armendariz and Morduch, 2005). In order to reduce transaction costs and the information asymmetry problem associated with uncollateralized micro-loans, micro-finance institutions have come up with innovations like joint liability lending (JLL)[2], which enables them to lend the poor with considerable degree of financial self-sufficiency and higher repayment rates (Ghatak and Guinnane, 1999).

The basic idea of micro-finance is that poor people are ready and are willing to pull themselves out of poverty if given access to economic inputs. The need for informality in credit delivery and easy access is demonstrated by the fact that Self-Help Groups (SHGs) and Micro-Finance Institutions (MFIs) constitute the fastest growing segment in recent years in reaching out to small borrowers. Micro-finance is a new development in which Indian institutions have acquired considerable expertise and where up-scaling holds great promise both to expand the nature of financial services offered to micro-enterprises and to make these the springboard for entrepreneurial development (Planning Commission, 2006).

The SHG movement is bringing about a profound transformation in rural areas of India. MFIs play a significant role in facilitating inclusion, as they are uniquely positioned in reaching out to the rural poor. Many of them operate in a limited geographical area, have a greater understanding of the issues specific to the rural poor, enjoy greater acceptability amongst the rural poor and have flexibility in operations providing a level of comfort to their clientele. It is roughly estimated that there are about 1,000 NGO-MFIs and more than 20 companies facilitating the activities in all-over India. There are today over 73 lakh such groups linked with banks out of which 60 per cent are women. The objective of the country is to enroll nearly 100 per cent rural women in India as members of SHGs over the next five years and link these SHGs to banks.

Apart from SBLP, MFI model of micro-finance is another important delivery channel, which has been operating in India over three decades but gained its momentum recently. The model shares 33.43 per cent against the total micro-finance client outreach of 93.9 million as on 2010-11 with an outstanding credit of ₹ 20,756 crore (Srinivasan, 2012).

Financial inclusion can be defined as a process that serves to remove the barriers and overcome the inabilities of some societal groups and individuals, including the poor and disadvantaged, to access and use low-cost, fair and safe formal financial services, such as credit, deposits, insurance and payments, whenever needed (Carbo, Gardener, and Molyneux, 2005; Conroy, 2005; Leyshon and Thrift, 1995; Mohan, 2006; Rangarajan Committee, 2008). In the context of financial institutions, financial inclusion concerns the spread of its activities among different sections of the population. The domain of activities of financial institutions can be quite large and it may vary across countries. For instance, in UK three major dimensions of financial inclusion are considered to be access to banking, access to affordable credit and access to face-to-face money advice. While these three dimensions are important for other countries as well, it seems to be important that a significant part of formal financial services in countries like India be directed towards priority sectors such as agriculture, small business activities, and economically backward sections of the population.

It is evident that financial inclusion is a multi-dimensional phenomenon. Moreover, it is well documented that performance of financial system significantly varies across different dimensions, across geographical regions as well as over time (Beck, Demirguc-Kunt, and Martinez Peria, 2007; Beck, Demirguc-Kunt, and Levine, 2007; Honohan, 2008; Pal and Vaidya, 2011). Thus, from individual dimensions one can get only partial information on financial inclusion. The position of a country may be quite good in one dimension of financial inclusion, but not in another dimension. It thus seems that micro-finance is a complementary tool of financial inclusion.

Micro-Finance Market in North-East India with Special Reference to Assam

Micro-finance, in India, is operating under two broad models[3], where Micro-finance Institutions (MFIs) model has gained momentum recently, albeit operational for over three decades. The model shares 25.53 percentages of the total micro-finance client outreach of 54.87 million as on 2007-08 with an outstanding credit of ₹ 6,124 crore (Srinivasan, 2009). The model has also been operating in Assam, which is a priority state in terms of SHG-Bank Linkage Programme[4] (SBLP) for a period of over one decade with infinitesimal share as compared to national total. The model shares only 0.98 per cent in terms of client outreach and 0.75 per cent in terms of loan portfolio (Srinivasan, 2009). It is thus an indication that there is a scope of increasing outreach and the assertion is justified with the coming up of new players in the market, which have hidden potentiality.

III

Micro-finance Demand in Assam

Micro-finance services are basically demanded by household, formal and informal sector enterprises. While household demand for micro-finance arises due to consumption smoothening and to cope up other inadvertent situations; micro-finance demand is also urged as fresh investment for livelihood in the form of small and micro-enterprises at individual level.

Despite the potential role as assumed to be played in the economy of Assam, there is hardly any official estimation on demand and supply of micro-finance sector. In the present study an approximation of micro-finance demand is calculated to substantiate the necessity in view of entrenched poverty in the state. Appropriate estimation of demand for particular market is really a bulky task, and the problem is more delicate in estimating demand for micro-finance. Although some analysts use some hypothetical ways to ballpark figure on micro-finance demand in various regions in the globe[5], the approaches are just an approximation since estimation of an exact micro-finance demand is not possible due to appropriateness of secondary data and reliability of some base indicators. However, specific demand estimates for Indian micro-finance are relatively non-existent. George *et al.* (2007) has provided an approximation towards the realistic estimation of micro-finance demand for India and the same method is acclimatized in this study.

In this study a slightly variant methodology as compared to George *et al.* (2007) has been exercised. While George *et al.* (2007) used incidence of poverty using population data and poverty ratios from Census 2011[6] to estimate micro-finance demand, the present study simply adopt India's poverty estimates for 2009-10 (Planning Commission, 2012) and mix market database. To calculate micro-finance demand, first, state wise number of poor person is calculated which is based on the latest Poverty Estimation for India (Planning Commission, 2012). Secondly, average loan portfolio is calculated from a database of 1,132 MFIs which were reported to MiX Market database as on 2010. To arrive at the final micro-finance demand, the number of poor is multiplied by the average loan size[7] which is fixed for all concerned regions. In addition, based on the customary micro-loan slab[8] of MFIs operating in Assam, it is also considered in estimating micro-finance demand. The rationale for adoption of such a simple methodology rest on two grounds; first, so far as Indian official data base on poverty is concerned, poverty estimates for 2009-10 is the latest database which was published in the year 2012. Secondly, the theoretical micro-finance exerts the notion that micro-finance are for poor people. Therefore, it implies that since micro-finance deals with the poor section of population, therefore, latest official database seems to appropriate for such estimation.

The estimation indicates that the demand for micro-finance in Assam ranges from ₹ 2,292 crore to ₹ 38,018.6 crore with an average demand of ₹ 8,824.2 crore. On the other hand, the demand for micro-finance for India ranges from ₹ 70,936 crore to ₹ 11,76,651 crore with an average demand of ₹ 2,73,104 crore. The estimated demand for Assam shares in the range of 2.6 to 43.2 percentages of NSDP and 1.2 to 20.1 percentage of GDP of India. Although the picture shows a bright micro-finance demand, is it predictive in nature? The answer is not such an easy binary type. It is apparent that the size of poverty in Assam has shown a declining trend during the period as compared to Indian scenario. Therefore, it implies that since micro-finance clients are basically people below the poverty line, as a result micro-finance demand will shrink in future. Contrary to this notion, as practical micro-finance broadened the coverage of clients by inclusion of people just above the poverty line, therefore, it seems that as an outcome of Government projects and policies, the BPL section may be upgraded to just above the poverty line and they may be in demand of micro-finance for better livelihood. Therefore, it is clear that although the estimation is not based on in-depth market research, it still provide a scenario of micro-finance demand structure in state.

However, there exists regional dispersion of micro-finance demand due to differences in the size of poverty. It is observed from Table 2.1, except the negative growth of micro-finance demand in Assam and NER, all other regions demonstrate positive growth of micro-finance demand for the period. Based on the methodology an estimation of micro-finance demand in Assam and India is made, which is shown in Table 2.1.

While Central regions show an increasing micro-finance demand, Northern region shows bulky demand. But, is the growth pattern really reflects demand pattern for the concerned regions? Table 2.2 shows a self-explicit answer to the question. It is apparent that the growth of micro-finance demand for the period is positive for both Assam and NER. Similarly, the share for the regions to all-India total has been increased for the period in concern. On the other hand, against a high positive growth of micro-finance demand, Northern regions demonstrate a depleting share to all-India total. It is worth mentioning that against a moderate increase in the micro-finance demand for Southern regions, it shares a commendable amount of all India total micro-finance demand next to Eastern region.

Table 2.1: Potential Micro-finance Demand for Assam and India for the Period 2009-10
(Based on National Poverty Estimates 2009-10)

Loan Size	*Potential Client*		*Micro-finance Demand (₹ crore)*		*Micro-finance Demand as a % of NSDP and GDP*	
	Assam	*India*	*Assam*	*India*	*NSDP (Assam)*	*GDP (India)*
2,000	11640000	354680000	2292	70936	2.6	1.2
5,000	(2.10%)	(3.14%)	5730	177340	6.5	3.0
10,000			11460	354680	13.0	6.0
15,000			17190	532020	19.5	9.1
20,000			22920	709360	26.0	12.1
25,000			28650	886700	32.5	15.1
7,700[a]			8824.2	273104	10.0	4.7
33,175[b]			38018.6	1176651	43.2	20.1

Notes: (a) Indian Average[9] and (b) Global average.

1. Average loan size indicates Gross Loan/Number of active borrowers, which was $ 710.7 as on 2010. Average loan size is based on the average of 1,132 MFIs as reported to Mix market database in 2010.
2. Exchange rate is based on the RBI reference rate as on 31st December, 2009 where ₹ 46.68 equal $ 1.
3. Figures in bracket indicates compounded annualized growth rate of poverty during the period 1999-2000 to 2009-10.
4. Gross Domestic Product (GDP) at factor cost (current prices) for India is considered for year 2008-09, stood at ₹ 58,68,331 crore and Net State Domestic Product (NSDP) at factor cost (current prices) for Assam for the same period was ₹ 88,023 crore.

Source: Calculation based on National Poverty Line 2009-10.

Table 2.2: Region-wise Potential Micro-finance Demand and Share
(1999-2000 to 2009-10)

State/ Region	*Micro-finance Demand (in ₹)*		*Share to all India Micro-finance Demand*		*Growth**
	1999-2000	*2009-10*	*1999-2000*	*2009-10*	
Assam	185016975000	386157000000	2.56	3.28	7.64
Northern	744778750000	450018875000	10.29	3.82	–4.91
NER	261949800000	500279000000	3.62	4.25	6.68
Eastern	2897205925000	3527199175000	40.02	29.98	1.99
Central	85725000000	3780291250000	1.18	32.13	46.03
Western	1363923775000	1354535250000	18.84	11.51	–0.07
Southern	1534974075000	1593859700000	21.21	13.55	0.38
All India	10009561000000	11766509000000			1.63

Notes: * Growth in terms of compounded annualized growth rate for the period 1999-2000 to 2004-05.

Source: National Poverty Estimate 1999-2000 and 2004-05, Planning Commission, Government of India.

Supply of Micro-Finance in Assam

In Assam, micro-finance is supplied basically *via* two broad models, e.g. Self-Help Bank Linkage Programme (SBLP) model and Micro-Finance Institutions (MFI) model. SBLP is a national micro-finance model of India which is under the supervision of NABARD. The model was initiated in 1992 by NABARD and till then it encompasses vast outreach in terms of client outreach and credit outstanding in all regions of the country. Although SHG approach is quite older practised non-formal version of micro-finance in India, the new version of the micro-financc approach by rural financial institutions assumed the form of the SBLP. While in this model basically credit is advanced by a number of commercial banks and government agencies; the route of delivery is channelized in various forms as such three widely practised models exist in India. This model has worldwide attraction as a possible way of delivery micro-finance services to poor that have been difficult to reach directly through banks or other institutions. Under the SHG-bank linkage programme, NGOs and banks interact with the poor, especially women, to form small homogenous groups not exceeding 20 members. These small groups are encouraged to meet frequently and collect small thrift amounts from their members and are taught simple accounting methods to enable them to maintain their accounts. This is the first step in establishing links with the formal banking system. Groups then, meet often and use the pooled thrift to impart small loans to members for meeting their small emergent needs. Gradually, the pooled savings grow and soon they are ready to receive external funds basically from the rural commercial banks. By aggregating their individual savings into a single deposit, self-help groups minimize the bank's transaction costs and generate an attractive volume of deposits.

MFI model on the other hand is a newer model in Assam as well as India. Under this model finance is provided by a micro-finance organization. Micro-finance organization also forms SHG not exceeding 20 members in the group and Joint Liability Group of 3 to 5 members. The creation and formation of such groups are under the discretion of respective branch managers of the MFIs. These MFIs are registered under Societies Registration Act, 1860, Section 25 Company and Non-Banking Financial Corporation Act. In Assam, Bosco Reach Out was the first of its kind which supports SHGs for better livelihoods. In subsequent period another five more prominent professional MFIs were emerged, out of which Credit and Savings Programme, RGVN and ASOMI and Bandhan have considerable depth and breadth of outreach.

In this analysis based on the database of MiX Market[9] and Bharat Micro-finance Quick Data 2010, 7 MFIs from Assam and 439 MFIs from India are considered for estimating supply of micro-finance.

A recent micro-finance supply scenario is portrayed in Table 2.3, where it is apparent that from the table that micro-finance supply in terms of total loan outstanding for the concerned period stands at ₹ 398.88 crore, which is 0.01 percentage of GDP of India. Further, the share of micro-finance supply of Assam is the least as compared to all other regions of the country, while southern region captures a lions' share of total micro-finance supply of India. The share of micro-finance supply under MFI model in southern region is 71.36 percentages.

The supply of micro-finance is basically catered by SBLP model, which shares commendably large portion of total micro-finance supply both in Assam and India. But the share of loan outstanding to total loan outstanding of micro-finance in Assam is comparatively higher (82.37 percentage) than the national share (65.51 percentage). It is estimated that the supply of micro-finance under MFI model is still lower as compared to SBLP model in Indian states as well as Assam. Since micro-finance under MFI model is a nascent delivery mechanism and the issues of equity funding and securitization emerged as coveted mechanism, therefore, it seems, the model could penetrate to the considerable depth of outreach in India and which results in better supply of micro-finance *via* this model. Instantaneously, in Assam there are a few professional MFIs and institutions like ASOMI able to receive foreign investment and now on the verge of finalization of securitization process. Similarly, premier MFI like SKS in India shows the way of receiving equity capital from open market.

Demand-Supply Gap of Micro-finance in Assam

In the previous sub-section the condition of demand for and supply of micro-finance are discussed separately. In this section it is tried to portray the mismatch between the two with the help of Table 2.4. It is clear from the table that for all loan sizes (except ₹ 2,000 and ₹ 5,000 in Southern region of India) micro-finance supply is deficient to meet micro-finance demand. As it is observed the gap is more prominent with the larger loan sizes than smaller loan sizes. Considering MiX Market average loan size, it depicts that micro-finance supply is 98.9 percentages deficient to meet the demand of micro-finance of Assam. Similarly, in India micro-finance supply only cater 3 percentages of total demand indicating a gap of 97.1 percentages.

Table 2.3: Region-wise Micro-finance Supply in India (as on 2009)

Region/State	*SBLP Model*		*MFI Model*		*Total*		*Regional Share to All India Total*		*Share of MFI Model*		*Share to GDP#*
	Client Outreach (in lakh)	*Loan Portfolio (in ₹ crore)*	*Client Outreach (in lakh)*	*Loan Portfolio (in ₹ crore)*	*Client Outreach (in lakh)*	*Loan Out-standing (in ₹ crore)*	*Client Outreach (in %)*	*Loan Out-standing (in %)*	*Client Outreach (in %)*	*Loan Out-standing (in %)*	*(in %)*
NR	24.98	678.92	2.92	290.56	27.90	969.48	3.34	2.80	10.47	29.97	0.02
Assam	**13.33**	**328.55**	**1.35**	**70.33**	**14.69**	**398.88**	**1.76**	**1.15**	**9.22**	**17.63**	**0.01***
NER	17.67	469.31	1.38	70.33	19.06	539.63	2.28	1.56	7.26	13.03	0.01
ER	140.02	3023.00	30.01	1150.30	170.04	4173.30	20.36	12.05	17.65	27.56	0.08
CR	49.82	2045.33	7.57	363.19	57.39	2408.52	6.87	6.96	13.19	15.08	0.05
WR	59.02	1551.15	5.84	273.63	64.86	1824.78	7.77	5.27	9.00	15.00	0.04
SR	342.14	14912.14	153.77	9793.30	495.91	24705.43	59.38	71.36	31.01	39.64	0.50
India	**633.65**	**22679.84**	**201.49**	**11941.30**	**835.15**	**34621.14**			**24.13**	**34.49**	**0.70**

\# Share to GDP indicates supply of micro-finance as percentage of GDP of India at current prices for the year 2008-09.

* Although the supply of micro-finance shares 0.01 percentage of GDP of India, it was 0.58 percentage of the Net State Domestic Product of Assam.

Note: Calculation done by author.

Source: Bharat Micro-finance Quick Data 2010, Sa-Dhan Micro-finance in India 2009, NABARD; MiX Market, Online Database (Accessed August 2010).

Table 2.4: Regional Demand and Supply Condition of Micro-finance in India

Micro-finance Demand and Supply	*Loan Size (₹)*	*Assam*	*Northern*	*NER*	*Eastern*	*Central*	*Western*	*Southern*	*All India*
Micro-finance Demand (₹ in lakh millions)	2,000	0.23	0.27	0.30	2.13	2.28	0.82	0.96	7.09
	5,000	0.58	0.68	0.75	5.32	5.70	2.04	2.40	17.73
	10,000	1.16	1.36	1.51	10.63	11.40	4.08	4.80	35.47
	15,000	1.75	2.03	2.26	15.95	17.09	6.12	7.21	53.20
	20,000	2.33	2.71	3.02	21.26	22.79	8.17	9.61	70.94
	25,000	2.91	3.39	3.77	26.58	28.49	10.21	12.01	88.67
	33,175	3.86	4.50	5.00	35.27	37.80	13.55	15.94	117.67
Micro-finance Supply (₹ in lakh millions)		0.04	0.10	0.05	0.42	0.24	0.18	2.47	3.46
Gap of Micro-finance Supply to Micro-finance Demand (in %)	2,000	–82.82	–63.14	–83.42	–80.25	–89.47	–77.96	157.06	–51.22
	5,000	–93.13	–85.26	–93.37	–92.10	–95.79	–91.18	2.82	–80.49
	10,000	–96.56	–92.63	–96.68	–96.05	–97.89	–95.59	–48.59	–90.24
	15,000	–97.71	–95.09	–97.79	–97.37	–98.60	–97.06	–65.73	–93.50
	20,000	–98.28	–96.31	–98.34	–98.02	–98.95	–97.80	–74.29	–95.12
	25,000	–98.63	–97.05	–98.67	–98.42	–99.16	–98.24	–79.44	–96.10
	33,175	–98.96	–97.78	–99.00	–98.81	–99.37	–98.67	–84.50	–97.06

Note: Calculation done by author.
Source: Bharat Micro-finance Quick Data 2010, Sa-Dhan Micro-finance in India 2009, NABARD, MiX Market, Online Database.

The gap is due to the absence of adequate number of MFIs in rural areas of the state in concern and the country as a whole. NABARD's effort in SHG financing is also unable to mitigate the demand gap since there are a large number of remote rural areas in Assam as well as India are untouched and as a result they are out of the coverage of micro-finance operation. Further SBLP is also plagued with a number of problems in catering finance to a considerable number of SHGs; out of which reluctance as expressed by public undertaking commercial banks to offer micro-finance in view of the problem growing NPA in micro-finance sector is the most prominent one.

Even more, there exists still a large rural area as geographically remote in the country and MFIs also reluctant to offer the services due to the absence of supportive financial infrastructure and high transaction and operational cost of the services. It, therefore, appears that both public and private initiative should be constructed in a positive way for the proliferation of the sector in the state.

IV

Financial Inclusion in North-East India

While there is large extent of financial exclusion in all parts of the country, the North-East, Eastern and Central regions contain most of the financially excluded population (Thorat, 2007). Therefore, it is imperative to analyze the policy initiative for financial inclusion.

Policy Initiative by Reserve Bank of India (RBI)

The RBI has adopted a structured, planned and integrated approach towards FI by focusing on both the demand and supply side constraints. Some of the defining features of RBI's approach to FI are:

- (i) Adoption of bank-led model for FI. However, non-bank entities are also permitted to partner banks in their FI initiatives.
- (ii) The self-sustainability and commercial viability of the FI initiatives.
- (iii) Leverage technology to attain greater reach and penetration while keeping the cost of providing financial services to the minimum.
- (iv) Adoption of innovative business models and delivery channels to expand their FI efforts.
- (v) RBI has adopted an integrated approach wherein efforts towards Financial Inclusion and Financial Literacy would go hand in

hand. Besides the various initiatives taken by RBI individually to encourage financial literacy, a *National Strategy for Financial Education* (NSFE) has also been finalized under the aegis of the Financial Stability and Development Council (FSDC) to coordinate efforts of various stakeholders involved in this process.

Moreover, RBI has adopted a number of initiatives in four broad areas, which are discussed below:

(a) Reach: In this endeavour the following policies are adopted:

(i) Branch expansion in rural areas — Branch authorization has been relaxed to the extent that banks do not require prior permission to open branches in centres with population less than 1 lakh, which is subject to reporting.

(ii) Agent banking through Business Correspondent/Business Facilitator Model was initiated in January 2006. RBI permitted banks to utilize the services of intermediaries in providing banking services through the use of business facilitators and business correspondents.

(iii) RBI permitted to have a combination of physical branch network and BCs for extending financial inclusion, especially in geographically dispersed areas.

(b) Access: A majority of unbanked population are excluded from formal financial services due to stringent banking norms, which basically prevent access. RBI has made a number of corrective measures to have better access and to increase financial inclusion. These are:

(i) Know Your Customer norms are relaxed with the following extent:

(a) Know Your Customer (KYC) requirements have been simplified to such an extent that small accounts can be opened with self-certification in the presence of bank officials.

(b) RBI has allowed 'Aadhaar' to be used as one of the eligible documents for meeting the KYC requirement for opening a bank account.

(ii) Roadmap for Banking Services in unbanked villages:

(a) In the first phase, banks were advised to draw up a roadmap for providing banking services in every village having a population of over 2,000 by March 2010.

(b) In the second phase, Roadmap has been prepared for covering remaining unbanked villages, i.e. with population less than 2000 in a time bound manner.

(c) Products: The following policy initiatives are adopted:

(i) Bouquet of Financial services: In order to ensure that all the financial needs of the customers are met, RBI advised banks to offer a minimum of four basic products, viz.

(a) A savings-*cum*-overdraft account;
(b) A pure savings account, ideally a recurring or variable recurring deposit;
(c) A remittance product to facilitate EBT and other remittances; and
(d) Entrepreneurial credit products like a General Purpose Credit Card (GCC) or a Kisan Credit Card (KCC).

(d) Transactions: Direct beneficiary transfer (DBT) is a recent introduction in this area. DBT, leveraging the Aadhaar platform, will help facilitate delivery of social welfare benefits by direct credit to the bank accounts of beneficiaries. In order to ensure smooth roll out of the Government's DBT initiative, banks have been advised to:

(i) Open accounts of all eligible individuals in camp mode with the support of local Government authorities.
(ii) Seed the existing and new accounts with Aadhaar numbers.
(iii) Put in place an effective mechanism to monitor and review the progress in implementation of DBT.

Moreover, RBI has encouraged banks to adopt a structured and planned approach to financial inclusion with commitment at the highest levels, through preparation of Board approved Financial Inclusion Plans (FIPs). The first phase of FIPs was implemented during the period 2010-13.

Table 2.5 depicts progress under financial inclusion plans. The table indicates that all the parameters mentioned in the table increase considerably over the period 2011-12. It is revealed in the table that total number of Customer Service Points deployment is increased by 91 per cent over the period. Similarly, banking outlets in villages have also increased considerably by 56 per cent during the period. It is interesting to note that Business Centre consists a lion's share (77%) in total banking outlets in villages in 2012.

Table 2.5: Progress under Financial Inclusion Plans

Sl.No.	*Particulars*	*As on March 2011*	*As on March 2012*
1.	Total no. of customer service points deployed	60,993	1,16,548
2.	Total banking outlets in villages, *of which*	1,16,208	1,81,753
	2.1 Branches	34,811	37,471
	2.2 BCs	80,802	1,41,136
	2.3 Other modes	595	3,146
3.	Urban Locations covered through BCs	3,771	5,891
4.	ICT-Based A/cs — through BCs (No. in millions)	32	57
5.	ICT-Based A/cs — Transactions (No. in millions)	84	141
6.	ICT-Based A/cs — Transactions (₹ billion)	58	93
7.	Number of No-Frill Accounts (in millions)	105	139
8.	Amount in No-Frill Accounts (₹ billion)	76	120
9.	Number of No-Frill Accounts with OD (in millions)	0.6	2.7
10.	Amount in No-Frill A/cs with OD (₹ billion)	0.3	1.1
11.	Number of KCCs-outstanding (in millions)	27	30
12.	Amount in KCCs-outstanding (₹ billion)	1,600	2,068
13.	Number of GCCs-outstanding (in millions)	1.7	2.1
14.	Amount in GCCs-outstanding (₹ billion)	35	42

Source: Trends and Progress of Banking in India, 2011-12.

Status of Financial Inclusion in North-East India

This section discusses the recent status of financial inclusion in North-East India *vis-à-vis* India. Table 2.6 portrays some of the popular parameters of financial inclusion. It is clearly depicted in the table that approximately 93 percentage of allotted villages are covered where 2.8 crore accounts opened as in February 2012.

The table reveals that North-East India shares an infinitesimal size of the all areas. However, it is interesting to note that Arunachal Pradesh has achieved the target faster as compared to the rest of the North-Eastern states of India. Out of 3,232 villages to be covered under FI programme, Assam considerably shares a large size (72%). However, Assam achieved 80 per cent target in this category.

Table 2.7 depicts, financial inclusion for different periods in Indian states. The table is adapted from Chakravarty and Pal (2012) to show the condition of financial inclusion in three different periods, such as pre-social banking[10], social banking[11] and post-social banking period.[12]

Table 2.6: Status of FIP Progress in North-East India (as on 29-02-2012)

Name of State/ Region	*Total No. of Villages Allotted*	*No. of Villages Covered*	*No. of Villages Yet to be Covered*	*Total No. of FI Accounts Opened*
North-East	3,232 (4.3)	2,589 (3.7)	643 (12.1)	10,52,377 (3.8)
Arunachal Pradesh	11 (0.0)	10 (0.0)	1 (0.0)	45,251 (0.2)
Assam	2,327 (3.1)	1,867 (2.7)	460 (8.6)	3,49,385 (1.2)
Manipur	186 (0.2)	100 (0.1)	86 (1.6)	1,781 (0.0)
Meghalaya	39 (0.1)	31 (0.0)	8 (0.2)	71,505 (0.3)
Mizoram	14 (0.0)	3 (0.0)	11 (0.2)	1,816 (0.0)
Nagaland	193 (0.3)	117 (0.2)	76 (1.4)	1,24,822 (0.4)
Sikkim	43 (0.1)	42 (0.1)	1 (0.0)	14,945 (0.1)
Tripura	419 (0.6)	419 (0.6)	0 (0.0)	4,42,872 (1.6)
Rest of India	71,169 (95.7)	66,489 (96.3)	4,680 (87.9)	2,69,36,947 (96.2)
India	**74,401**	**69,078**	**5,323**	**2,79,89,324**

Source: SLBC Convenors.

Table 2.7 considers 17 states of India, where only two North-Eastern States, viz. Assam and Tripura are included. It is clearly revealed from the table that two states of North-Eastern region of India failed to keep the target of financial inclusion during the mentioned period, which is revealed by Index of Financial Inclusion (IFI). While, Kerala topped the march for financial inclusion in all the mentioned period, Assam remains in the bottom place during social banking period and post-social banking period.

The table does not portray a comparative picture of financial inclusion. Therefore, to make a comparative analysis, IFI is calculated for North-Eastern state based on the methodology of Sarma and Pais (2008). Table 2.7 portrays IFI of 7 NER states, where it depicts that Manipur leads the march for financial inclusion, which is followed by Meghalaya. Nagaland is far lagging behind in terms of financial inclusion.

Table 2.7: Financial Inclusion for Different Periods in Indian States

State/Region	Mean of Financial Inclusion Index (I)					
	Pre-Social Banking Period 1972-1976		Social Banking Period 1977-1990		Post-Social Banking Period 1991-2009	
	$I_{pre\text{-}ob}$	Rank	I_{ob}	Rank	$I_{post\text{-}ob}$	Rank
Andhra Pradesh	0.129	9	0.310	10	0.433	8
Assam	0.040	16	0.168	17	0.286	17
Bihar	0.090	12	0.252	12	0.360	12
Gujarat	0.221	5	0.334	8	0.403	10
Haryana	0.142	8	0.315	9	0.428	9
Himachal Pradesh	0.122	10	0.336	7	0.485	6
Karnataka	0.228	4	0.406	3	0.520	5
Kerala	0.244	1	0.495	1	0.648	1
Madhya Pradesh	0.076	14	0.231	14	0.328	15
Maharashtra	0.238	2	0.376	5	0.525	4
Orissa	0.031	17	0.210	16	0.341	14
Punjab	0.236	3	0.451	2	0.589	2
Rajasthan	0.088	13	0.226	15	0.316	16
Tamil Nadu	0.217	6	0.386	4	0.536	3
Tripura	0.042	15	0.238	13	0.351	13
Uttar Pradesh	0.102	11	0.261	11	0.381	11
West Bengal	0.201	7	0.356	6	0.453	7
Range	**0.213**		**0.327**		**0.362**	
All-India	**0.152**		**0.307**		**0.419**	

Note: Financial inclusion index is measured by considering $r = 0.75$.
Source: Chakravarty and Pal, 2012.

Table 2.8: Financial Inclusion Index for North-Eastern States (as on 2012)

State	Index of Financial Inclusion
Arunachal Pradesh	0.190
Assam	0.188
Manipur	0.427
Meghalaya	0.259
Mizoram	0.205
Nagaland	0.183
Tripura	0.250

Source: Calculated by author.

V

Issues of Micro-finance in Financial Inclusion and Conclusion

Tables 2.7 and 2.8 reveal that NER states are lagging far behind in achieving the objective of financial inclusion. Although both Central and State Governments have been adopting a number of states, the desired results differ context to context. Moreover, the banking sector now-a-days has moved to priority sector, which help in achieving the goal of financial inclusion to some extent.

In the context of financial inclusion there is an ongoing debate over the issue of micro-finance as a strategy of financial inclusion. While some group favour the case of micro-finance as a tool of financial inclusion, others defy its potentiality as a tool of financial inclusion by showing the failure of micro-finance in combating poverty.

The overviews suggested some issues regarding micro-finance as a tool of financial inclusion. These are outlined below:

(i) *Transaction Cost:* The issue of transaction cost is equally important for both demand and supply side. From demand side, customers have still to incur an amount before realization of credit. This is due to the formality of loan application procedure. The cost associated with the loan sometimes create problem within the group. Similarly, transaction cost is a big issue in micro-finance operation especially under MFI model. Larger transaction cost has an impact on the rate of interest rate and thus cost of capital for the borrowers will become higher.

(ii) *Non-Repayment and NPA Problem:* Another serious problem associated with micro-finance operation is non-repayment and NPA problem. Non-repayment has an impact on financially sustainability and thus it may hamper on the sustainable operation of the programme.

(iii) *Client Exit:* Client exit in terms of exhausted demand is also an issue in this concern.

(iv) *Exploitation of Vulnerability:* Since micro-finance is designed for poor, they are exploited in terms of security money and higher annualized tax rate.

(v) *Over Debt and Multiple Debt:* The issue of over and multiple debt is also important issue related to the issue of financial inclusion. The case of Andhra Pradesh crisis and some study revealed that micro-finance sustainability would be in stake if demand side is completely overlooked. Borrower run is also a similar problem in this regard.

In conclusion, it can be maintained that in an economy with the vast majority of the people living in the rural areas, if development is to take place and become self-sustaining, it should start in the rural areas in general and the agricultural sector in particular (Todaro and Smith, 2003). The statement is equally applicable in case of North-East India, where rural population dominates the population size (Census of India, 2011). The present study indicates that financial inclusion is required to be geared up in North-Eastern states. In this endeavour apart from banking institutions micro-finance sector has a major role to play, since there is high micro-finance demand in the North-East India. But, envisaging micro-finance as a tool of financial inclusion has to be carefully instrument and monitored. The Micro-finance Development and Regulation Bill, 2012 have an immense role if it becomes an Act. The Bill provides security for both the supply and demand side and equally it has provision of financial inclusion in terms of setting up micro-finance equity fund.

NOTES

1. According to Asian Development Bank, micro-finance services are supplied by three types of sources. These are: formal institutions (i.e., rural banks and cooperatives); semi-formal institutions (i.e., non-governmental organizations); and informal sources (i.e., moneylenders and shopkeepers). Institutional micro-finance includes micro-finance services provided by both formal and semi-formal institutions. Micro-finance institutions are institutions whose major business is the provision of micro-finance services.
2. Joint liability lending is the provision of a private goods in return for a public goods (Matin, 1997). It involves the provision of loans to a group of individuals such that they are jointly liable to the repayment of the loan.
3. Self-Help Group model and Micro-finance Institutions models are two dominant models in India.
4. Self-Help Group Bank Linkages Programme is a huge micro-finance programme under the aegis of National Bank for Agricultural and Rural Development, which covers 8.6 crore poor households as on 31st March, 2009 in India.
5. For example, Guangwen (2010) estimated micro-finance demand in China and George *et al.* (2007) estimated micro-finance demand for India.
6. Since most of the data of Census 2011 are provisional in nature, the present study avoid adoption of these data.
7. Average loan size of the 1,132 MFIs was calculated at $710.68 as against $533.4 which was equivalent to ₹ 33,175. This is due to the fact that where the former is actual average loan size; the latter is average loan balance per borrower.
8. By micro-loan slab, it meant that in India loan under micro-finance sector is fragmented by the performance of the clients and by client group. The range of loan is ₹ 2,000 — 25,000, where ₹ 2,000 is the lower ceiling of micro-loan which is basically advanced for a fresh group or client. It is basically more prominent in SHGs rather than JLGs. As the client or group become trustworthy through outstanding repayment performance the group or client becomes eligible for an advanced tier of loan.
9. Indian average is based on the average loan portfolio of 88 MFIs reported to MIX Market database.
10. Pre-social banking period indicates period from 1972 to 1976.
11. Social banking period indicates period from 1977 to 1990.
12. Post-social banking period indicates period after 1991.

3

FINANCIAL INCLUSION IN NORTH-EAST INDIA: An Outline

Jyoti Bikash Chakma

Introduction

Financial Inclusion has emerged as a tool for the socio-economic development of the society. The basket of financial services under Financial Inclusion will create an opportunity to capture the underserved market fulfilling corporate social responsibility thereby driving the economic growth of the country. Financial inclusion has become one of the most critical aspects in the context of inclusive growth and development of a region or a country. The importance of an inclusive financial system is widely recognized in policy circles and has become a policy priority in many countries. Several countries across the globe now look at financial inclusion as the means to more comprehensive growth, wherein each citizen of the country is able to use earnings as a financial resource that can be put to work to improve future financial status and adding to the nation's progress.

The concept of financial inclusion in India can be traced back to the year 1904 when cooperative movement took place in India. It gained momentum in 1969 when 14 major commercial banks of the country were nationalized and lead bank scheme was introduced shortly thereafter. Branches were opened in large numbers across the country and even in the areas which were hitherto being neglected. Even after all these measures a sizable portion of the population of the country could not be brought under the fold of banking system. In fact, there is a severe gap in financial access which needs special attention.

Financial Inclusion: An Overview

Financial inclusion is delivery of banking services at an affordable cost to the vast sections of underprivileged and low income groups. By financial inclusion we mean the provision of affordable financial services, viz. access to payments and remittance facilities, savings, loans and insurance services by the formal financial system to those who tend to be excluded. RBI defines financial inclusion as "a process of ensuring access to appropriate financial products and services needed by all sections of the society in general and vulnerable groups such as weaker sections and low income groups in particular, at an affordable cost in a fair and transparent manner by regulated mainstream institutional players." Rangarajan Committee (2008) viewed financial inclusion as "the process of ensuring access to financial services and timely and adequate credit where needed by vulnerable groups such as weaker sections and low income groups at an affordable cost." The financial services include the entire gamut — savings, loans, insurance, credit, payments, etc. By providing these services, the aim is to help them come out of poverty.

Thus, financial inclusion needed for equal opportunities to all sections of people in country, inclusive growth, economic development, social development and business opportunity.

The access to finance could be divided into five segments:

(i) The proportion of the population that uses a bank or bank like institution,
(ii) Population which uses services from non-bank "other formal" financial institutions, but does not use bank services,
(iii) The population which only uses services from information financial service providers,
(iv) Percentage of population transacting regularly through formal financial instrument, and
(v) The population which uses no financial services.

Financial Inclusion in India

Financial Inclusion in India is not a new one. Nationalization of banks, priority sector lending stipulations, the lead bank scheme, establishment of Regional Rural Banks, launch of Self-Help Groups-banks linkage programmes were all part of the Reserve Bank of India's initiative to provide financial access to the unbanked and under-banked masses. However, the momentum gathered after 2005, when the regulator highlighted the need for financial inclusion in its Annual Policy Statement, and a symbolic beginning was made in the same year, Indian Bank brought all households in Mangalam Village in Pondicherry within its fold. The Reserve Bank of India's vision for 2020 has envisaged on opening of nearly 600 million new customers' accounts and service them through a variety of chann·i by leveraging on Information Technology. However, illiteracy and the low income savings and lack of bank branches in rural areas continue to be a road block to financial inclusion in many states.

The importance of financial inclusion arises from the problem of financial exclusion of nearly 3 billion people from the formal financial services across the world. With only 34 per cent of population engaged in formal banking, India has 135 million financially excluded households, the second highest number after China. Further, the real rate of financial inclusion in India is also very low and about 40 per cent of the bank account holders use their accounts not even once a month. Financial Inclusion has far reaching consequences, which can help many people come out of abject poverty conditions. Therefore, India being a socialist, democratic republic, it is imperative on the policies of the government to ensure equitable growth of all sections of the economy. The financially excluded sector in India consists largely of landless labourers, oral lessees, marginal farmers, unorganized sector work-force, urban slum residents and socially excluded groups. With 82 per cent of India's poor households located in rural locations, vast majority of rural India can be considered as financially excluded. Some of the important causes of relatively low extension of institutional credit in the rural areas are risk perception, cost of its assessment and management, lack of rural infrastructure, and vast geographical spread of the rural areas with more than half a million villages, some sparsely populated (Mohan, 2006).

Table 3.1 indicates that, out of 3,29,02,390 total current accounts and savings accounts of banking services in All India, 27.44 per cent of total accounts are in South India, 20.71 per cent of total accounts are in

Table 3.1: Coverage of Banking Services in India

Sl. No.	*Region*	*Current Accounts*	*Saving Accounts*	*Total Population*	*Total No. of Accounts*	*Total No. of Accounts (%)*
1.	North	4215701	52416125	32576462	56631826	17.65
2.	North-East	476603	6891081	38495089	7367684	2.3
3.	East	1814219	47876140	227613073	49690359	15.48
4.	Central	2202217	64254189	255713495	66456406	20.71
5.	West	3178102	49525101	149071747	52703203	16.42
6.	South	4666014	83386898	223445381	88052912	27.44
	All India	**16552856**	**304349534**	**1027015247**	**320902390**	**100.00**

Sources: National Sample Survey Organization (2012).

Central India, 17.65 per cent of total accounts are in North India, 16.42 per cent of total accounts are in West India, 15.48 per cent of total accounts are in East India and 2.3 per cent of total accounts are in North-East India. So, it is concluded that, the maximum number of 27.44 per cent of total accounts are in South India.

Some key statistics regarding the extent of financial inclusion in India are as follows:

- 41 per cent of the Indian population is unbanked (80 million households). Out of this, 40 per cent are unbanked in urban areas and 60 per cent in rural areas. Only 14 per cent of adult population has credit accounts with formal financial institutions.
- Out of 203 million households in India, 147 million households are located in rural India. Out of these rural households, 89.3 million households are farmer households. 66 per cent of farmer households are marginal farmer households.
- 51.4 per cent farmer households (45.9 million out of 89.3 million) are financially excluded from both formal and informal financial sources.
- 27 per cent farmer households have access to formal sources of credit. Among non-cultivator households nearly 80 per cent do not access credit from any source
- North-East, Eastern and Central India account for 64 per cent of all financially excluded farmer households in India. Overall indebtedness to formal finance sources is 19.66 per cent in these three regions.
- Geographically, 256 districts (out of 640 districts) representing 40 per cent of total districts in India, spread over 17 states and 1 UT have critical credit exclusion thresholds in respect of access to formal credit.
- The proportion of people having some form of life insurance cover stands at 10 per cent and people with any form of non-life insurance cover stands at less than 1 per cent. There are only 3.1 policies per thousand people in India (2007).

North-East India and Its Current State of Financial Inclusion

The North-East India comprises contiguous eight states of Arunachal Pradesh, Assam, Nagaland, Manipur, Meghalaya, Mizoram, Tripura and Sikkim — is geographically, ethnically and culturally different from the rest of the country. While significant initiatives have been taken by the government towards inclusion of the financially excluded in the country, the challenge gets accentuated for the north-eastern region due to its inherent characteristics that make it difficult to implement or replicate the inclusion models adopted elsewhere in the country. In fact, the banking development in North-East India was, only a post-nationalization phenomenon. Prior to nationalization of banks in 1969, no bank branch of commercial banks existed in Arunachal Pradesh and Mizoram. Only two branches of commercial banks served the entire state in Manipur and Nagaland. Assam, however, with tea and oil industries was historically better served by banks among the states in the region. Since nationalization of banks in 1969, a remarkable progress was made in the banking development both geographically and demographically. Though starting from a low base, the branch network of commercial banks expanded significantly in the region. However, banking development is still lagging far behind all other states in India. Even within the region, the inequalities in the availability of banking services are found to be very wide and glaring.

Table 3.2 reveals that the number of rural bank branches ranged from 37 in Nagaland to 791 in the state of Assam. Population per branch shows that Manipur has the highest whereas Sikkim got a population of 8252 per bank branch which seems a got sign of financial inclusion in the state. The Credit-Deposit ratio ranged from 24 in Mizoram to 41 in Manipur which is lower than the national average of 73. The regional

Table 3.2: Major aspects of Financial Inclusion in North-East India (as on March 2010)

States	*Bank Branches (Number)*		*Population per Branch (Number)*	*Bank Branches per 1000 sq.km.*	*C-D Ratio*	*Ratios of Deposit and Credit Accounts to Population (2009-10)*		*Per Capita Deposits and Credit (Amount in ₹)*	
	Total	*Rural*				*Deposit*	*Credit*	*Deposit*	*Credit*
A.P.	80	51	17282	1	27	37.7	4.1	29843	8218
Assam	1477	791	21103	19	36	36.8	4.2	15590	5892
Manipur	81	35	33602	3	41	18.1	2.7	9917	4170
Meghalaya	213	126	13916	9	26	30.9	3.9	25785	6605
Mizoram	98	54	11133	4	24	29.7	5.4	20525	10916
Nagaland	90	37	22007	5	30	24.3	4.6	21140	6406
Sikkim	74	48	8252	10	37	56.9	7.2	51561	19188
Tripura	192	114	19120	22	25	46.2	8.3	20319	5999
NER	2342	1256	19465	9	35	39.8	4.9	16879	6255
All India	86960	32627	13916	26	73	60.7	9.8	37688	27642

Source: http://www.mdoner.gov.in/content/financial-inclusion

average of 9 in respect to the bank branches per 1000 km^2 is comparatively much lower than the All India average of 26, which signify the low standard of financial inclusion in the region. Hence, all these banking development indicators show the slow progress of banking and resultant low level of financial outreach in North-East India.

Development of North-East India has been high on the agenda of the Central and the respective State governments. Recognizing the special requirements of the region and the need for significant levels of government investment, North-East India has been recognized as Special Category Region. The Government of India and the Reserve Bank have initiated various measures for spread of banking and promotion of financial inclusion. Nevertheless, to accelerate the pace of growth in North-East India, some of the challenges that lie ahead are highlighted hereunder:

- First, weak market linkages are a major constraint in the development of the region. For this reason, urgent attention needs to be paid to developing roads, air links, telecommunications and other components of transport and communications. Investment in infrastructure could be scaled up through the Public-Private Partnership model.
- Second, initiatives need to be taken to promote sustainable industrial development compatible with the unique bio-diversity of the region. Agro-based industries, food processing, wood products, traditional textiles and light manufacturing industries can be encouraged to come up in the region.
- Third, there is a need to increase agricultural productivity and promote diversification into horticulture and floriculture for which the agro-climatic conditions in the region are well-suited.
- Fourth, a sustainable growth paradigm will not only help further acceleration in growth but will also improve fiscal sustainability by helping to lower the debt-GSDP ratio.
- Fifth, the high level of literacy and human development levels coupled with bio-diversity provides ample opportunity for development of tourism and exports.
- Sixth, a deterrent for bank lending is the high level of non-performing assets (NPAs) in the region. This has been, in part, due to unavailability of some of the activities financed by banks and lack of adequate engagement with the borrowers. There is, therefore, a need to improve credit culture in which financial education could play a vital role.

- Seventh, in any plan for financial sector development, the physical presence of a bank branch is important. But the topography of the region, the dispersal of population, transport bottlenecks and law and order conditions in some areas inhibit branch expansion other than in certain commercial centres. Hence, all the stakeholders — banks, State governments and the Reserve Bank — need to work in close coordination for increasing banking penetration and promoting financial inclusion in the region.

The regional economy of the north-east is largely dependent on agriculture, and most other economic activity is small-scale and heavily dependent on traditional skills of weaving and handicraft. Inadequate infrastructure is another major challenge that isolates the region from the rest of the country. This has led to the development of a diversely-organized informal financial market in the region, which reflects the creativity of local communities to meet their specific needs. The solution lies in developing low-cost banking models, by leveraging technology and forging local partnerships, and this is an opportune time to actualize execution of the financial inclusion strategy for the north-eastern region (Kapoor, 2011). While significant initiatives have been taken by the government towards inclusion of the financially excluded in the country, the challenge gets accentuated for the north-eastern region due to its inherent characteristics that make it difficult to implement or replicate the inclusion models adopted elsewhere in the country. The financial inclusion strategy for North-East India needs to be built around the existing developments and trends in the region, and initiatives being taken by the government.

Factors Affecting the Access of Financial Inclusion

Following are the factors that affect the basic access of financial inclusion in India:

- **Psychological and Cultural Barriers:** Many people voluntarily excluded themselves due to psychological barriers and they think that they are excluded from accessing financial services.
- **Lack of Legal Identity:** Lack of legal identity like voter Id, driving licence, birth certificates, employment identity card, etc.
- **Level of Income Decides Financial Access:** Low income people generally have the attitude of thinking that banks are only for the rich.

- **Various Terms and Conditions:** While getting loans or at the time of opening accounts, banks place many conditions, so the uneducated and poor people find it very difficult to access financial services.
- **Lack of Customized Products:** As people differ in their perception, opinions and thoughts so does their needs, the banking industry has to understand this basic philosophy and develop customer centric innovative products. The whole banking industry is offering generic products matching the needs of urbanized population and arsenal of other services whereas the unbanked still remains to see the light of the dawn.
- **Lack of Financial Literacy:** Financial literacy and lack of basic education prevent people to have access from financial services. Low literacy rate has been a great impediment for financial inclusion as ignorance caused low levels of awareness causing difficulty to communicate the necessity for banking habits and what savings can do to enrich their living standards.
- **Language Barrier:** One of the major hitch in financial inclusion being non-availability of printed literature in regional vernaculars which is otherwise a prerequisite for reaching the masses. As most of the literature in the banking industry are in bilingual mode (Hindi/English), with large demographic spread are habitually jeopardize by the ignorance of language which creating a fear psychosis.
- **Geographical Remoteness:** Commercial banks operate only in profitable areas. Banks set their branches and offices only in those commercial areas. Therefore, people living in underdeveloped areas find it very difficult to go for any bank transaction in other area again and again. Hence, they don't go for any bank services.
- **Infrastructural Requirements:** With the liberalization branch opening under new branch authorization policy of RBI which encourages the opening of branches in underbanked or unbanked areas. Infrastructural deployments are not that enthusiastic to run even a satellite operation which requires power, telecommunication services and roads for geographical access.

Initiatives Undertaken for the Growth of Financial Inclusion

Reserve Bank of India and Government play an important role in promoting financial inclusion for economic growth to increase the banking penetration in the country. Before 1990s, several initiatives have been undertaken which included creation of State Bank of India in 1955; nationalization of commercial banks in 1969 and 1980; initiating the Lead Bank Scheme in 1970; was a big step to expand financial inclusion. Priority sector lending norms, branch licensing norms with focus on rural and semi-urban branches, National Bank for Agriculture and Rural Development (NABARD) was set up in 1982 mainly to provide refinance to the banks extending credit to agriculture, establishment of regional rural banks in 1975 are also the major steps for same aim which encourage branch expansion in rural area (Raman, 2012).

The Reserve Bank of India is navigating the path to financial inclusion by means of regulations and guidance. It has initiated several measures to help bank the unbanked. Some of them are:

- **Opening of No-frills Accounts:** Basic banking no-frills account is with nil or very low minimum balance as well as charges that make such accounts accessible to vast sections of the population. Banks have been advised to provide small overdrafts in such accounts.
- **Relaxation on Know Your Customer (KYC) Norms:** KYC requirements for opening bank accounts were relaxed for small accounts in August 2005, thereby simplifying procedures by stipulating that introduction by an account holder who has been subjected to the full KYC drill would suffice for opening such accounts. The banks were also permitted to take any evidence as to the identity and address of the customer to their satisfaction.
- **Overcoming Language Barrier:** Large sections of the Indian population are not familiar with English and Hindi, the languages mostly used in bank forms. Banks are, therefore, required to provide forms pertaining to account opening disclosure, etc. in the regional language as well.
- **Simplification of Savings Bank Account Opening Form:** To ease the opening of bank account by the migratory labour, street hawkers and other poorer sections of the society, "Simplified Account Opening Form" has been designed. Banks have been requested to put in place a system to enable the customer to fill the account opening form on an 'online' mode.
- **Engaging Business Correspondents (BCs):** RBI permitted banks to engage business facilitators (BFs) and BCs as intermediaries for providing financial and banking services. The BC model

allows banks to provide doorstep delivery of services, especially cash in-cash out transactions, thus addressing the last-mile problem.

- **Opening of Branches in Unbanked Rural Centres:** To further step up the opening of branches in rural areas so as to improve banking penetration and financial inclusion rapidly, the need for the opening of more bricks and mortar branches, besides the use of BCs, was felt.
- **Simplified Branch Authorization:** To address the issue of uneven spread of bank branches, in December 2009, domestic scheduled commercial banks were permitted to freely open branches in tier III to tier VI centres with a population of less than 50,000 under general permission, subject to reporting. On the other hand, banks can open branches in any centre — rural, semi-urban or urban — in the North-East without applying for permission each time, again subject to reporting.
- **Electronic Bank Transfer:** The introduction of Information and Communications Technology (ICT) facilitates the electronic transfer of social security benefits directly to the beneficiaries. This reduces dependence on cash, thereby lowering the transaction costs and minimizing the chances of fraud by unscrupulous middlemen.
- **Financial Education:** Financial literacy will go a long way in achieving financial inclusion. Accordingly, the RBI has initiated several financial education measures. For example, it publishes comic strips to explain the concept of savings.

Special Financial Inclusion Measures for NES

Highlights of some of the special financial inclusion measures initiated by the Government of India for North-East India:

First, in December 2009, the Reserve Bank relaxed the branch authorization policy and permitted domestic scheduled commercial banks (other than RRBs) to open branches in rural, semi-urban and urban centres in North-East India without having the need to take permission from the Reserve Bank in each case, subject to reporting.

Second, to improve banking penetration in the North-East India, the Reserve Bank requested the state governments and banks to identify centres where there is a need for setting up either full-fledged branches or those offering foreign exchange facilities, handling government business or for meeting currency requirements.

Conclusion

Financial inclusion is the road which India needs to travel towards becoming a global player. As people invest and save more and more will remove vicious circle of poverty and unemployment, it also act as a source of empowerment, better control of finance and allow people to participate more effectively in the economic and social process thereby increase per capita income. The issue of financial inclusion has received large importance in India during the recent years. India had invested considerable amount of resources in expanding its banking network with the objective of reaching to the people. During the last 40 years huge infrastructure has been created in the banking sector. While urban India has been getting access to, and avails itself of banking services at a rising rate, large areas of rural India are still severely underbanked, especially the North-Eastern region of India. Therefore, in achieving complete financial inclusion and for inclusive growth, there is a need for coordinated action between the banks, the government and others to facilitate access to bank accounts amongst the financially excluded so that the financial inclusion can be taken forward. In addition to cooperating with other stakeholders, policymakers who believe that micro-finance can help them to speed up financial inclusion in their respective states should fund financial education programmes that allow their citizens to realize the economic potential of micro-finance. Basic financial literacy programmes can help achieve better results in poverty alleviation. Thus, financial inclusion has enough scope for economic growth, raising living standard of people of a particular region.

REFERENCES

Arulmurugan, P., Karthikeyan, P. and Devi, N. (2013). "Financial Inclusion in India: A Theoretical Assessment", *Indian Journal of Applied Research*, Vol. 3, Issue 3, March, pp. 217-22.

Kapoor, R. (2011). "Enabling Financial Inclusion in North-East", *The Economic Times*. economictimes.indiatimes.com/opinion/view-point/enabling-financial-inclusion-in-north-east/articleshow/8524456.cms accessed on 19th July, 2013.

Mohanty, Deepak, *Economic and Financial Developments in the North-Eastern States*, Speech delivered at Gauhati University on March 24, 2011.
www.rbi.org.in/scripts/BS_SpeechesView.aspx?Id=554 accessed on 15th October, 2013.

Mohan, R. (2006). "Agricultural Credit in India: Status, Issues and Future Agenda", *Economic and Political Weekly* (March), pp. 1013-23.

Rajdeep Sahrawat, *Financial Inclusion — From Obligation to Opportunity*, TCS White Papers.

Raman, A. (2012). "Financial Inclusion and Growth of Indian Banking System", *IOSR Journal of Business and Management* (IOSRJBM), Vol. 1, Issue 3, May-June, pp. 25-29.

Rangarajan, C. (2008). *Report of the Committee on Financial Inclusion in India*, Government of India.

Swamy, V. and Vijayalakshmi (2013). *Role of Financial Inclusion for Inclusive Growth in India — Issues and Challenges*, accessed on 19th September.

4

REACHING THE UNREACHED
Traversing the Issues and Roadmap of Financial Inclusion

Rajashree Dutta Purkayastha

The concept of financial inclusion is long practiced in India. Also, socio-economic developments were treated imperatives for broader financial inclusion and economic growth. Government of India through bank nationalization initiated the attempt to bring financial services within the reach of all segments of the nation. Following which, priority sector lending requirements for banks, lead bank scheme, establishment of regional rural banks (RRBs), service area approach, self-help group-bank linkage programme, etc., were introduced with a view to serve the so long excluded groups and empowering the downtrodden masses. As a result of which a large number of bank branches were set-up aiming to encompass every nook and corner of the country, but in vain. Yet a large group of people, estimated to be around 60 per cent of total Indians do not have access even to the simplest type of formal financial services, i.e. bank account. The proportion of people having any kind of life insurance cover is as low as 10 per cent and proportion having non-life insurance is abysmally low at 0.6 per cent. People having debit cards comprise only 13 per cent and those having credit cards only a marginal 2 per cent of the population (Chakraborty, 2012).

The basic idea of financial inclusion entails the spread of access of formal financial services, products, and facilities to the low income and marginally excluded groups at an affordable cost. *Rangarajan Committee* (2008) viewed financial inclusion as "The process of ensuring access to financial services and timely and adequate credit where needed by vulnerable groups such as weaker sections and low income groups at an affordable cost." Thus, the aim of this concept is to cover all unbanked and underbanked regions and cater to the need of everyone. Measurement of financial inclusion implies to evaluate the extent of accessibility, availability and usage of financial services (Kumar and Mishra, 2011). RBI, in December 2009 explained that financial inclusion is not restricted to mere opening of bank accounts but also includes other facilities as well. Thus, savings, loans, insurance, payments, and remittance facilities, financial counseling were considered under the aegis of financial services. Studies have proved that lack of inclusion or rather exclusion from the banking system results in a loss of 1 per cent to the GDP (Chattopadhyay, 2011). Among the developed nations, UK was one of the earliest to realize the importance of financial inclusion (Kempson, 2004, Collard *et al.*, 2001). Understanding the gravity of the problem, Reserve Bank in its Mid Term Review of Monetary Policy of 2005-06, urged the banks to make financial inclusion as one of their prime objectives. Despite all these efforts, there is lack of equitable financial access across all regions of the country. The major objective of this chapter is to analyze the present status of financial inclusion in North-Eastern states of India.

Literature Review

A good number of studies have been carried out on financial inclusion in academia. According to Chakraborty (2010) financial inclusion is no longer a policy choice but it is a policy compulsion today. Gupta (2011) discussed the steps taken by Reserve Bank of India to foster the needs of weaker sections of the society under the corpus of financial inclusion. It also examines the role of Information and Communications Technology (ICT) in expanding financial inclusion in India. Paramasivan and Ganeshkumar, 2013 outlines the status of financial inclusion in India. Massey (2010) said that, role of financial institutions in a developing country is vital in promoting financial inclusion. Sarma and Paise (2008) suggest that the issue of financial inclusion is a development policy priority in many countries. Using the index of financial inclusion developed in levels of human development and financial inclusion in a country move closely with each other, although a few exceptions exist. Among socio-economic factors, as expected, income is positively associated with the level of financial inclusion. Further physical and electronic connectivity and information availability, indicated by road network, telephone and internet usage, also play positive role in enhancing financial inclusion.

Ananth and Oncu (2013) tries to explore the challenges faced by the financial institutions in Andhra Pradesh with regard to financial inclusion. It further explicates the fact that the inability of formal financial institutions to meet the specific needs of the poor has enabled informal service providers to fill the vacuum. Chattopadhyay (2011) attempts to examine the extent of financial inclusion in the state of West Bengal. An index of financial inclusion is developed in the study which divulged that except Sikkim all the eastern, north-eastern, and central states are in the low level of financial inclusion. Further, out of 7 North-Eastern States, three states, *viz.* Assam, Nagaland and Manipur, score the lowest rank of financial inclusion. It further reveals that despite various measures have been undertaken for financial inclusion, the success is not found to be considerable.

Objectives

This chapter is an attempt to analyze the status of financial inclusion in North-Eastern states. Moreover, it attempts to envisage the steps taken by RBI to foster financial inclusion and to suggest way out for harnessing the negative phenomenon.

Financial Inclusion in India — An Overview

Sarma (2008:3) defines financial inclusion "as a process that ensures the ease of access, availability and usage of the formal financial system for all members of an economy." The World Bank (2008:2) considers financial inclusion as access to financial services. It "implies an absence of obstacles to the use of these services, whether the obstacles are price or non-price barriers to finance." If we mull over the comparative position of India *vis-à-vis* other states in financial inclusion, the following picture gets revealed, where India stands much behind its other counterparts (Table 4.1).

Further analysis upon various parameters of financial inclusion indicates India's position in financial inclusion and also the extent of usage of technology which is having mundane scope in advancing prompt inclusion in the country.

The Economist revealed the status of mobile banking usage among various countries, which shows except South Africa (where only 9% of total adult population are regular user), all other countries have a meagre percentage (hardly 1% or 2%) of population who use mobile banking for various transactions.

Table 4.1: Select Indicators of Fi.ancial Inclusion — Cross Country Comparison

Country	*Number of Branches (per 0.1 million adults)*	*Number of ATMs (per 0.1 million adults)*	*Bank Loan as per cent of GDP*	*Bank Deposits as per cent of GDP*
India	**10.64**	**8.90**	**51.75**	**68.43**
Australia	29.61	166.92	128.75	107.10
Brazil	46.15	119.63	40.28	53.26
France	41.58	109.80	42.85	34.77
Mexico	14.86	45.77	18.81	22.65
United States	35.43	—	46.83	57.78
Korea	18.80	—	90.65	80.82
Philippines	8.07	17.70	21.39	41.93

Source: Financial Access Survey, IMF, 2011.

Further World Bank in 2011 pointed out a sheer gap among total credit, deposit participant of population and those from formal institutions which is revealed in Table 4.2 suggesting wider scope of improvement in service and expansion in the formal channels for ensuring inclusion to a broader perspective. The comparative position reveals the weaker status of India in the aspect of financial inclusion, which is miles behind its other foreign counterparts.

Table 4.2: World Bank's Financial Inclusion Index: Select Indicators on Financial Inclusion, 2011 (*Proportion of Population of Age 15+*)

Indicator's Name	*United States*	*United Kingdom*	*Ger-many*	*Russian Federation*	*Brazil*	*China*	*India*
(1)	*(2)*	*(3)*	*(4)*	*(5)*	*(6)*	*(7)*	*(8)*
Credit							
Loan from a financial institution in the past year	20.1	11.8	12.5	7.7	6.3	7.3	7.7
Loan from a financial institution in the past year, income, bottom 40%	17.6	11.1	12.3	6.3	3.5	7.7	7.9
Loan from a financial institution in the past year, income, top 60%	22.3	13.2	13.7	8.7	8.2	7.0	7.5
Loan in the past year	44.6	28.8	25.3	31.9	23.8	29.4	30.6
Loan in the past year, income, bottom 40%	45.1	28.1	25.4	32.1	19.7	32.4	35.7
Loan in the past year, income, top 60%	44.2	30.2	24.6	31.7	26.6	27.3	24.9
Insurance							
Personally paid for health insurance	NA	NA	NA	6.7	7.6	47.2	6.8

(*Contd.*)

Table 4.2 (*Contd.*)

(1)	*(2)*	*(3)*	*(4)*	*(5)*	*(6)*	*(7)*	*(8)*
Purchased agriculture insurance (% working in agriculture, age 15+)	NA	NA	NA	3.7	11.2	7.2	6.6
Payments							
Checks used to make payments	65.5	50.1	7.2	5.2	6.7	1.8	6.7
Electronic payments used to make payments	64.3	65.3	64.2	7.7	16.6	6.9	2.0
Mobile phone used to pay bills	NA	NA	NA	1.7	1.3	1.3	2.2
Savings							
Saved at a financial institution in the past year	50.4	43.8	55.9	10.9	10.3	32.1	11.6
Saved at a financial institution in the past year, income, bottom 40%	32.1	43.5	55.1	8.8	5.8	18.3	10.4
Saved at a financial institution in the past year, income, top 60%	66.5	44.3	60.0	12.4	13.3	41.7	12.9
Saved any money in the past year	66.8	56.7	67.3	22.7	21.1	38.4	22.4
Saved any money in the past year, income, bottom 40%	51.5	56.2	67.1	18.9	12.1	23.3	19.4
Saved any money in the past year, income, top 60%	80.2	57.7	68.1	25.4	27.1	48.9	25.8

NA = Not available.
Source: IMF's Financial Inclusion Survey, 2012.

It is believed that financial inclusion primarily should ensure every citizen at least having a bank account. So, banks were compelled to expand their reach even to the remote areas. Hence, the concept of brick and mortar branch, single man branch concepts were divulged.

Table 4.3: Growth of the Banking Sector Since the First Nationalization (*Scheduled Commercial Banks, including Rural and Regional Banks*)

	March 1969	*March 1991*	*March 2012*
Number of banks	73	272	165
Number of bank branches	8,262	60,220	99,884
Deposits at banks (billion ₹)	43.38	1,925.41	59,090.82
Credits at banks (billion ₹)	33.96	1,163.01	46,118.52
Deposits per branch (million ₹)	5.25	31.97	591.59
Credits per branch (million ₹)	4.11	19.31	461.72
Deposits per capita (thousand ₹)	0.08	2.16	47.60
Credits per capita (thousand ₹)	0.06	1.30	37.15

Source: Reserve Bank of India (Banking) and World Bank (Population).

However, even after being aware about the fact of limited outreach of banking facility and to cover rural households with at least 2000 population huge number of bank branches were opened in these years, but there is lack of equitable establishment among various regions in the country.

Table 4.4: Region-wise and Population Group-wise New Bank Branches Opened during 2011-12

Region	*Rural*	*Semi-urban*	*Urban*	*Metropolitan*	*Total*
Central	543	483	240	119	1,385
Eastern	301	352	217	89	959
North-Eastern	43	60	49	—	152
Northern	450	425	187	205	1,267
Southern	647	871	315	247	2,080
Western	269	387	122	297	1,075
Total	2,253	2,578	1,130	957	6,918

Source: RBI, 2012.

It is imperative that there needs to have special focus on NER for financial inclusion. In this regard a thematic representation of various new windows, their status in NER and the SWOT analysis of the region with respect to financial inclusion is presented hereafter.

Financial Inclusion in North-Eastern India

Popularly known as the land of seven sisters this picturesque region does not depict a rosy picture in terms of financial inclusion rather identified as being the states coming under the category of low financial inclusion. Various researchers like Chattopadhyay (2011), Kumar and Mishra (2011) have justified this argument by preparing an index of financial inclusion and assigning ranks with respect to the states. These studies have quite adequately revealed low level of financial inclusion in north-eastern states as some of these even occupied the last and lowest rank status out of all Indian states. For calculating the index Banking penetration, availability of banking services and usage are considered as important dimensions, which were calculated as below:

Banking Penetration (Dimension 1)

Considering this as one of the most important indicators of financial inclusion this measure is calculated as the number of adult population having a bank account. In the absence of the data on banked population, number of bank accounts as a proportion of the total population is treated as an indicator of this dimension. However, both deposit account and loan account are taken as the indicators of banking penetration.

Availability of Banking Services (Dimension 2)

For calculating the availability of services the number of bank outlets (per 1,000 population) and/or by the number of ATM per 1000 people, or the number of bank employees per customer, number of BCs appointed are treated as important measures. In the absence of data on the number of ATMs and number of BCs appointed, the number of bank branches per 1,000 adult population and also number of branches per square km is used.

Usage (Dimension 3)

In order to calculate this dimension, outstanding credit and deposit are considered as two basic services of the banking. Accordingly, the volume of outstanding deposit and credit as proportion of the Net District Domestic Product (NDDP) has been used to measure this dimension.

Table 4.5 depicts the state-wise index of financial inclusion and their respective ranks.

Table 4.5: State-wise Index of Financial Inclusion

Name of the State	*Banking Penetration*	*Availability of Banking Services*	*Usage*	*Index of Financial Inclusion*	*Rank in Terms of IFI*
Assam	0.17	0.17	0.07	0.13	22
Arunachal Pradesh	0.20	0.16	0.14	0.17	18
Manipur	0.00	0.01	0.01	0.01	24
Meghalaya	0.21	0.28	0.14	0.21	14
Mizoram	0.13	0.26	0.09	0.16	19
Nagaland	0.03	0.04	0.07	0.05	23
Tripura	0.31	0.22	0.08	0.20	15

Source: Financial Inclusion in India: A Case Study of West Bengal, 2011.

By considering different parameters of measuring financial inclusion as identified by Rangarajan, 2008 the status of various indicators in NE region is expressed in Table 4.6.

Table 4.6: Indicators of Financial Inclusion in NE States of India

Name of the State	*Total No. of Bank Branches*	*Branches per Person*	*Credit-Deposit Ratio (in %)*	*Bank Credit/ State GDP Ratio*	*Life Insurance Pene-tration (in %)*	*Insurance Density (in ₹)*	*No. of Districts having Non-life Insurance Offices*	*% of Districts Covered with Non-life Insurance*
Assam	1707	0.047	36	20	1.05	387.9	25	93
Arunachal Pradesh	95	0.063	23	15	0.61	415.7	14	87
Manipur	94	0.034	33	13	0.72	268.4	2	22
Meghalaya	230	0.078	24	16	0.36	213.6	4	57
Mizoram	108	0.089	43	19	NA	246.9	1	13
Nagaland	107	0.036	23	12	0.86	525.6	3	27
Tripura	218	0.057	31	16	0.58	312.0	3	75

Source: Compiled by author.

Table 4.7: Financial Inclusion by Postal Network (as on 31-03-2012)

Postal Circles	*No. of Post Offices*	*Area Covered (in sq.km.)*	*Population/ Post Office*
Assam	4,007	19.57	7,784
North-Eastern (except Assam)	3,121	58.87	4,620
All India	1,54,822	21.23	7,817

Source: Compiled by author.

From the above tables, it is quite evident that there needs to have significant improvement in terms of bank branch expansion, Insurance penetration and population coverage under postal networks for attaining better financial inclusion. Out of all seven states no state is doing exceptionally good in these aforesaid parameters. Smaller and more geographically dispersed states like Arunachal Pradesh, Manipur, Nagaland and Mizoram are more backward in terms of financial inclusion in these respective states. Although Government of India and Reserve Bank of India is paying prime focus on this North-Eastern region and trying to follow the path to financial inclusion. The advancements under the new action plan in this region reflects sea change in terms of growth in the region. Banking penetration in villages using various modes like branch opening, BC/BF outlet and other modes has increased 3.9 times in March 2012 compared to 2010, which is even higher than all-India position.

Road Map for Improvement

Being located in the geographically isolated and remote location of India, North-Eastern region has lagged in various ways; in case of financial inclusion parameters the comparative position is quite weak with reference to all-India standards. Thus, the ways and means to uncover existing level of financial exclusion is an important challenge.

Despite several initiatives like assigning special emphasis on NE region taken by RBI in order to normalize the scenario, the improvement in the status of financial inclusion seems to be far reaching. A dig into the number of newly opened bank branches in the region unleashes the picture. It, therefore, stresses for more stringent measures on the part of regulators as well as collaborative participation of various related entities.

In order to prepare the action plan it will be prudent to have a clear understanding about the strength and weakness of the region so as to foresee the exact shortcomings. An attempt made in this regard is as follows:

Table 4.8: SWOT Analysis of Financial Inclusion in North-Eastern Region

Strength	*Weakness*	*Opportunity*	*Threat*
(1)	*(2)*	*(3)*	*(4)*
Huge potential of expansion	Reach of formal institution is quite limited	Increasing level of mass awareness as a result of chit fund frauds, yet a lot to be done to motivate masses to channelize their savings in formal institutions	Yet a large number of masses lack required information on savings and credit
Moderate level of Financial literacy, thereby giving chance to venture	A good number of people are yet to get awareness about other forms of financial institutions	Increased use of Mobile phone can help to facilitate mobile banking network	Improper knowledge of technology can lead the common men prone to be cheated
Demand for formal financial instruments on the rise	Some people are yet reliant upon informal or fraudulent mechanism	Opening of single man branch and engagement of Business Correspondents under the RBI dictum of opening at least 25 per cent of new branches in unbanked area	A huge chunk of population is yet to consider formal channels as dependable contrary to traditional system of savings and investment

(Contd.)

Table 4.8 (*Contd.*)

(1)	*(2)*	*(3)*	*(4)*
Untapped market in certain area, others yet to saturate	Financial services available only in some selected centres	Largely unbanked population can be satisfied with the simplest form of financial services	Common men largely prefer the word of mouth information for financial planning instead of informed decision
Better demographic dividend	Lack of innovativeness in the service, absence of liaison between various government initiatives, private entity and common men	Increased financial need of youngsters at convenience can be met by better Information and Communication Technology	The luster of some informal schemes attracts common men to make easy money and subsequent loss
Huge network of post offices and presence of postal branches	Poor communication, lack of infrastructure, connectivity, and co-operation. Improper security arrangement and insurgency problem are also responsible for low financial inclusion	Widespread postal network can be promulgated to help in expanding financial inclusion and provide required financial services	The traditional financial schemes of India post are gradually loosing competitiveness

In the light of above, the future course of action can be designed so as to have better improvement in the scenario of financial inclusion in the region. A brief outline is provided hereunder:

- Collective effort involving all stakeholders should be undertaken in order to increase the financial awareness of masses.
- Financial outreach through formal institutions should be extended even to the remote localities by involving Business correspondents, banking on wheel, single man branch, adopting ICT model, using mobile banking network and the like.
- Spread of meaningful information related to savings, investment and credit should be divulged on an adequate and timely way encompassing all media.
- Innovative financial products should be devised in order to attract common as well as informative masses. Moreover achieving confidence of common men is an apt necessity.
- Postal network should be used in more meaningful way as well as spreading financial inclusion in the region.

REFERENCES

Ananth, S. and Oncu, T.S. (2013). "Challenges to Financial Inclusion in India: The Case of Andhra Pradesh", *Economic and Political Weekly* (*EPW*), Vol. xlviii, No. 7, February, pp. 77-83.

Chakraborty, K.C., Speech (2012). "Bank for International Settlements — Central Bank of Malaysia Workshop on Financial Inclusion Indicators", Kuala Lumpur, 5th November.

Chattopadhyay, S.K. (2011). *Financial Inclusion in India: A Case Study of West Bengal*, WPS (DEPR): 8 July, RBI Working Paper Series.

Collard, S.; Kempson, E.; and Whyley, C. (2001). *Tackling Financial Exclusion*, Bristol: Policy Press.

Dixit, R. and Ghosh, M. (2013). "Financial Inclusion for Inclusive Growth of India — A Study of Indian States", *International Journal of Business Management and Research* (IJBMR), Vol. 3, Issue 1, March, pp. 147-56.

Gupta, S.K. (2011). "Financial Inclusion — IT As Enabler", *Reserve Bank of India Occasional Papers*, Vol. 32, No. 2, Monsoon 2011.

Kempson, E.; Atkinson, A. and O. Pilley (2004). *Policy Level Response to Financial Exclusion in Developed Economies: Lessons for Developing Countries*, Report of Personal Finance Research Centre, University of Bristol.

Kumar, C. and Mishra, S. (2011). *Banking Outreach and Household Level Access: Analyzing Financial Inclusion in India*, 13th Annual Conference on Money and Finance in the Indian Economy, February.

Massey (2010). "Role of Financial Institutions in Financial Inclusion", *Banking and Finance Journal*, FICCI.

Paramasivan, C. and Ganeshkumar (2013). "Overview of Financial Inclusion in India", *International Journal of Management and Development Studies*, Vol. 2, Issue No. 3, March.

Sarma, M. (2008), *Index of Financial Inclusion*, Indian Council for Research on International Economic Relations, Working Paper No. 215, June.

Sarma, M. and Pais, J. (2008). "Financial Inclusion and Development: A Cross Country Analysis", *Indian Council for Research on International Economic Relations*, pp. 1-28.

World Bank (2008). *Finance for All?: Policies and Pitfalls in Expanding Access*, World Bank Policy Research Paper, World Bank.

Government of India (2008). "Report of the Committee (Chairman: C. Rangarajan) on the Financial Inclusion", January.

RBI, *Annual Report*, 2002-2012.

Annual Report of India Post, 2012-13.

IRDA, *Annual Report*, 2010-2012.

5

VENTURE CAPITAL FINANCING FOR ENTREPRENEURIAL DEVELOPMENT
Prospects and Challenges

N. Rokendro Singh

Introduction

Venture capital financing is one of the important innovative financial services in the financial system of an economy. It is a fund based financial service. Venture Capital is a form of equity financing especially designed for funding high risk and high reward projects. VC fund is an instrument for bringing about industrial development, it exploits vast and untapped potentialities and promotes growth of the knowledge based industries. Development of small and medium enterprises (SMEs) and microenterprises has been accepted in India as a strategy for rapid industrialization and also for generation of employment opportunities, particularly among educated unemployed youth. VC finance helps those potential entrepreneurs to become successful entrepreneurs, by providing seed money, start-up money and money at a later stages. Venture Capital Fund (VCF) supports first generation entrepreneurs by providing equity capital needed for starting up the enterprises. SEBI introduced SEBI (VCF) Regulation in 1996 for regulating and promoting activities of domestic venture capital funds. And in 2000 SEBI (Foreign VCF) Regulation was introduced enabling foreign venture capital and private equity investors to register with SEBI.

Research Objectives

1. To understand the concept of venture capital.
2. To understand venture capital industry in India.

3. To study the need of venture capital in India with a view of NER for entrepreneurship development.
4. To understand regulation of venture capital in India framed by SEBI.
5. To find out the opportunities and challenges of venture capital financing in India.

Main Features of Venture Capital (VC)

Features of venture capital differentiate it from other capital investments. It is basically equity finance in relation to new enterprises relatively high risk and possibility of high return. VC finance has the following main features:

High Degree of Risk: VC represents financial investment in highly risky projects with the objective of high rate of return.

Equity Participation: VC financing is, invariably, an actual or potential equity participation wherein the objective of VC capitalist is to make capital gain by selling the shares once the firm becomes profitable.

Long-term Investment: VC financing is a long term investment. It generally takes a long period to encash the investment in securities made by the Venture Capitalists.

Participation in Management: In addition to providing capital, VC funds (VCF) take an active interest in the management of the assisted firms. The approach of VCF is different from that of a traditional moneylenders or banker. It is also different from ordinary stock market investors who merely trade in the shares of companies without participating in the management. VCF combines the qualities of banker, stock investor and entrepreneur in one.

Achieve Social Objective: It is different from the development capital provided by the Central and State level Government bodies in that the profit objective is the motive behind the financing. But VCF projects generate employment and balanced regional growth indirectly due to setting up of successful new businesses.

Investment is Illiquid: A VCF is not subject to repayment on demand as it is with an overdraft or following a loan repayment schedule. The investment is realized only when the company is sold or achieves a stock market listing. It is lost when the company goes into liquidation.

Areas of VC Investment

The areas of investment that are favoured by a lot of venture capital companies are:

- Biotechnology,
- Medical services,
- Communications,
- Electronic components and software companies,
- Media,
- Health and pharmaceuticals,
- Agri-business,
- Retailing, and
- E-commerce/E-marketing.

Investors in VCF

Venture capital can be formed as a trust, a company or a corporate body. Investors in VCF are:

- Financial institutions.
- Banks.
- Pension funds.
- Corporations.
- High net-worth individuals.

Venture capitalist raises money/funds from these investors and they again invest in start up of companies/entrepreneurs.

Significances of VC Financing

- VCF or VC companies provide the necessary risk capital to the entrepreneurs who lack capital to be risked but want to start having high potential for earning profit.
- VCF provides seed capital for industrial start-ups and at various stages of growth.
- VCF helps in Research and Development projects for the promising high return business firms.
- VC finance helps or involve actively in the management of the firms which helps to the development of various entrepreneurs.
- VCF generates employment by setting up new enterprises.
- Venture capital is also useful to the society in regard to balance regional growth.
- VCF also provides capital to mature enterprises for expansion, diversification and restructuring.
- Venture capital also provides capital to new entrepreneurs in foreign operations.

Stages of VC investment

Early Stage Investment

Seed Capital and Research and Development: Venture capital funds keen to encourage in seed finance and research and development. It helps and gives finance before starting up an enterprise for conducting research and development and seed capital.

Start-ups: The start-up is widely recognized as the essence of venture capital activity. Start-up term is usually used in the launching of a new enterprise. VCF is playing a great role in this stage by proving finance for start-ups.

Second Round Finance: In this stage capital is provided for marketing and meeting working capital needs of an enterprise that has commenced the production, but does not have positive cash flows or sufficient to take care of its growth.

Later Stage Investment

Expansion and Diversification: VCF provides finance for expansion of the business and for diversification of products or area. It is normally finance for one to three years period in such stages of VC financing.

Replacement: It means substituting one shareholder for another, rather than rising of new capital which results in the change of ownership pattern. VCF purchases shares from the entrepreneurs. VCF also buys ordinary shares from non-promoters and convert it to preference shares with fixed dividend coupon.

Turnarounds: It is a rare form of finance in the later stage financing. Most of the VCFs avoid this due to higher degree of risk. This requires specialized skills. It may need renegotiation, change in management or even change in ownership.

Table 5.1: Venture Capital Spectrum

Stages of Investment	*Time Scale (years)*	*Degree of Risk*
Early Stage Investment		
Early stage	7-10	Extreme
Start-ups	5-10	Very high
Second round	3-7	High
Later Stage Investment		
Expansion	1-3	Medium
Replacements	1-3	Low
Turnarounds	3-5	Medium
Buy outs	3-5	Low

Buy Outs: It involves the creation of a separate business by separating it from its existing owners. A buy out will involve the existing or a new management team and a set of assets which may be just a trade name or a group of people.

Venture Capital Funds in India: An Overview

VCF is a new type of financial intermediary which emerged during 1970s in United States. Up to 1975 the concept of venture capital in India was almost nil. In 1972, a committee on Development of Small and Medium Enterprises highlighted the need to foster venture capital as a source of funding new entrepreneurs. Risk Capital Foundation, sponsored by IFCI, was set-up in 1975 to promote and support new technologies and businesses. Seed Capital Scheme and the National Equity Scheme were set-up by IDBI in 1976. Programme for Advancement of Commercial Technology (PACT) Scheme was introduced by ICICI in 1985.

In 1986, Government of India announced the setting up of VCF to encourage the enterprises based on indigenous technology and upgradation of existing technology. Government of India guidelines for overseas venture capital investment came out on September 20, 1995. SEBI Venture Capital Regulation came in 1996 and SEBI Foreign Venture Capital Investor's Regulation came in 2000.

Venture capital providers in India can be divided into the following categories:

(i) Specialized financial institutions and their financing schemes — IFCI, IDBI, ICICI, UTI (UTI Venture Capital Unit Scheme) are major institutions. They engage in financing high technology new ventures.

(ii) Funds promoted by state level institutions — such as APIDC-Venture Capital Ltd., wholly owned by Andhra Pradesh Industrial Development Corporation Ltd. for promoting technology innovation in the state; Gujarat Venture Finance Ltd. for improvement in product quality and energy conservation, etc.

(iii) Funds promoted by public sector banks — like Canbank Financial Services Ltd.

(iv) Private Agencies — for example, Credit Capital Venture Fund, 20th Century VCF, India Investment Fund, Indus Venture Capital Fund, etc.

(v) Overseas Venture Capital Funds.

Regulations and Guidelines of Venture Capital in India

The Government of India took a policy initiative and announced guidelines for venture capital funds (VCFs) in India in 1988. Laws relating to venture capital funds in India are:

SEBI (Venture Capital Funds) Regulations, 1996

The venture capital fund regulations by the Securities and Exchange Board of India are a comprehensive set of laws to be followed by the venture capital funds in India. From the registration of venture capital funds to the action to be taken in case of default, the regulation has been divided in VI chapters.

Registration of Venture Capital Funds: A Venture capital fund can either be a fund established as a trust under the Indian Trust Act or a company as defined under Companies Act, 1956.

The regulations provided for the registration of a company or a trust which either was functioning as a venture capital fund before the commencement of this Act or proposed to do so after the commencement of this Act.

A company or trust (which functioned as a venture capital fund before the commencement of these regulations) shall cease to function as a venture capital fund if it does not apply to SEBI for registration within 3 months from the commencement of the regulations.

Procedure to be Followed for Registration

(i) An application for grant of certificate to be made to SEBI in Form A along with a fee of ₹ 25,000. The fee shall be paid through a draft.

(ii) There are certain conditions which must be fulfilled before the certificate of registration is granted by SEBI:

(a) In case of a company, the MOA of the company shall have the business of venture capital fund as its main object, and invitation to public shall be expressly barred by the MOA and AOA, in addition to this, any officer of the company shall be involved in any litigation connected to the security market or should not have been convicted of an economic offence.

(b) In case of a trust, the trust is in form of a deed and has been duly registered under the Indian Registration Act.

Carrying the business of venture capital fund is its primary objective. Any trustee of the trust is not involved in a litigation connected with security market and has not been convicted of any economic offence.

(c) In case of a body corporate, it should be formed under the laws of Central or State legislature and it is permitted to venture in the field of venture capital funds.

(iii) The application for registration shall be complete in all respect. If SEBI discovers anything in the application that renders it incomplete, it shall give the applicant a time of thirty days to remove the loophole, failing which the application can be rejected by the Board.

(iv) SEBI after finding the applicant to be eligible, shall inform the applicant about it, after receiving the information the applicant shall tender to SEBI the registration fee which is ₹ 5 lakh, after receiving which SEBI shall issue the Certificate of Registration.

Conditions and Restrictions on Investments: The regulation has applied a lot of conditions and restrictions to the amount of investment to be made in and by the venture capital fund in India.

An investment in the venture capital fund can be made by any person whether Indian, Foreigner or NRI, but no investment which is less than ₹ five lakh can be allowed in the venture capital fund. This, however, does not apply to investment made by the employees, directors or the principal officers of the company or by the trustee where the venture capital fund is a trust.

The investment strategy at the time of registration shall be disclosed by the venture capital fund. The venture capital fund shall also disclose the duration of its life-cycle. Not more than 25 per cent of the fund shall be invested in a single venture capital undertaking. Investment to be made in the following manner:

(i) At least 66.67 per cent of the fund shall be invested in unlisted equity shares or other instruments linked to equity shares of the venture capital undertaking.

(ii) Not more than 33.33 per cent of the investible fund shall be invested by the way of IPO of a venture capital undertaking whose shares are proposed to be listed, the debt instrument of the venture capital undertaking in which the venture capital fund has already invested, preferential allotment of equity shares of a listed company, equity shares or equity linked instrument of a financially weak company and SPVs which have been created by the venture capital fund.

No venture capital fund shall get its units listed on any recognized stock exchange till the expiry of three years from the date when they were issued to the investors by the venture capital fund. The venture capital funds shall also not invite any member of the public by way of advertisement to subscribe to its units. The venture capital fund may receive investments only through private placements of its units.

Venture Capital and Entrepreneurship Development with a View of NER

The development of the organized venture capital industry in India, as is in existence today, was slow. Most entrepreneurs had to rely on their own financial resources, and those of their families and well-wishers or private financiers to realize their entrepreneurial dreams. For entrepreneur-ship development in the country there is a need to foster venture capital as a source of funding new entrepreneurs.

In India, the Venture Capital plays a vital role in the development and growth of innovative entrepreneurships. Venture Capital activity in the past was possibly done by the developmental financial institutions like IDBI, ICICI and State Financial Corporations. These institutions promoted entities in the private sector with debt as an instrument of funding. For a long time funds raised from public were used as a source of Venture Capital.

Venture capital fund will be significant financial service in North-East India for entrepreneurial development. In North-East India majority of the industrial enterprises are in MSME sector. Venture capital concept is poor in the region. In the list of registered Venture Capital Funds (VCFs) under SEBI, most of them are initiated outside the North-Eastern Region. North-East India needs some VCFs for development of entrepreneurial activities in various sectors of the economy.

VCFs play an important role in development of entrepreneurship and help in the technological progress of an economy by providing the seed capital required for various industries with limited access to conventional source of finance.

Registered VCFs under SEBI

The role of VCF gain importance on account of limited availability of funds through conventional institutions, non-banking financial companies etc. During the years between 2007 to 2013 there is an increase in the number of registration of VCFs both domestic and foreign. The number of VCF increased from 90 in 2006-07 to 211 in the year 2012-13. The number of Foreign Venture Capital Investors (FVCIs) increased from 78 in 2006-07 to 168 in 2012-13. Table 5.2 and Fig. 5.1 show the number of VCFs and FVCIs registered during 2006-07 to 2012-13.

Table 5.2: Number of Registered Venture Capital Funds as on Respective Years

As on Date	*VCFs*	*FVCIs*	*Total*
31-3-2007	90	78	168
31-3-2008	106	97	203
31-3-2009	133	129	262
31-3-2010	158	143	301
31-3-2011	184	153	337
31-3-2012	207	175	382
31-3-2013	211	182	393

Source: SEBI Annual Reports 2007-08 to 2013.

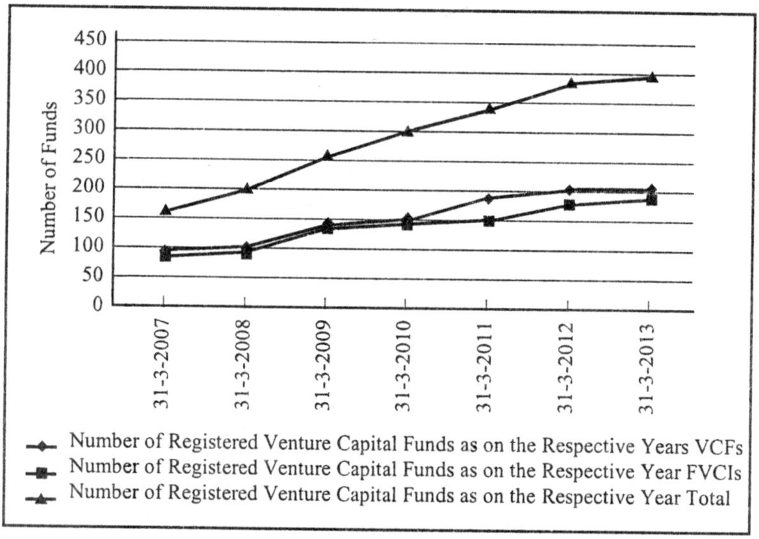

Figure 5.1: Number of Registered VC Funds and FVCIs in India.

Venture Capital Investments in India

The venture capital investment in India during the years from 2006-07 to 2008-09 was continuously increasing and thereby found reduced in 2009-10 and again increased till 2011-12. FVCIs figure of investment show a continuous upward trend during the last six years from 2006-07 to 2011-12. Table 5.3 and Fig. 5.2 show investment of VCFs and FVCIs during 2006-07 to 2011-12.

Table 5.3: Investment of VCFs and FVCIs During 2006-07 to 2011-12 (Cumulative Net Investment at the End of the Year) (*₹ crore*)

Year	*VCFs*	*FVCIs*	*Total Investment*
2006-07	11270	7856	19126
2007-08	19955	16705	36660
2008-09	22771	23047	45818
2009-10	18273	28894	47167
2010-11	25576	35593	61169
2011-12	28839	39492	68331

Source: SEBI Annual Report, 2013.

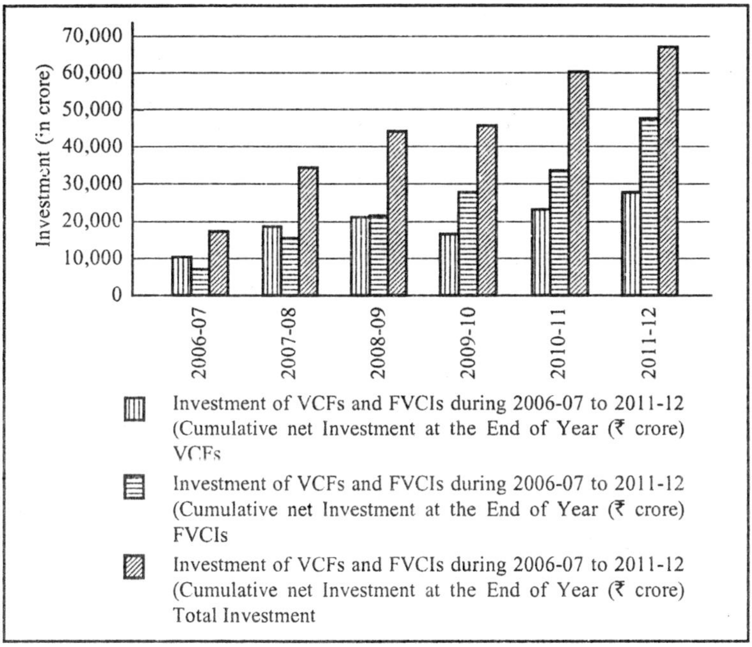

Figure 5.2: Investment of VCFs and FVCIs in India.

Alternative Investment Funds (AIFs)

SEBI notified Alternative Investment Funds (AIF) Regulation, 2012, on May 21, 2012. AIFs are basically funds established or incorporated in

India for the purpose of pooling in capital from Indian and Foreign investors for investing. During 2012-13, 42 AIFs have been registered with SEBI.

Out of 42 registered AIFs, Category I, II and III AIFs are 13, 22, and 7 respectively. Further out of 13 Category I there are five, three, three and two AIFS in VCF, Infrastructure, SME and Social AIFs respectively.

Prospects of Venture Capital Financing

- Many State governments have also set-up venture capital funds for the IT sector in partnership with the local state financial institutions and SIDBI. These include Andhra Pradesh, Karnataka, Delhi, Kerala and Tamil Nadu.
- In the year 2000, the Finance Ministry announced the liberalization of tax treatment for venture capital funds to promote them and to increase job creation. This is expected to give a strong boost to the non-resident Indians located in the Silicon valley and elsewhere to invest some of their capital, knowledge and enterprise in these ventures.
- A Bangalore based media company, Graycell Ltd., has recently obtained VC investment totalling about $ 1.7 million. The company would be creating and marketing branded web based consumer products in the near future.
- Existence of a globally competitive high technology.
- Globally competitive human resource capital.
- Second largest English speaking, scientific and technical manpower in the world.
- Vast pool of existing and ongoing scientific and technical research carried by large number of research laboratories.
- Initiatives taken by the Government in formulating policies to encourage investors and entrepreneurs.
- Initiatives of the SEBI to develop a strong and vibrant capital market giving the adequate liquidity and flexibility for investors for entry and exit.

Challenges Ahead for Venture Capital Financing in India

Problems or challenges to be faced in the process of Venture Capital Financing are as follows:

- VCF is in its nascent stages, just coming to existence and beginning, in India. In other words, Venture Capital in India is still at its early stage.

- The emerging scenario of global competitiveness has put an immense pressure on the industrial sector to improve the quality level with minimization of cost of products by making use of latest technological skills. The implication is to obtain adequate financing along with the necessary hi-tech equipments to produce an innovative product which can succeed and grow in the present market condition.
- The necessary capital can be obtained from the venture capital firms who expect an above average rate of return on the investment.
- The financing firms expect a sound, experienced, mature and capable management team of the company being financed. Since the innovative project involves a higher risk, there is an expectation of higher returns from the project.
- The payback period is also generally high (5-10 years).
- In addition to the challenge of raising Funds in tough market situations, the biggest challenge for a VC in India is to find the right set of passionate resources for each of their portfolio companies to support their growth at early stages. The reason many companies fail at early stages is not only because they are not able to mobilize Funds at initial stages, but because they are not able to attract the right talent to work with them and to guide them.
- The other various problems/challenges can be outlined are: Requirement of an experienced management team; Uncertainty regarding the success of the product in the market; Questions regarding the infrastructure details of production like plant location, accessibility, relationship with the suppliers and creditors, transportation facilities, labour availability, etc.; The category of potential customers and hence the packaging and pricing details of the product; The size of the market, market share, Major competitors; etc.

Conclusion

The world is becoming increasingly competitive. Companies are required to be super efficient with respect to cost, productivity, labour efficiency, technical back-up, flexibility to consumer demand, adaptability and foresightedness. There is an impending demand for highly cost-effective quality products and hence, the need for right access to valuable human expertise to guide and monitor along with the necessary funds for financing the new projects.

The Government of India in an attempt to bring the nation at par and above the developed nations has been promoting venture capital financing to new, innovative concepts and ideas, liberalizing taxation norms, providing tax incentives to venture firms, creation of local pools of capital and holding training sessions for the emerging VC investors. Development of Small and Medium Enterprises highlighted the need to foster venture capital as a source of funding new entrepreneurs. Risk Capital Foundation, sponsored by IFCI, was set-up in 1975 to promote and support new technologies and businesses. Seed Capital Scheme and the National Equity Scheme were set-up by IDBI in 1976. Programme for Advancement of Commercial Technology (PACT) Scheme was introduced by ICICI in 1985.

There is development in venture capital financing in India. During the years between 2007 to 2013 there is an increase in the number of registration of VCFs both domestic and foreign. The number of VCF increased from 90 in 2006-07 to 211 in the year 2012-13. The number of Foreign Venture Capital Investors (FVCIs) increased from 78 in 2006-07 to 168 in 2012-13.

REFERENCES

Debbie Ariyo (2000). "The Growth and Prospect for Venture Capital Activities in Nigeria", *Africa Economic Analysis*.

Government of India, Planning Commission, New Delhi (2012). "Creating a Vibrant Entrepreneurial Ecosystem in India", *Report of The Committee on Angel Investment and Early Stage Venture Capital*.

Ms. Ridhima Meher (2008). *Venture Capital: Challenges and Scope Ahead in India*.

P. Mohana Rao (2002). "Financial Services: An Overview", in P. Mohana Rao and R.L. Hyderabad (eds), *Financial Services — Text, Cases and Strategies*, Deep and Deep Publishers, New Delhi, pp. 89-98.

Shashi K. Gupta, Nisha Agarwal and Neeti Gupta (2009). *Financial Services — Including Financial Markets and Services*, Kalyani Publishers, New Delhi, pp. 13.1-13.21.

V. Balu (2002). "Financial Services to SSI Sector — A Study on Support System", in P. Mohana Rao and R. L. Hyderabad (eds), *Financial Services — Text, Cases and Strategies*, Deep and Deep Publishers, New Delhi, pp. 1-12.

SEBI Annual Reports, 2007 to 2013.

http://www.nextbigwhat.com/vikram-gupta-ivycap-ventures-297/14-11-2013.

6

FINANCIAL INCLUSION AND SUSTAINABLE DEVELOPMENT

A. Sundaram

Introduction

Credit is one of the key inputs of economic development. The timely availability of credit at an affordable cost has a big role to play in contributing the well-being of the weaker sections of the society. Proper access to finance to the rural people is a key requisite to employment, economic growth and poverty alleviation which are primary tools of economic development. Micro-Finance, Self-Help Groups and Financial Inclusion are the three dimensional approaches to achieve inclusive growth in the economy. A socio-economic speed of development of economy as a whole or a region in particular is depending on the availability of all kinds of infrastructure. Among various kinds of infrastructure, active presence of financial infrastructure is necessary for rapid economic progression of a country or region. The focus of financial inclusion is on promoting sustainable development and generating employment for a vast majority of the population especially in the rural areas. In this context, the objectives of the study are to understand the present status of North-East India's financial inclusion, to estimate the financial inclusion index for various states in North East India and to study the relationship between Financial Inclusion Index and Socio-Economic Development.

The main aim of this chapter is to understand the interrelation between financial inclusion and its overall contribution to economic growth. The study analyzes the importance, need, status, impacts, shortcomings, issues, challenges involved in financial inclusion for inclusive growth and economic development in North-East india. Finally, this chapter suggests some policy choices for successful implementation of the policy of financial inclusion for sustainable growth of North-East Indian economy.

The Need and Importance of Financial Inclusion in NE States

Financial development is pro-poor not only in the sense that economic growth lifts households above the poverty line, but also in a relative sense because it narrows income differentials. If financial inclusion leads to a healthier household and small business sector, it could also contribute to enhanced macro-economic (and financial system) stability.

Financial inclusion is a key driver of economic growth and poverty alleviation, as access to finance can boost job creation, reduce vulnerability to shocks and increase investments in human capital. Despite some progress, there is still a major scope for improvement in financial inclusion.

The concept of financial inclusion bringing the large segment of the productive sectors of the economy under formal financial network could unleash their creative capacities besides augmenting domestic demand on a sustainable basis driven by income and consumption growth from such sectors. Financial inclusion efforts do have multiplier effect on the economy as a whole through higher savings pooled from the vast segment of the bottom of the pyramid population by providing access to formal savings arrangement resulting in expansion in credit and investment by banks.

Deeper engagements of the underbanked population in the economy through the formal financial system could lead to improvement of their financial conditions and living standards, enabling them to create financial assets, generate income and build resilience to meet macro-economic and livelihood shocks. Government also immensely benefits by way of efficient and leakage-proof transfer of vast amounts of welfare benefits to the targeted, disadvantaged groups of population. Financial inclusion contributes towards growth in income thus decreasing the vulnerability of the poor. This facilitates poverty reduction and growth with equity. Financial inclusion links more economic resources to the formal economic system thus leading to overall economic growth and development, especially in the developing nations. Through financial inclusion it is possible, over a period of time, to transform these economically deprived people into a large section of society that actively contributes to the economic development of the nation thus making true inclusive growth a reality.

With financial inclusion, banks gain business, providing a further impetus to the economy. Financial inclusion is an effective tool for poverty reduction if applied strategically. With reduction in poverty, at least a part of the huge amount of public resources spent on provision of basic needs for the poor can be used for other purposes. Further financial inclusion checks pilferage of funds. This can bring into the mainstream economy major funds which are otherwise lost to the unaccounted black economy. Financial inclusion opens up access to a large market. This will attract global market players and foreign investment, increasing employment and business opportunities in developing countries.

Financial inclusion is a must for inclusive economic growth. Though the banking industry has grown both horizontally and vertically but the branch penetration has not been that enthusiastic with population load even after passing decades of nationalization, whose rationale was to shift the focus from class banking to mass banking. It paves the way for establishment of an account relationship which helps the poor to avail a variety of savings products and loan products for housing, consumption, etc. An inclusive financial system facilitates efficient allocation of productive resources and thus can potentially reduce the cost of capital.

This also enables the customer to remit funds at low cost. The government can utilize such bank accounts for social security services like health and calamity insurance under various schemes for disadvantaged. From the bank's point of view, having such social security cover makes the financing of such persons less risky. Reduced risk means more flow of funds at better rates. Access to appropriate financial services can significantly improve the day-to-day management of finances. For example, bills for daily utilities (municipality, water, electricity, and telephone) can be more easily paid by using cheques or through internet banking, rather than standing in the queue in the offices of the service. Transfer of money can be done more safely and easily by using the cheque, demand draft or through internet banking.

A bank account also provides a passport to a range of other financial products and services such as short term credit facilities, overdraft facilities and credit card. Further, a number of other financial products, such as insurance and pension products, necessarily require the access to a bank account.

The single gateway of a banking account can be used for several purposes and represents a beneficial situation for all the economic units in the country. Improvements in rural infrastructure in terms of availability of electricity, improvement in connectivity through provision of rural roads and telecommunications, and construction of warehouses, are expected to lead to better overall supply chain management, enhance productivity of physical resources in the rural areas and greater addition in agriculture. These developments would lead to much greater demand for banking activity in rural areas.

With higher financing needs of such new activities *vis-à-vis* traditional ones, the overall financing intensity of agriculture is likely to experience a manifold rise. Along with growth in rural infrastructure, there is also likely to be an increase in rural non-farm activities, such as repair activities, education, housing, restaurants and medical services. These activities, both traditional and emerging ventures, would be available for financing by the banking sector. Thus, as the economy begins to grow rapidly, the rate of financial intermediation is expected to increase further. In other words, the banking system will be expected to increasingly provide larger quantum of funds to existing and emerging enterprises.

Deepening the financial system and widening its reach is crucial for both accelerating growth and for equitable distribution, given the present stage of development of our country. There has been a burst of entrepreneurship across the country, spanning rural, semi-urban and urban areas. This has to be nurtured and financed. It is only through growth of enterprises across all sizes that competition will be fostered. A small entrepreneur today will be a big entrepreneur tomorrow, and might well become a multi-national enterprise eventually if given the comfort of financial support.

As poverty levels decline and households have greater levels of discretionary incomes, they will be first time financial savers. They will, therefore, need to have easy access to formal financial systems to get into the banking habit. Banks will need to innovate and devise newer methods of including such customers into their fold. The importance of 'no-frills' account and expanding the range of identity documents that is acceptable to open an account without sacrificing objectivity of the process in this milieu can never be overemphasized.

Banks will need to go to their customers, rather than the other way around. The micro-credit and the Self-Help Group movements are in their infancy but are gathering force. More innovation in the form of business facilitators and correspondents will be needed for banks to increase their outreach for banks to ensure financial inclusion. New entrants to the banking system need households at their doorstep.

With increasing liberalization and higher economic growth, the role of banking sector is poised to increase in the financing pattern of economic activities within the country. To meet the growing credit demand, the banks need to mobilize resources from a wider deposit base and extend credit to activities hitherto not financed by banks. The trend of increasing commercialization of agriculture and rural activities should generate greener pastures, and banks should examine the benefits of increasing penetration therein. Financial inclusion will strengthen financial deepening and provide resources to the banks to expand credit delivery.

North-East region, though rich in her natural beauty, is considered to be the most backward in economic term. There has been lack of avenues of income and investment in the region leading to widespread unemployment. Compared to other regions of the country, NER lacks entrepreneurism. Economic development of the region is largely dependent on the efficiency of the banks operating in the region. It is the efficiency of banks that helps to a great extent in mobilizing savings and investing the same into profitable channels of investment in order to uplift the economic conditions of the people in the region.

The Report of the Committee on "Financial Inclusion" (January 2008) stated that 72.7 per cent of India's 89.3 million and 95.91 per cent in NE farmer households are excluded from formal sources of finance. So, it is imperative to bring the unbanked population within the ambit of banking. Invariably financially excluded people depend on moneylenders even for their day-to-day needs, borrowing at exorbitant rates to finally get caught in a debt trap. On the other hand, these people are completely ignorant of financial products like insurance, which may protect them in adverse circumstances. Moreover, the rural poor suffer from financial impediments due to their seasonal income, irregularity of work and job related migration. In the light of such issue, the need of the hour is a financial inclusion to meet their living standards ensuring the growth of the North-East economy as a whole. The North-East poses a more complex challenge for financial inclusion because of difficult terrain, lower population densities, poor infrastructure, inadequate communication facilities and law and order disruptions. So, it is necessary and important to ensure that financial inclusion in NER is at par with that in the rest of the country.

Status of Financial Inclusion in North-East India

It is estimated that, globally, over two billion people are excluded from access to financial services, of which one-third is in India. "The Report of the Committee on Financial Inclusion" (January 2008) stated that 72.7 per cent of India's 89.3 million farmer households are excluded from formal sources of finance. The highest percentage of farmer households excluded from formal source of finance is 95.91 per cent in the North-Eastern States.

There are 3,250 villages in the North-Eastern Region (NER) falling into this category of over 2,000 population with as yet no banking facility. Of these, only about 1,031 villages were covered by end September 2011. North-East is the most financially excluded region in the country. The banking and finance infrastructure in the region is very weak, with North-East lagging in almost all critical banking outreach indicators.

This is evident from the low banking penetration (higher average population per branch) in NES as compared with the all-India average, though there were significant variations across states in the region with Mizoram and Meghalaya having much better ratios. In June 2009, average population per commercial bank branch for north-east was as high as 21,000, 40 per cent higher than the national average of 15,000. Manipur in particular had an average population of 33,000 per commercial bank branch which was highest for any state in the country.

The region offers low investment opportunity which is reflected by low credit-deposit ratio. Since deregulation in 1992, the CD ratio in all the years is consistently far below the national average. The CD ratio in NER has decreased from 45 to 35 in 2010 and increased from 62 to 73 at the national level.

Among the states, Mizoram accounts for the highest CD ratio of 58.7 in 2009 whereas the state of Arunachal Pradesh accounts for the lowest CD ratio of 24.8. Likewise the Investment plus CD ratio is also highest at 83.2 in Mizoram in 2008 and lowest in the state of Arunachal Pradesh at 40.3 in the same year. Farm households not accessing credit from formal sources as a proportion total farm households is especially high at 95.91 per cent, in the North-East. Thus, apart from the fact that exclusion in general is large, it also varies widely across regions, social groups and asset holdings. The poorer the group, the greater is the exclusion. Even as credit expanded at a faster pace than deposits in the last decade, the gap remained very wide.

The average growth rate of 1.81 in the region is also far below the national growth rate of 2.45. Sikkim is a clear outlier amongst the North-Eastern states, with a developed financial system where credit supply exceeds demand. The extent of financial inclusion varies from a minimal 7 per cent in Meghalaya to a respectable 37 per cent in Mizoram, averaging approximately 19 per cent. Clearly, some states require far more support over the next 5 years.

It also shows that the growth rate of the North-Eastern bank branches at 2.02 is much below the all-India growth rate of 3.71. There has always been a wide disparity between deposit mobilization and credit advancement in the region. Total percentage of deposit account comes out to be around 2.53 per cent.

The financial exclusion in the region by 2015 over one-third of the low income families will be financially included in the region. Agriculture is one of the key priority sectors for lending by banks; under the priority sector lending sector, banks are required to ensure that at least 18 per cent of their advances goes to agriculture. By 2015, the total loan outstanding of micro-finance should be close to ₹ 17.5 billion in North-East. This much gross loan outstanding will be needed to cater to approximately one-third of the total low income households in North-East.

These indicators clearly show the extent of financial exclusion in the region. The gap could not be amply filled by the MFIs too, as micro-finance in the region has not taken off yet. The SHG-Bank linkage has limited outreach, shows erratic growth and suffers from quality issues with high NPAs.

Impact of Financial Inclusion on Economic Development in North-East India

The Impact of financial inclusion reflects through macro-economic indicators which are generally used to reveal the economic strength and status of North-Eastern states. In fact, it includes growth rate of state domestic product, per capita income, size of deficit in the state budget and also the burden of public debt on the state. Real per capita income is being used as the base of consumption expenditure which reveals the economic status of an individual in the each state.

Since nationalization of banks in 1989 and deregulation in 1992, a remarkable progress was made in economic development in NE States. The data on net state domestic product (NSDP) over the 8-year period, from 2001 to 2008, the weighted average NSDP growth in NES was at 5.2 per cent and 7.1 per cent at the all-India level. The average NSDP growth in NES was lower as compared with the all-India level.

There were, however, significant inter-state variations within NES with the growth performances of three states, except Mizoram, Sikkim

Tripura all other States in NE are lower than the all-India average due to the poor performance of agriculture and industry. While the growth rate in agriculture has been particularly low in Assam and Mizoram, the growth rate of agriculture in Nagaland was high.

The composition of GSDP of North-Eastern States is characterized by dominance of Primary and Tertiary sectors while Secondary sector specially manufacturing remains subdued. Primary sector has contracted but is still higher than national percentages. The tertiary sector is growing due to expansion of public administration, confirming the fact that outside agriculture, Government is the main employer. The need, therefore, is to place a greater emphasis on promoting the growth of the industrial sector in the region.

Agriculture in North-East has remained a subsistence activity. Productivity has remained below the agricultural potential of the region. On the industrial front, Industries are underdeveloped and hardly there are any large industries. Entrepreneurship is yet to be adequately developed among the people of the region. During the period 2004-05 to 2009-10 the annual average growth rate of Industries for the NE region as a whole was just 3.94 per cent while all-India industrial growth rate was 10.42 per cent.

The annual average growth rate of Gross State Domestic Product at factor cost in NE States has increased from 3.85 per cent in 1981 and has increased to 7.80 per cent in 2011. Gross State Domestic Product at Factor Cost (Constant Prices) during 2004-05 to 2010-11 grew at 10.73 per cent for India. The structural changes among the states in the region during the time period has been a fall in the sectoral contribution of the primary sector (–10.42%). This has been compensated by an increase in the tertiary sector (7.88%) followed by the secondary sector (2.53%). The region, therefore, exhibits a trend of transformation where primary sector is not replaced by the secondary sector but by the tertiary sector.

The trends in fiscal indicators such as revenue deficit and outstanding debts are viewed as indicators of fiscal discipline. Gross fiscal deficit of NES reveals that in the year 2000-01, it was 6 per cent of GSDP, which subsequently declined to 0.2 per cent in the year 2008-09 and suddenly shot up to 10.5 per cent due to increase in liability on account of implementation of Sixth Pay Commission and impact of slow down realized. The revenue deficit has been started declining from the year 2001-02 due to measures undertaken for fiscal consolidation that resulted into surplus in revenue from 2003-04 to 2008-09.

Although it is a good sign of fiscal discipline but other side of observation is that these states might not be spending more on social and economic schemes or may not be investing in capital assets. Surge in revenue account occurred mainly because of resources transfer from Central Government to NES and not because of state tax collection efforts. The portion of debt on NES is observed below the 43 per cent of GSDP which is quite good but it also depicts that NESs are not taking risk in investing in infrastructural facilities and state enterprises.

The pattern of change in per capita consumption expenditure during 1993-94, 1999-2000 and 2004-05 has shown more stability as compared to per capita income. The coefficient correlation between income and consumption has declined from 0.59 in 1999-2000 to 0.15 in 2004-05. Surprisingly, fast growing State like Tripura in fact saw decline in consumption whereas high levels of consumption is maintained in States like Nagaland and Mizoram irrespective of the level and growth of per capita income.

Among the all NES, real PCI of Assam, Manipur, and Tripura are found below the NES average real per capita income and lesser by ₹ 5000 of the all India average real PCI in 2007-08. However, states such as Arunachal Pradesh, Meghalaya and Nagaland's real PCI remains above the NES average. Average growth rate of net state domestic product (NSDP) for the period 2000-01 to 2007-08 is recorded much below in the states of Assam; Manipur was at around 4.3 per cent, which is even lower than NES and all-India average growth rate of NSDP. It is clear that among all NES, Assam and Manipur remained on back foot due to the poor performance of agricultural and industrial sectors. In order to bring NES at equal level of all-India growth rate plunk, special efforts through sectoral policy of development for these states should be implemented on urgent basis.

The rate at which HDI scores improved between 1993-94 and 2004-05 also seem to reject the economic performance of these States' post-liberalization. The economic performance of States like Tripura and Sikkim in recent years take their per capita incomes (NSDP) well above those of other North-Eastern States. While it is true that income distribution pattern will determine the extent to which high per capita income will translate into human well-being and that growing income of these States have translated into improved performance in HDI scores. A remarkable feature is that the number of States having per capita income above the national average declined from four in 1993-94 to just one in 1999-2000, and increased to five in 2009-10. This indicates that

North-Eastern States, in general, have recovered from the adverse initial impact of economic liberalization.

Many studies have focused largely on the impact of financial development on growth, income inequality, and poverty reduction. The evidence strongly indicates that, when effectively regulated and supervised, financial development spurs economic growth, reduces income inequality, and helps lift households out of poverty. Recent researches in this area have provided intriguing new insights into the micro-economic underpinnings of the relationship between financial inclusion and economic development, using applied general equilibrium modelling.

As for credit, there is some evidence that access to credit is associated with a decline in poverty (Burgess and Pande, 2005); greater investment in business durables, increases in the number of businesses started, and improvements in the profitability of existing ones (Banerjee and Others, 2010); positive effects on consumption, economic self-sufficiency, some aspects of mental health and outlook (Karlan and Zinman, 2010). Other studies found that micro-credit increases consumption or income (Pitt and Khandker, 1998 and Khandker, 2005). One area of strong interest in recent work on financial inclusion is better identification of specific transmission channels through which it contributes to income equality and poverty reduction. Thus, Micro-economic evidence indicates that well developed financial systems have a strong positive impact on economic growth in North-Eastern States over long time periods.

Impact of Financially Excluded Masses

They pay higher charges in the absence of financial transactions like money transfer and cheque cashing, etc. They take credit from non-institutional creditors at exorbitantly higher rate which exacerbate the harm already caused due to poverty. The small business may suffer due to loss of access to middle class and higher-income consumers, higher cash handling costs and delays in remittances of money. Saving potential remains unexploited and unproductive from social point of view. There is a general decline in investments.

Challenges of Financial Inclusion in North-East India

There are number of factors affecting access to financial services by weaker section of society in North-East India. The lack of awareness, low incomes and assets, social exclusion, illiteracy are the barriers from demand side. The distance from bank branch, branch timings, cumbersome banking procedure and requirements of documents for opening bank accounts, unsuitable banking products or schemes, language, high transaction costs and attitudes of bank officials are the barriers from supply side. Hence, there is a need for financial inclusion to build uniform economic development, both spatially and temporally, and ushering in greater economic and social equity.

SHG-Bank linkage has issues related to quality, increasing NPAs and erratic growth; direct micro-finance has not even begun in most of the states. There are not enough MFIs and small NGO-MFIs have issues related to capacity and funding. The outreach of MFIs has largely been limited to parts of Assam, Manipur and to a small extent, Tripura.

Constraints in SHG-Bank Linkage

(i) *Growth:* If we compare the performance of SHG-bank linkage growth has been lopsided.
(ii) *Portfolio Quality:* Portfolio quality of SHG-Bank linkage is 10 per cent and very low.
(iii) *Difficulty in Linkage:* Self-help Promoting Institutes (SHPIs) still face a lot of difficulty in linking SHGs to banks.
(iv) *Quality of SHGs:* Weak SHGs which are not able to sustain as institutions, as they lack reliable financial records and often default on their loans. This is reflected in the high NPAs in SHG-Bank linkage in the region.

Constraints in Direct Micro-finance: Direct micro-finance has its own set of constraints, which are related to outreach, capacity, funds and human resource:

(i) *Outreach:* The outreach of MFIs in the region is still very limited to parts of Assam, Manipur and Tripura. The MFIs are mostly concentrated in Assam and their operations are densely situated in limited geographic areas. Most of the MFIs are operating in and around Guwahati. In Meghalaya, Tripura, Arunachal Pradesh, Mizoram there are still no MFIs.
(ii) *MFI Capacity:* These small NGO-MFIs lack capacity and guidance to establish and scale up their micro-finance operations. They are unable to effectively manage and sustain operations in the initial phase, in large part because of limited human resource ability and weak internal processes.

(iii) *Legal Forms:* Most of the MFIs in North-East are still operating under not-for-profit forms. There are only a few NBFCs in North-East. Even some of the big MFIs have been struggling to transform to NBFC. Lack of suitable legal form severely constraints the growth prospects of the MFIs due to their inability to mobilize loans and equity.

(iv) *Difficult for MFIs External to the Region to Operate:* Due to strong ethnic identities and weak infrastructure it is generally difficult for a MFI to operate in another state or region. Outside MFIs find it difficult to get acceptance among local people due to strong cultural identities. This is also important as there are often cultural conflicts among different ethnic groups.

(v) *Lack of Access to Market:* Economic activity in the region is limited by the lack of market access. People do not have sufficient investment opportunities, which make scalability difficult and growth almost impossible. The credit absorption capacity may get restricted beyond a certain level unless markets are developed and livelihood opportunities are created.

(vi) *Inability to Mobilize Funds:* MFIs in North-East face a lot of problems in raising funds. The region itself is considered high risk by the banks, the banking infrastructure is weak, and MFIs still do not have scales or systems to be attractive to banks. The level of underdevelopment is both a cause and a symptom of this problem.

(vii) *Credit Rating:* Despite various constraints which are unique to North-East, the MFIs in the region get measured with same yardsticks as applied to MFIs in other states such as Andhra Pradesh, Karnataka, etc. by rating agencies. The MFIs in North-East do not fare well on most of these indicators of cost, efficiency and profitability which are more appropriate for other parts of the country. This restricts the funding opportunities for MFIs, and drives them to operate in more densely populated and well-connected areas rather than venturing into more remote and inaccessible locations.

(viii) *Higher Cost of Operations:* Due to low population density, poor infrastructure, and the high diversity of local cultures, the cost of operations in North-East is high. MFIs thus have difficulty breaking even, and are forced in some cases to pass on those costs in the form of high interest rates.

(ix) *Lack of Representative Body for Micro-finance:* There has been a lack of a representative body for micro-finance in North-

East to raise region-specific issues at the national level, to carry out policy advocacy and to mobilize the sector.

(x) *Other Constraints:* There are several other social, economic, political and geographic peculiarities of the region that inhibit the growth of micro-finance in North-East. These reasons are:

(a) The region has typical geographical characteristics. The terrain is hilly which makes it difficult to operate in the region. The region is also prone to natural disasters such as floods, which are quite common in Assam, this increases the risk for micro-finance. Rough and sometimes virtually unknown terrain makes it difficult even for state-led initiatives to reach people and achieve the desired results.

(b) The low connectivity of the region in general and the physical isolation of some parts is a big constraint on outreach.

(c) The infrastructure in the region is poor. Underdevelopment of communications, transportation, banking facilities, and an unpredictable power situation makes it difficult for any industry or agency to operate in the region.

(d) The region has low population density with some states such as Arunachal as low as 13 persons/sq.km. Coupled with poor infrastructure, this dispersion of people increases the cost of operations for MFIs, which ultimately results in high costs for the clients.

(e) The decline in agricultural growth and stagnant industrial and service sector has led to limited livelihood options. This poses a challenge to link micro-credit activities to livelihood generation.

(f) The area is marked by the presence of a large tribal population. The presence of multi-ethnicity, multiple languages and heterogeneous cultures act as a constraint. The cost of aggregating people in the North-East is much higher.

(g) Although the region has a strong pool of natural resources, a mismatch between resources, control over resources and scientific management of the same are hindering growth and development of the region.

(h) North-Eastern region has many diverse traditional systems and even geographical conditions across different states.

These make it difficult to replicate the successful initiatives of one state into another. Sometimes, it is difficult even to replicate it within the state.

(i) For decades now, the region has had an ongoing problem of insurgency. This acts as a huge impediment for government, other agencies and institutions to operate in the region.

(j) The financial institutions deem the region to be of high risk, therefore, funding is difficult.

(k) There have been limited experiments in technology suiting the needs of the region. On a regular basis, technological advancements achieved in the main and are lifted and adopted, which lie down largely owing to unsuitability in the hilly regions.

Suggestions and Policy Choices for Financial Inclusion

Suggestions and policy choices for successful financial inclusion for inclusive growth and economic development in North-East India may be enumerated as follows:

(i) *A New Financial Architecture to Suit the Needs of Inclusive Growth:* Keeping in view the dynamics of the changing economy, there is a strong need to restructure the financial system particularly the rural financial system.

(ii) *Coordination with UIDAI:* There needs to be proper systematic coordination with UIDAI in order to make the best use of it for the purpose for financial inclusion.

(iii) *Formation of National Financial Inclusion Mission:* The formation of National Financial Inclusion Mission on the lines of National Literacy Mission to carry out systematic and coordinated drive for financial inclusion.

(iv) *Involvement of Education Sector for Furthering Financial Inclusion:* Involving educational institutions, particularly college students for financial inclusion drive would not only be cost-effective but also would create wide public awareness.

(v) *Establishment of Financial Counselling Centres:* Financial Inclusion drive should not be shortlived; instead a systematic effort should be structured by establishing FCCs (Financial Counselling Centres) on the lines of e-Seva centres in Andhra Pradesh for providing financial services.

(vi) *Building Client Capacities:* As the saying goes "teach him to fish instead of giving him fish", it should be the effort of all the concerned (particularly the financial institutions) to develop these poor people as prospective customers. Building client capacities would definitely help all the stakeholders and would be a vibrant financial system.

(vii) *Partnership with Dedicated NGOs and MFIs:* Partnering with trustworthy and acclaimed people's organizations would definitely accelerate the process of financial inclusion especially in the rural areas. Specific financial as well as non-financial incentives have to be designed for the spirited involvement of such organizations.

(viii) *Financial Inclusion as a Part of Course Curriculum in High Schools:* Financial Inclusion should be imbibed into the course curriculum in high schools so that the students would understand the importance of financial inclusion for inclusive growth in the economy which in turn would motivate them to automatically participate in the financial system.

(ix) *Digitize the Documentation Process for Opening of Bank Accounts:* One of the often stated reasons for slow pace of financial inclusion has been the hassles involved in opening of bank accounts and availing of loans from financial institutions due to the long process of documentation. To overcome this, there is a need to digitize the public records for dual purpose of easy accessibility and storage.

(x) *Strategize the Provision of Bank Credit:* Need is felt to strategize the provision of bank credit to the rural farmer households. Majority of the marginal farmer households are not at all covered by the formal finance. As such public sector banks and the cooperative banks in the rural areas have to sensitize about the need for provision of timely and cheaper credit to these segments. Reserve Bank of India in consultation with NABARD should come out with a comprehensive strategy for revitalizing the quiescent rural credit mechanism.

(xi) *Exclusive Focus on the Socially Excluded and the Poor:* It is imminent to encompass the socially excluded sections and the poor like, tenant farmers, oral lessees and share croppers, marginal farmers with small uneconomical landholdings, agricultural labourers, rural artisans and people involved in making handicrafts and also majority of weavers in handloom Sector.

(xii) *Extensive Use of Cooperatives:* PACS (Primary Agricultural Cooperative Societies) could provide valuable services to their members with a sense of belongingness. Accordingly, there is a need to revitalize these cooperatives as per the Vaidyanathan Committee recommendations and use them extensively for financial inclusion in the rural areas.

(xiii) *Undoubtedly a Greater Role for NABARD:* NABARD has to play a proactive role by partnering with the rural credit institutions in the field and identify new initiatives that will contribute to effectively improving the extent of financial inclusion involving SHGs, MFIs, etc.

(xiv) *Procedural/Documentation Changes:* It is inevitable on the part of the regulators to find out an easy way of procuring the documents for opening of bank accounts and availing loans. The present guidelines are more tedious and result in huge costs for the poor in accessing the banks for any kind of services. Simplifying Mortgage Requirements, Exemption from Stamp Duty for Loans to Small and Marginal Farmers, Serial Documentation for Agricultural Loans.

(xv) *Proactive Role of Government:* State Governments should be asked by the Central Government to play a proactive role in facilitating Financial Inclusion. Issuing official identity documents for opening accounts, creating awareness and involving district and block level functionaries in the entire process, meeting cost of cards and other devices for pilots, undertaking financial literacy drives are some of the ways in which the State and district administration should involve themselves.

(xvi) *A Role for Rural Post Offices:* Post Offices in rural areas can be asked to provide their services in accelerating the financial inclusion activity. In view of the postman's intimate knowledge of the local population and the enormous trust reposed in him post offices can be used in the process of financial inclusion.

(xvii) *Effective Use of Information Technology Solutions:* The use of IT enables banks to handle the enormous increase in the volume of transactions for millions of households for processing, credit scoring, credit record and follow-up. The use of IT solutions for providing banking facilities at doorstep holds the potential for scalability of the Financial Inclusion initiatives.

(xviii) *Adequate Publicity for the Project of Financial Inclusion:* In a huge country like India, there needs to be huge publicity for popularizing the concept and its benefits to the common man. In this direction, a comprehensive approach has to be developed involving all the concerned at all levels to impress upon the need for financial inclusion for accelerating the economic growth in the country.

(xix) *Financial Inclusion as a Corporate Social Responsibility of all the Banks and Financial Institutions:* It should be the endeavour of all the financial institutions to adopt financial inclusion as a corporate social responsibility and chalk out strategies in tune with the national policy on financial inclusion.

(xx) *Role of RBI:* Reserve Bank needs to take a proactive role in accelerating financial inclusion by involving all the stakeholders in the financial system by using its power of moral suasion as well as regulatory powers.

(xxi) *Political Will:* Political will is an all important aspect in any developmental effort. Political leadership should accord adequate importance for financial inclusion in order to motivate and mobilize all the weaker sections of the society in favour of financial inclusion for their economic upbringing.

(xxii) *Ensure Financial Inclusion is Part of the New UN Development Framework:* The UN High level Panel and member states should consider how increased access to financial inclusion could be a measure of progress towards more equitable and inclusive economic growth.

Conclusion

The economic status of NES in context of all India financial and fiscal indicators was found extremely weak. However, it is not because of lack of natural resources and manpower but it seems to be the non-implementation of regional plan and special strategy for fostering industrial development in these states. The interplay between agricultural and industrial development can promote inclusive growth in these states. The spillover effect of industrialization and tourism development would act as catalyst for achieving the goal of economic inclusion in general and financial inclusion in particular in NES.

In order to develop NES in all respect, an integrated policy of development should put in place for infrastructure development to harness the local potential so that food processing, wood products and traditional textile industries can be developed on large scale. Broad initiative is needed for stepping up agricultural productivity along with further development of horticulture, floriculture, animal husbandry is possible. All these efforts may push further the inclusive growth and financial inclusion in NES of India. Financial inclusion is the integration of below poverty line people into the mainstream economy. Financial inclusion is a necessary step in ensuring inclusive economic development.

REFERENCES

Bhatnagar, S.D. (2007). "Emerging Knowledge-based innovations with special reference to Micro-Credit", *The Journal of Indian Institute of Banking and Finance*, July-September 2007, Vol. 78, No. 3, pp. 50-58.

Devaki, Muthukrishnan (2008). "Financial Inclusion", *The Journal of Indian Institute of Banking and Finance*, April-June, pp. 30-33.

Gadewar, A.U., "Financial Inclusion: Issues and Challenges", *Vinimaya*, Vol. XXVII(4), 2006-07, pp. 49-56.

Government of India (2008). *Report of the Committee on the Financial Inclusion*, January 2008.

Leeladhar, V. (2005). "Taking Banking Services to the Common Man: Financial Inclusion", Commemorative Lecture by Shri V. Leeladhar, Deputy Governor, RBI, Fedbank Hormis Memorial Foundation, Ernakulam, December 2, 2005.

Mahendra Dev, S. (2006), "Financial Inclusion — Issues and Challenges", *Economic and Political Weekly*, Vol. 41(41), October 14-October 20, 2006.

Mathew, Joseph, "Financial Inclusion for Inclusive Growth", *Vinimaya*, Vol. XXVIII.

Muthukrishnan, Devaki "Financial Inclusion", *The Journal of Indian Institute of Banking and Finance*, April-June 2008, pp.30-33.

NABARD, *Status of Micro-finance in India 2008 to 2011*.

North-Eastern Council (2006). *Basic Statistics of NER*, 2006, Shillong, Meghalaya: North-Eastern Council Secretariat.

Rao, Srinivasa K. (2009). "Micro-credit Engine for Inclusive Growth", *The Indian Banker*, September 2009, Vol. 4, No. 9, pp. 40-43.

Ramanathan, Narayanan Laxmi (2011). "Socio-Economic Impact of SHG-Bank Linkage on Members: An Assessment", *Southern Economist*, March 2011, pp. 13-16.

RBI, *Report on Trend and Progress of Banking in India*, 2010-11.

Sarkar, A.N. and Singh Jagjit (2006). "Savings-Led Micro-finance to Bank the Unbankables: Sharing of Global Experience", *Global Economic Review*, July 2006, Vol. 7, No. 2, pp. 271-95.

Trivedi, Pratima, "Financial Inclusion: A Must for Financial Stability", *Vinimaya*, Vol. XXIX(2), 2008-09, pp. 59-64.

7

FINANCIAL INSTITUTIONS AND SELF-HELP GROUPS IN TRIPURA

Navin Kumar Rajpal and *A.K. Agarwal*

Financial institution plays a leading role not only in transfer of resources to cater the needs of individual and enterprises, but also in developing the thrust areas of economy. The higher concentration of financial institutions in urban areas has not only regional disparity in development, but also increased the level of poverty and unemployment. Further, there exists migration of people towards the concentrated areas. The nationalization of the commercial banks and the extensive policies of RBI have given a new dimension to development and coverage of financial sectors in India. Even after having widest banking coverage India's half of the population not having saving account with any financial institution (Rangarajan Committee Report, 2008). Moreover, only 9 per cent have credit account with banks. The non-coverage of the vast section of population was a matter of concern not only for government but also for policy makers and researchers. Various studies show the major reason behind this vast exclusion is lack of designed product as per needs of poor. The poor people basically lack on several ground among which the collateral security, non-maintenance of account and higher minimum balance ratio was the major one. Further, other factors like lack of identity, non availability of proper address, small loan, high maintenance cost, and bad behaviour of bank officials have served strong hindrance in proper functioning of banking services towards the poor and vulnerable sections. The introduction of SHG based micro-finance programme has given a new hope not only to government in providing credit at cheaper rate but also to poor and vulnerable section of society to access the credit without collateral security. The Self-help Groups are basically the homogeneous group of poor, women, user, etc.

which are voluntarily formed for the common interest of their development. The group meets together for addressing their common problems and make voluntary thrift on regular basis. Further, this reported money is pooled to make small interest bearing loans to individual members in need. The basic idea of micro-finance is to provide access to basic financial services including credit which enables to poor entrepreneurs to start their own micro-enterprise through which they move out from the clutches of poverty and unemployment.

The present study highlights the growth and performance of SHG programme in India and its different regions. It also examines the financial status of SHGs programme in different states of NER and Tripura. This chapter also highlights the role played by various financial institutions in promoting SHG programme in Tripura and their relative contributions.

Growth and Performance of SHGs Programme in India — An Overview

The SHG based micro-finance programme started in India with the initiative of NABARD, RBI and MYRADA during 1992 by linking 225 SHGs with various Banks. The restless effort of various governmental and non-governmental agencies like APMAS, WCD, MYRADA, PRADHAN, SEWA, MISSION SHAKTI, TRIPTI, DRDA, ITDA, ICDS, STREE SHAKTI, various government departments, Banks, etc. have created a milestone not only by achieving the results greater than the targeted but also in achieving the major goal of economic upliftment and social empowerment of deprived section of society. The growth and performance of SHGs in India and NER is explained in Table 7.1. Due to lack of availability of data pertaining to status of micro-finance in India in terms of saving, credit and outstanding and NPA, the study focuses on data available in details since 2007-08.

SHG-Saving Linkage

The growth of SHG-saving linkage over the years is explained in terms of saving linkage facility available to SHGs along with saving amount. The study found that during the year 2007-08, 50.09 lakh SHGs were provided saving linkage facility with different financial institutions along with saving amount of ₹ 3,785.38 crore. While in NER, the number of SHGs provided saving linkage facility was only 2.03 lakh with saving amount of ₹ 86.33 crore holding share of 4.05 per cent and

Table 7.1: Growth and Performance of SHGs in India and NER

(Amount in ₹ in crore)

Year	*Particulars*	*Saving of SHGs with Banks (India)*	*NER*	*Loan Disbursed (India)*	*NER*	*Bank Loan Outstanding with SHGs (India)*	*NER*
2006-07	No. of SHGs	4160584	N.A.	1105749	N.A.	2894505	N.A.
	Amount	3512.71	N.A.	6570.39	N.A.	12366.49	N.A.
2007-08	No. of SHGs	5009794	203045	1227770	29119	3625941	103424
	Amount	3785.38	86.33	8849.26	148.71	16999.91	355.63
Growth rate 2007-08 (In %)	**No. of SHGs**	**20.41**	—	**11.04**	—	**25.27**	—
	Amount	**7.76**	—	**34.68**	—	**37.47**	—
2008-09	No. of SHGs	6121147	240093	1609586	35506	4224338	117812
	Amount	5545.61	102.10	12253.51	246.41	22679.84	469.30
Growth rate 2008-09 (In %)	**No. of SHGs**	**22.18**	**18.24**	**31.10**	**21.93**	**16.50**	**13.91**
	Amount	**46.50**	**18.26**	**38.47**	**65.69**	**33.41**	**31.96**
2009-10	No. of SHGs	6953250	292188	1586822	49307	4851356	133785
	Amount	6198.70	121.67	14453.30	287.16	28038.28	673.47
Growth rate 2009-10 (In %)	**No. of SHGs**	**13.59**	**21.69**	**–1.41**	**38.86**	**14.84**	**13.55**
	Amount	**11.78**	**19.16**	**17.95**	**16.53**	**23.63**	**43.50**
2010-11	No. of SHGs	7461946	324739	1196134	39307	4786763	150021
	Amount	7016.30	131.04	14547.73	320.95	31221.17	695.25
Growth rate 2010-11 (In %)	**No. of SHGs**	**7.31**	**11.14**	**–24.6**	**–20.28**	**–1.3**	**12.13**
	Amount	**13.2**	**7.70**	**0.01**	**11.76**	**11.4**	**3.23**
2011-12	No. of SHGs	7960394	366718	1147878	51003	4354442	159416
	Amount	6551.41	152.51	16534.76	451.28	36340.00	993.26
Growth rate 2011-12 (In %)	**No. of SHGs**	**6.7**	**12.92**	**–4.01**	**29.75**	**-9.0**	**6.26**
	Amount	**–6.7**	**16.38**	**13.7**	**40.60**	**16.4**	**42.86**
2012-13	No. of SHGs	7317551	323896	1219821	25168	4451434	143660
	Amount	8217.25	130.10	0585.36	180.21	39375.29	796.75
Growth rate 2012-13 (In %)	**No. of SHGs**	**–8.07**	**–11.67**	**6.26**	**–50.65**	**2.22**	**–9.88**
	Amount	**25.42**	**–14.69**	**24.49**	**-60.06**	**8.35**	**–19.78**

Source: Status of Micro-finance in India, 2007, 2008, 2009, 2010, 2011, 2012 and 2013.

2.28 per cent respectively. In the year 2010-11, the number of SHGs provided saving linkage facility was 74.61 lakh along with saving linkage amount of ₹ 7,016.30, while in NER the saving linkage facility available to SHGs was 3.24 lakh along with saving amount of ₹ 131.04 crore holding a share of 4.60 per cent and 1.86 per cent respectively. During the year, 2012-13, 73.17 lakh SHGs were provided saving linkage facility along with saving amount of ₹ 8,217.25 crore which clearly reflects the decline in SHG saving linkage facility, but increase in terms of saving amount made by SHGs. As the NER concern the study found 3.23 lakh SHGs were provided saving linkage facility along with saving amount of ₹ 130.10 crore holding share of 4.42 per cent and 1.58 per cent respectively. This clearly indicates over the years, the share of SHGs of NER region in terms of saving linkage has not increased above 5 per cent of India's total while the saving amount has shown declining tendency from 2.28 per cent to 1.58 per cent which shows increasing trend at national level.

SHG-Credit Linkage

As the matter of SHG-Credit linkage concern, the study found during the year 2007-08, 16.09 lakh SHGs were provided credit linkage facility along with credit amount of ₹ 12,253.51 crore. In NER, the SHGs availed credit linkage facility was 3.55 lakh with credit amount of ₹ 246.41 crore holding share of 2.20 per cent and 2.01 per cent respectively. In the year 2010-11, the credit linkage facility to SHGs had declined to 11.96 lakh along with credit amount of ₹ 14,547.73 crore. In NER, the number of SHGs provided credit linkage facility was 39307 along with credit amount of ₹ 320.95 crore holding share of 3.26 per cent and 2.20 per cent respectively. But in the year 2012-13, the number of SHGs provided credit linkage facility was 12.19 lakh along with credit amount of ₹ 20,585.36 crore while in NER the SHGs provided credit linkage facility was only 0.25 lakh along with credit amount of ₹ 180.21 crore holding share of 2.06 per cent and 0.87 per cent respectively. The study clearly indicates that the lower share of NER in credit linkage programme ranging between 2-3.26 per cent while in terms of credit amount the share has declined to 0.87 per cent in 2012-13 from 2.01 per cent during 2007-08.

Loan Outstanding

In the year 2007-08, 36.25 lakh SHGs have loan outstanding with different financial institutions along with outstanding amount of

₹ 16,999.91 crore, while in NER only 1.03 lakh SHGs have loan outstanding along with outstanding amount of ₹ 355.63 crore holding share of 2.85 per cent and 2.09 per cent respectively. With the moving years, the outstanding amount has increased both in national as well as in North-Eastern region (except 2012-13). In the year 2010-11, 47.86 lakh SHGs have outstanding loan along with outstanding amount of ₹ 31,221.17 crore while in NER, 1.50 lakh SHGs have outstanding loan constituting amount of ₹ 695.25 crore holding share of 3.13 per cent and 2.22 per cent respectively. Further, the study found in the year 2012-13, 44.51 lakh SHGs have loan outstanding with different financial institutions along with outstanding amount of ₹ 39,375.29 crore while in NER it was 1.43 lakh SHGs with amount outstanding of ₹ 796.75 crore holding share of 3.22 per cent and 2.02 per cent respectively. It has been observed that the SHGs loan outstanding has shown declining trend over the years at national level whereas the outstanding amount has shown positive trend almost in every year. But in NER the situation is somehow different, as compared to national level the growth of SHGs loan outstanding and amount was lower as compared to national level. Moreover, during 2012-13, both aspects have shown negative trend in NER while at national level it has shown positive trend.

Growth of SHGs in Different States of NER

The North-Eastern Region usually comprises 8 states as per classification made by NABARD while in terms of geographical location it is termed as seven sisters (Sikkim is included in eastern region). The SHG programme has not shown any significant improvement over the years as compared to other regions of India. Table 7.2 shows the growth of SHG Saving linkage programme in different states of NER. The study found during 2007-08, in every state of NER there is existence of SHG-Saving linkage programme, but it was highest in Assam followed by Tripura and Meghalaya while lowest in Sikkim followed by Arunachal Pradesh and Nagaland. Till 2012-13 same tendency has been observed, i.e. Assam and Tripura have shown highest saving linkage facility towards SHGs. In terms of Saving linkage amount in the year 2007-08, it was highest in Assam with ₹ 58.00 crore followed by Tripura (₹ 11.29 crore) and Mizoram (₹ 7.92 crore) while lowest in Arunachal Pradesh (₹ 0.53 crore), Sikkim (₹ 0.60 crore) and Nagaland (₹ 1.19 crore). Same tendency of higher saving amount has been observed in Assam and Tripura over the years except in 2012-13 where the saving was highest in Sikkim in addition to Assam. The study further found that during

Table 7.2: Growth of SHG-Bank Saving Linkage in NER

(*Amount in crore*)

Year	*Particulars*	*Assam*	*Meghalaya*	*Nagaland*	*Tripura*	*Arunachal Pradesh*	*Mizoram*	*Manipur*	*Sikkim*
2007-08	No. of SHGs	149719	14199	3405	19904	2001	4225	7945	1647
	Amount	58.00	3.09	1.19	11.29	0.53	7.92	3.67	0.60
2008-09	No. of SHGs	180996	9625	6057	22811	5148	4230	9474	1752
	Amount	62.96	3.27	1.57	28.58	0.93	1.84	1.91	0.99
Growth rate (in %)	No. of SHGs	20.89	–32.21	77.88	14.60	157.27	0.11	19.24	6.37
	Amount	8.55	5.82	31.93	153.14	75.47	–76.76	–47.95	65.0
2009-10	No. of SHGs	218352	11787	5926	31349	6418	5097	10831	2428
	Amount	73.59	3.60	3.34	33.35	1.64	2.51	2.18	1.41
Growth rate (in %)	No. of SHGs	20.63	31.22	–2.16	37.42	24.66	20.49	14.32	38.58
	Amount	16.88	10.09	112.73	16.68	76.34	36.41	14.13	42.42
2010-11	No. of SHGs	245120	10653	9866	34312	7079	4592	10306	2811
	Amount	81.96	3.76	3.62	33.95	1.86	1.78	2.40	1.68
Growth rate (in %)	No. of SHGs	12.25	–9.62	66.48	9.45	10.29	–9.90	–4.84	15.77
	Amount	11.37	4.44	8.38	1.79	13.41	–29.08	10.09	19.14
2011-12	No. of SHGs	276565	14091	10711	34021	8363	4976	12711	5280
	Amount	98.45	4.14	3.74	33.77	1.86	5.72	2.19	2.60
Growth rate (in %)	No. of SHGs	12.82	32.27	8.56	–0.84	18.13	8.36	23.33	87.83
	Amount	20.11	10.10	3.31	–0.53	0.00	221.34	–8.75	54.76
2012-13	No. of SHGs	271072	9573	8478	10438	5033	3117	12656	3529
	Amount	107.50	5.15	1.85	2.19	4.12	6.12	2.35	7.90
Growth rate (in %)	No. of SHGs	–1.98	–32.06	–20.84	–69.31	–39.81	–37.35	–0.4	–33.16
	Amount	9.19	24.39	–50.53	–93.51	121.50	6.99	7.30	203.84

Source. *Status of Micro-finance in India*, 2007, 2008, 2009, 2010, 2011, 2012 and 2013.

2009-10, in terms of growth of saving linkage the growth was highest in Arunachal Pradesh while in saving amount it was highest in Tripura. With the moving years, the pattern of growth has shown different trends. In the year 2012-13, the study found negative growth trend in every state of NER in terms of SHG-saving linkage facility while in saving linkage amount the study found negative growth except in Mizoram and Nagaland.

SHG-Credit Linkage in Different States of NER

Table 7.3 shows the growth of SHG-Credit linkage programme in different states of NER. The study found during the year 2007-08, the number of SHGs has been provided credit linkage facility was highest in Assam followed by Tripura and Meghalaya while lowest in Nagaland, Manipur and Sikkim. With the moving years same pattern has been observed, i.e. Assam and Tripura stood initial status. In the year 2012-13, the SHGs has been provided credit linkage facility was highest again in Assam and Tripura whereas lowest in Arunachal Pradesh and Meghalaya. As the growth rate concern, the study found during 2008-09 Tripura and Manipur stood initial position in terms of SHG-Credit linkage while Tripura and Sikkim in terms of Credit amount. Over the years uneven growth has been observed both in credit linkage and credit amount in every State of NER.

In 2012-13, all States of NER have shown negative trend in terms of SHG-Credit linkage programme. Moreover, negative trend is again observed in every State of NER except Nagaland and Mizoram.

Financial Institutions and SHG-Bank Linkage in Tripura

Tripura is a state of North-East India which shares its borders with Bangladesh, Mizoram and Assam. It is surrounded by Bangladesh in north, south and west covering 856 km in length. The total area of the state is 10,491.69 sq.km. with population 36,73,917. The United Bank of India serves as the lead Bank in all districts of Tripura. The study found that all major financial institutions, i.e., Commercial Banks, RRBs and Cooperative banks are engaged in providing linkage facility to SHGs. Table 7.4 shows the growth of SHG-Saving linkage programme under different financial institutions in Tripura. The study found that since 2007-08 the Regional Rural Bank (commonly known as Tripura Gramin Bank) plays a major role in providing saving linkage facility to SHGs followed by Commercial Banks and Cooperative Banks. Similar pattern has been observed relating to the amount of saving made by

Table 7.3: Growth of SHG-Bank Credit Linkage in Different States of NER

Year	*Particulars*	*Assam*	*Meghalaya*	*Nagaland*	*Tripura*	*Arunachal Pradesh*	*Mizoram*	*Manipur*	*Sikkim*
2007-08	No. of SHGs	20318	2143	543	2365	1459	775	578	668
	Amount	88.69	13.62	3.87	16.66	10.04	8.93	2.47	4.39
2008-09	No. of SHGs	26448	1003	94	4766	391	919	903	982
	Amount	156.96	5.09	2.00	54.28	2.29	8.38	4.86	12.52
Growth rate (in %)	No. of SHGs	30.17	–53.19	–82.68	101.52	–73.20	18.58	56.22	47.00
	Amount	76.97	-62.62	–48.32	225.81	–77.19	–6.15	96.76	185.19
2009-10	No. of SHGs	39058	1895	603	5424	919	417	538	906
	Amount	195.73	8.84	6.37	62.70	3.18	4.66	3.01	5.29
Growth rate (in %)	No. of SHGs	47.67	88.93	541.48	13.80	135.03	–54.62	–40.42	–7.73
	Amount	24.70	73.67	218.5	15.51	38.86	–44.39	–38.06	–57.74
2010-11	No. of SHGs	29094	1113	657	6015	956	420	721	331
	Amount	227.15	7.58	5.19	68.35	4.52	2.86	3.51	1.74
Growth rate (in %)	No. of SHGs	–25.51	–41.26	8.95	10.89	4.02	0.71	34.01	–63.46
	Amount	16.05	–14.25	–18.52	9.01	42.13	–38.62	16.61	–67.10
2011-12	No. of SHGs	28012	691	862	19029	130	575	1308	396
	Amount	187.46	4.89	6.21	231.41	1.57	6.90	8.57	4.23
Growth rate (in %)	No. of SHGs	–3.71	–37.91	31.20	216.35	–86.40	36.90	81.41	19.63
	Amount	–17.47	–35.48	19.65	238.56	–65.26	141.25	144.15	143.10
2012-13	No. of SHGs	21497	400	796	801	112	544	659	359
	Amount	137.55	4.62	9.74	12.50	1.32	8.27	4.05	2.12
Growth rate (in %)	No. of SHGs	–23.25	–42.11	–7.65	–95.79	–13.84	–5.39	–49.61	–9.34
	Amount	–26.62	–5.52	56.84	–94.59	–15.92	19.85	–52.74	–49.88

Source: Status of Micro-finance in India, 2007, 2008, 2009, 2010, 2011, 2012 and 2013.

SHGs. During 2011-12, 16,696 SHGs have been provided saving linkage facility by Tripura Gramin Bank holding saving amount of ₹ 27.36 crore while the Cooperative Banks though shown lower saving linkage to SHGs but the saving amount was highest (₹ 38.8 crore) as compared to other institutions. As the average saving per SHG concern it has been observed that during 2007-08 the average saving was highest in RRBs (₹ 6,163.00) followed by Commercial Banks (₹ 4,868.31) and Cooperative Banks (₹ 3,774.87). In the year 2011-12, the average saving per SHG was again highest in RRBs (₹ 16,387.15) followed by Cooperative Banks (₹ 6,820.17) and Commercial Banks (₹ 2,165.69).

Table 7.4: SHG-Saving Linkage with Different Financial Institutions in Tripura

(Amount in crore)

Year	*Particulars*	*Commercial Banks*	*Regional Rural Banks*	*Cooperative Banks*
2007-08	No. of SHGs	5012	13435	1457
	Amount	2.44	8.28	0.55
2008-09	No. of SHGs	5697	15059	2055
	Amount	2.62	25.06	0.90
2009-10	No. of SHGs	11244	15832	4273
	Amount	5.74	26.60	1.00
2010-11	No. of SHGs	10979	17644	5689
	Amount	2.44	27.62	3.88
2011-12	No. of SHGs	11636	16696	5689
	Amount	2.52	27.36	3.88
2012-13	No. of SHGs	10438	N.A.	N.A.
	Amount	2.19	N.A.	N.A.

Source: Status of Micro-finance in India, 2007, 2008, 2009, 2010, 2011, 2012 and 2013.

SHG-Credit Linkage with Different Financial Institutions in Tripura

Table 7.5 shows the share of different financial institutions in SHG-Credit linkage programme in Tripura. The study found that in the year 2007-08, the RRBs stood initial position in providing credit linkage facility to SHGs followed by Commercial Banks and RRBs. Similar pattern has been observed with credit linkage amount. The average loan available to per SHG during the year was highest with Cooperative Banks (₹ 1,56,140.35) followed by RRBs (₹ 69,612.06) and Commercial Banks (₹ 29,323.30). With the moving years the continuous growth has been observed on part of both RRBs and Cooperative Banks in providing credit linkage facility while on part of Commercial Banks uneven trend has been observed. In the year 2011-12, again the RRBs holds greater share in credit linkage programme including linkage amount followed by Cooperative Banks and Commercial Banks. The average loan available to each SHG was highest in Commercial Banks (₹ 1,56,612.31) followed by RRBs (₹ 1,19,434.39) and Cooperative Banks (₹ 1,19,642.85).

Table 7.5: SHG-Credit Linkage with Different Financial Institutions

(Amount in crore)

Year	*Particulars*	*Commercial Banks*	*Regional Rural Banks*	*Cooperative Banks*
2007-08	No. of SHGs	665	1856	114
	Amount	1.95	12.92	1.78
2008-09	No. of SHGs	1791	2799	176
	Amount	5.91	44.16	4.20
2009-10	No. of SHGs	1292	2929	1203
	Amount	13.68	39.58	9.44
2010-11	No. of SHGs	1300	3091	1624
	Amount	8.71	40.21	19.43
2011-12	No. of SHGs	1104	16301	1624
	Amount	17.29	194.69	19.43
2012-13	No. of SHGs	801	N.A.	N.A.
	Amount	12.50	N.A.	N.A.

Source: Status of Micro-finance in India, 2007, 2008, 2009, 2010, 2011, 2012 and 2013.

SHG-Loan Outstanding with Different Financial Institutions in Tripura

Table 7.6 shows the year-wise growth of SHG-Loan outstanding with different financial institutions in Tripura. The study found that in the year 2007-08, the loan outstanding and amount with SHGs was highest in RRBs followed by Commercial and Cooperative Banks.

Table 7.6: SHG-Loan Outstanding with Different Financial Institutions

(Amount in crore)

Year	*Particulars*	*Commercial Banks*	*Regional Rural Banks*	*Cooperative Banks*
2007-08	No. of SHGs	1642	3065	333
	Amount	4.07	12.82	3.38
2008-09	No. of SHGs	2456	7419	526
	Amount	6.84	25.88	4.82
2009-10	No. of SHGs	5404	7467	1709
	Amount	27.55	60.08	9.23
2010-11	No. of SHGs	7928	10173	2667
	Amount	40.61	37.90	24.53
2011-12	No. of SHGs	6845	15652	2677
	Amount	54.13	174.50	24.53
2012-13	No. of SHGs	6860	N.A.	N.A.
	Amount	55.98	N.A.	N.A.

Source: Status of Micro-finance in India, 2007, 2008, 2009, 2010, 2011, 2012 and 2013.

While in terms of average loan outstanding per SHG concern, it was highest with Cooperative Banks (₹ 1,01,501.50) followed by RRBs (₹ 41,827.07) and Commercial Banks (₹ 24,786.84). With the moving years increasing trend has been observed in loan outstanding with SHGs on part of RRBs and Cooperative Banks while in terms of outstanding amount increasing trend has been observed with Commercial and Cooperative Banks. In the year 2011-12, again the major share in outstanding holds by RRBs followed by Commercial and Cooperative Banks. The average outstanding with each SHG during the year was highest in RRBs (₹ 1,11,487.34) followed by Cooperative Banks (₹ 91,632.42) and Commercial Banks (₹ 79,079.67).

Growth of SHGs under Different Commercial Banks in Tripura

As per NABARD report 2012-13, out of the existing banks, only 8 scheduled commercial banks are engaged in formation and promotion of SHGs in Tripura. Further among these banks only few banks are seriously engaged in providing saving and credit facility to SHGs.

Table 7.7 shows the growth of SHG-Saving linkage along with saving amount under different scheduled commercial banks in Tripura. The study found during the year 2007-08 only three scheduled commercial banks, i.e. United Bank of India, State Bank of India and Central Bank of India are having saving account of SHGs. With the moving years several other scheduled commercial banks have engaged themselves in promotion of SHGs programme, but their performance was negligible. Moreover, the Vijaya Bank, Indian Bank and Union Bank have shown stagnant position in providing saving linkage facility to SHGs over the years.

In the year 2012-13, 6,295 SHGs were provided saving linkage facility by United Bank of India followed by SBI, UCO Bank and Central Bank of India. The average saving amount per SHG was highest with Vijaya Bank (₹ 38,000) followed by Bank of Baroda (₹ 16,666.66) and Central Bank of India (₹ 14,705.88) while lowest in United Bank of India (₹ 1,032.72), UCO Bank (₹ 2,569.59) and Indian Overseas Bank (₹ 2,941.17).

Table 7.8 shows the growth of SHG-Credit linkage programme under different Scheduled Commercial Banks in Tripura. The study found the condition more worst as compared to national and NER. During the year 2007-08 only two scheduled commercial banks were engaged in providing credit linkage facility to SHGs. Moreover, the

Table 7.7: Growth of SHG-Saving Linkage in Tripura

(*Amount in ₹ lakh*)

Sl.No.	*Bank*	*Particulars*	*2007-08*	*2008-09*	*2009-10*	*2010-11*	*2011-12*	*2012-13*
1.	Bank of Baroda	No. of SHGs	0	13	16	18	19	30
		Amount	0	3.17	4.57	9.45	1.34	5.00
2.	Central Bank of India	No. of SHGs	81	100	144	159	164	170
		Amount	22.00	22.18	22.83	22.99	24.00	25.00
3.	Indian Bank	No. of SHGs	0	0	1	44	20	2
		Amount	0	0	0.01	0.09	0.44	0.02
4.	Indian Overseas Bank	No. of SHGs	0	0	23	46	26	34
		Amount	0	0	1.00	2.00	2.00	1.00
5.	State Bank of India	No. of SHGs	2984	3096	3970	4170	4811	3345
		Amount	90.02	94.28	123.00	131.00	146.00	107.00
6.	UCO Bank	No. of SHGs	0	215	345	499	530	546
		Amount	0	3.25	10.22	13.75	13.93	14.03
7	Union Bank of India	No. of SHGs	0	0	3	26	9	15
		Amount	0	0	0.32	1.60	1.20	1.90
8.	United Bank of India	No. of SHGs	1947	2273	6742	6017	6057	6295
		Amount	132.74	139.24	412.39	63.22	63.77	65.01
9.	Vijaya Bank	No. of SHGs	0	0	0	0	0	1
		Amount	0	0	0	0	0	0.38

Source: *Status of Micro-finance in India*, 2007, 2008, 2009, 2010, 2011, 2012 and 2013.

Table 7.8: Growth of SHG-Credit Linkage in Tripura

(Amount in lakh)

Sl.No.	Bank	Particulars	2007-08	2008-09	2009-10	2010-11	2011-12	2012-13
1.	Bank of Baroda	No. of SHGs	0	13	13	3	9	3
		Amount	0	2.50	3.18	7.38	2.37	0.90
2.	Central Bank of India	No. of SHGs	9	14	13	11	11	11
		Amount	3.00	3.50	4.50	14.39	14.82	15.34
3.	Indian Bank	No. of SHGs	0	0	0	0	0	0
		Amount	0	0	0	0	0	0
4.	Indian Overseas Bank	No. of SHGs	0	0	15	11	0	0
		Amount	0	0	9.00	9.00	0	0
5.	State Bank of India	No. of SHGs	661	358	873	199	407	269
		Amount	192.00	590.71	1263.00	264.00	649.00	439.00
6.	UCO Bank	No. of SHGs	0	26	54	124	26	14
		Amount	0	26.00	7.19	38.35	0.91	8.93
7.	Union Bank of India	No. of SHGs	0	0	3	3	3	5
		Amount	0	0	0.60	0.58	1.73	1.75
8.	United Bank of India	No. of SHGs	0	513	321	949	648	499
		Amount	0	567.10	81.20	537.35	1060.46	784.75
9.	Vijaya Bank	No. of SHGs	0	0	0	0	0	0
		Amount	0	0	0	0	0	0

Source: Status of Micro-finance in India, 2007, 2008, 2009, 2010, 2011, 2012 and 2013.

credit amount available to SHGs was only ₹ 33,333.33 (Central Bank of India) and ₹ 29,046.89 (State Bank of India).

Over the years, no progressive achievement has been observed by many of scheduled commercial banks. Moreover, no credit linkage facility has been provided by Indian Bank and Vijaya Bank over the years. During 2012-13, out of existing 8 scheduled commercial banks, 3 banks have not lend any credit to SHGs in the State. Further the average loans made available to SHGs was highest in SBI (₹ 1,63,197.36) followed by United Bank of India (₹ 1,57,264.52), Central Bank of India (₹ 1,39,454.54) while lowest in Bank of Baroda (₹ 30,000) and Union Bank of India (₹ 35,000).

Conclusion

The growth and performance of SHG programme is a matter of concern both in NER as well as in Tripura. The lower saving and credit facility along with amount available to SHG members has served as the major factors behind this backwardness. Further in Tripura the dominant role is played by Tripura Gramin Bank whereas the number of commercial banks has not taken any interest in promoting SHG programme in the State.

8

FINANCIAL INCLUSION AND MICRO-ENTREPRENEURS IN MIZORAM

Lalhunthara and *N.V.R. Jyoti Kumar*

Introduction

The North-East Region (NER) in India is quite different from the rest of the country due to its socio-economic, geographical and cultural diversities. The problems faced by the industrial sector in this region are also different from their counterparts in the other parts of the country. The industrial sector in this region suffers from a number of innate constraints such as entrepreneurial, geographical, financial, social, political and infrastructure. In spite of the huge potential for different types of resources based industries, the process of industrialization is very slow because of the unique geographical location, inadequate infrastructure, worried investment climate, lack of entrepreneurial skill and remoteness of market (Vepa, 1988). Due to the steep slopes of the hills in the NER, road transport and railways are not well developed. The region also suffers from lack of sufficient plain areas to be used for industrial purpose. Frequent racial clashes, extortion of money by the insurgent groups, etc. create an insecure investment environment which discourages the national and multinational companies in investing in the region and ultimately go against the interest of the industrial development (Lingaiah, 1998).

The limitations and constraints which hinder the growth of micro and small enterprises at the national level are more or less equally applicable to this sector in the NER. The enterprises which are run by an individual or a few partners usually suffer from some innate deficiencies like poor capital base, lack of proper technical know-how, weak bargaining power, poor marketing capacity of products, etc. (Deb, 1993).

In this backdrop, an attempt has been made to study the financial problems faced by the micro-entrepreneurs in Aizawl district, Mizoram, a small state in North-East.

The Present Study

Mizoram is one of the most industrially backward states in India. The entire state has been notified as backward and is categorized as 'No Industry State' due to non-existence of large and medium industries (*Economic Survey: Mizoram*, 2007-08). Mostly micro-enterprises exist in Mizoram while big industries are almost absent. The disadvantages due to topographical and geographical condition of the State coupled with underdeveloped infrastructure and transport bottlenecks are the main hurdles for the first generation entrepreneurs of the State to move towards industrialization. The growth and performance of the manufacturing sector has been poor. The share of industry, consisting registered and unregistered units, to the state GSDP could marginally increase from 1.2 per cent at the beginning of Tenth Five Year Plan to 1.5 per cent at the terminal year (2006-07). The State has witnessed a low scale of migration of workforce from agriculture to non-agricultural sector. Business activities like tailoring, furniture making, automobile repairs, steel making, bakery, handloom weaving, blacksmithy, etc. account for 80 per cent of the total number of business enterprises in the state. There is little scope for big enterprises and as such micro-enterprises dominate the industrial scenario acquiring a prominent place in the socio-economic development of the State (*Economic Survey: Mizoram*, 2008-09).

About 60 per cent of the total workers in the State were engaged in agricultural activities mostly by practicing shifting cultivation (also known as *jhuming*). However, the share of agriculture to the GSDP was hardly seven per cent at current prices during 2008-09 (*Economic Survey: Mizoram*, 2008-09). There is a discontentment among the farmer community, they do not want to remain in the traditional sector and are very much keen to find out an alternative occupation to support the growing needs of their expanding family members (Laskar, 2010). Therefore, the micro-enterprises have specific role to play in the context of the economy of Mizoram. This sector requires less amount of capital and low level of technical skill. The vast natural resources and local raw materials can be utilized more efficiently by strengthening the micro-enterprises in the State thereby creating employment opportunities mainly to the underprivileged people and local artisans, which in turn, would help in realizing the planned goal of inclusive development.

Review of Literature

In this section, an attempt has been made to review some important studies in brief relating to the financial problems faced by entrepreneurs in Indian context.

Rao (1986) conducted a study in coastal Andhra, aiming at evaluating the impact of the programme of industrial estates on the emergence of entrepreneurship and growth of small units. The study also examined the socio-economic background of the entrepreneurs, forces behind the spirit of entrepreneurship, growth of enterprises in industrial estates and the various problems faced by the entrepreneurs. His study identified the shortage of working capital as an important financial problems.

Murthy (1992) carried out a field study of small entrepreneurs in Chittoor district of Andhra Pradesh. His study revealed that among the various problems associated with finance, working capital problem appeared to be the most important.

Murthy (1998) made an attempt to analyze the magnitude of financial assistance to SSI sector in Karnataka. The study found that the availability of institutional finance to SSI has not been sufficient to meet their needs nor in proportion to the volume of activity generated by the sector.

Dhameja (2004) undertook a study on women entrepreneurs in the States of Punjab, Haryana and Union Territory of Chandigarh. The study aimed at finding out entrepreneurial performance, problems and a host of other issues related to women in business. The study revealed that 45.7 per cent were found to be facing financial problem. Of all, reluctance by financial institutions to extend credit to women was the biggest financial problem.

Chanambam (2006) conducted a study of women entrepreneurs in the three states of Manipur, Nagaland and Tripura. She found that over two-third of the women entrepreneurs in Manipur, Nagaland and Tripura were suffering from financial problems.

Ramswamy (2012) in her study on micro handloom enterprises predominantly run by women in a remote tribal cluster, Thenzawl in Mizoram, identified the sources of fixed capital for the enterprises and the problems faced by them related to finance.

From the above review of literature, it is observed that most of the studies have been conducted on different managerial problems faced by Micro, Small and Medium Enterprises (MSMEs) in different parts of the country. Very few studies have been conducted in the context of NER. The present study on financial problems faced by micro-enterprises in Mizoram is an attempt to fill-up the research gap.

Objectives and Methodology

The objectives of this chapter are to study some financial aspects in respect of micro-enterprises in Aizawl district, Mizoram. The study covers diverse range of micro-enterprises in Aizawl district. Since it is an exploratory study, it is mostly based on primary data collected from the entrepreneurs of micro-enterprises. As per the Third Census of Small Scale Industries (2001-02), there were 2,718 registered small scale industries in Mizoram, out of which 2,027 were in Aizawl district (1914 were in Aizawl urban and 113 were in Aizawl rural). Precisely all these enterprises constituted the population from which the sample for the purpose of the present study had to be chosen. The number of entrepreneurs engaged in activities like manufacturing, printing/ publications, food processing, handlooms, tailoring, etc. are found to be abundant in Aizawl district of Mizoram. Almost 75 per cent of the registered enterprises (2,027 out of 2,718) are located in Aizawl district. Therefore, it was thought that Aizawl district represents the whole of Mizoram. The size of the sample was fixed at 20 per cent of the enterprises in Aizawl district. Accordingly, a total of 406 enterprises (383 enterprises in Aizawl urban and 23 enterprises in Aizawl rural) were covered. Then the sample was drawn by using random sampling technique. However, in the course of identifying the sample enterprises in the field study it was found that some of the enterprises were either non-functional or closed units. In such instances, those sample units were selected randomly again. Another practical problem faced at the time of selection of sample units was relating to the nomenclature used in the records kept by the Directorate of Industries, Government of Mizoram. In these records 'micro' and 'small enterprises' were not differentiated because such data were based on the nomenclature used prior to the enactment of the MSMED Act, 2006. Hence, the researchers had to take the difficulty of eliminating 'small enterprises' from the list with a view to confine to only 'micro-enterprises'. It was to be noted that such type of small enterprises are very few in the data provided by the Third Census of Small Scale Industries in respect of Mizoram.

Information from the sample entrepreneurs was collected in 2007 and 2008 by administering a schedule. Data were collected at the place of work of the entrepreneurs. The data thus collected were further supplemented by unstructured interviews with the entrepreneurs.

The sample units, drawn on the basis of random sampling technique, fall under seven groups of business activities as shown in Table 8.1. They are:

- *Food Processing:* This includes enterprises engaged in food items and other related products like milk and milk products, biscuits, bakery and other food items.
- *Wooden:* This group includes enterprises engaged in making and repairing wooden objects and structures, cane and bamboo products.
- *Repair Services:* All types of repair services are included here ranging from small electronic items to big machinery.
- *Steel/Metal:* This includes the enterprises who engaged in making, fabricating, repairing, constructing or manufacturing steel structures.
- *Printing/Publication:* This group includes those who engaged in all types of printing and publishing activities.
- *Handlooms:*The enterprises who engage in weaving of clothes and resale them to the market through middlemen or directly to the customers are included in this group.
- *Tailoring:* All enterprises involved in sewing of clothes made from cotton, wool, embroidery, etc. and used to make clothes or curtains, are included here.

Table 8.1: Distribution of Sample Enterprises

Sl.No.	*Entrepreneurial Activity*	*Sample Size*
1.	Food items	20
2.	Wood products	110
3.	Repair services	69
4.	Steel/Metal products	85
5.	Printing/publication	19
6.	Handloom	34
7.	Tailoring	69
	Total	406

Discussion and Results

Problems of Finance

Without the availability of adequate financial resources the smooth running of the business will be in a standstill. Usually, small entrepreneurs started well in the initial stage but somewhere down the line in their operation they miss the route to success. In more than half of such cases, the reasons identified can be attributed to financial mismanagement. At times such entrepreneurs had a feeling they are doing financially well but the year end consolidation of accounts indicate a different picture, i.e. loss or almost on the verge of losing (Pathak, 1991). One of the most difficulties for the entrepreneurs and prospective entrepreneurs is non-availability or scarcity of finance to meet their requirement. Financial support as well as financial viability are the most important considerations of any business proposition (Dhameja, 2004).

Due to financial constraints, the micro-entrepreneurs find it difficult to promote their products and services. In addition to financial problems, competition from well established firms, was one of the major problems faced by the sample entrepreneurs. Consequently, lack of competitiveness would lead to loss of markets for their products. This might have adverse effect on the growth of entrepreneurship in Mizoram. The nature of financial problems faced by the entrepreneurs, under the study, is shown in Table 8.2.

Table 8.2: Problems of Finance Faced by Entrepreneurs

Problems	*Entrepreneurs' Ranking of Financial Problems*					
	Number One	*Number Two*	*Number Three*	*Weighted Score*	*Rating (%)*	*Rank*
High rate of interest	149	96	81	720	36.8	1
Meagre assistance from government agencies	76	76	58	438	22.4	2
Red-tapism in government agencies	35	62	63	292	14.9	4
Red-tapism in banks	69	70	87	434	22.2	3
Any other problems (Please specify)*	14	12	7	73	3.7	5
No. of entrepreneurs not responded	—	27	47	—	—	
Total	343	343	343	1957	100.0	

* Other problems include credit sales and bad debts.
Note: 63 enterprises were reported not facing the problem of finance.
Source: Field Survey.

High rate of interest was rated as the most serious problem (36.8% of rating), followed by meagre assistance from government agencies (22.4% of rating), red-tapism in banks (22.2% of rating) and, red-tapism in government agencies (14.9% of rating). In other words, 43.4 per cent of the entrepreneurs indicated high rate of interest as the number one problem. Over 30 per cent of the entrepreneurs felt high interest rate as the second most important problem, and 27.3 per cent of them considered red-tapism as the third most important problem. The scarcity of finance poses serious challenges to the development of entrepreneurship in Mizoram. The capital base of the enterprises in the state is typically weak and they generally run their business on the basis of sole proprietorship.

Recognizing the need and importance for smooth credit flow for the development of micro and small enterprises sector, the Government of India set up State Financial Corporations (SFCs) and Small Industries Development Bank of India (SIDBI) to look after the financial needs of the small scale sector. Banks were mandated to provide 40 per cent of their lending to priority sector including micro and small enterprises. However, banks claim to meet their lending target on paper but in reality they are reluctant to lend to the micro and small entrepreneurs due to low recovery rate and higher cost of lending to them. Moreover, banks insist on collateral security against the spirit of Reserve Bank of India (RBI) guidelines. Sometimes, the market value of collateral could be as high as five times the value of the outstanding loan or credit limit. The micro and small enterprises are hardly in a position to offer the guarantee required by the banks. Small loans can be raised from government agencies but the procedure is so cumbersome that most of the entrepreneurs hesitate to avail these facilities (Laskar, 2010). There were 108 bank branches in Mizoram as on December 31, 2008 including 60 branches of Mizoram Rural Bank (MRB), 26 branches of State Bank of India (SBI), 11 branches of Mizoram Cooperative Apex Bank (MCAB). Besides, development financial institutions like NABARD, SIDBI and NEDFI also have their branches in Mizoram. Only 18 per cent of the total loans and advances were disbursed to the industrial sector during 2006-07. The same was 15.8 per cent in 2007-08; it was 7.56 per cent in 2008-09 and 5.84 per cent in 2009-10 (*Economic Survey: Mizoram*, 2010-11).

This implies the poor performance of banks in providing assistance to the micro and small enterprises. Moreover, Mizoram has no State Financial Corporation (SFC) to provide funds to the industrial sector in the State. Most of the sample entrepreneurs in the present study do not maintain proper books of accounts to record their business transactions. At the time of applying for loans, banks and other agencies ask them to produce financial information, but the entrepreneurs are not always in a position to do so because of non-maintenance of proper records. In addition, those entrepreneurs who could get loans find it difficult to repay the loans due to improper financial planning and management. Therefore, banks and financial institutions hesitate to provide loans to the entrepreneurs because of risk of creating non-performing assets. The recovery rate of bank loans during 2005-06 was 59.79 per cent; it was 69.95 per cent during 2006-07, 64.34 per cent in 2007-08, 70.2 per cent in 2008-09 and 70 per cent in 2009-10 (*Economic Survey: Mizoram*, 2009-10). The loan recovery rates under different centrally sponsored schemes reflect the similar situation. For example, during 2007-08, the recovery rate under PMRY scheme was only 11.62 per cent; it was 46.57 per cent under SGSY, 11.64 per cent under SJSRY (*Economic Survey: Mizoram*, 2007-08). As observed by Laskar (2010), poor loan recovery has prevented many educated youth of Mizoram from benefiting from the loans offered by various financial institutions. Moreover, District Industries Centres (DICs) make recommendations to the banks from time to time regarding the requirements of funds by the entrepreneurs. It was found that the banks and financial institutions in the State do not give due importance to those recommendations forwarded to them by DICs. The specialized bank branches like IDBI, SIDBI, NEDFI, NABARD, etc. are located only in the State Capital at Aizawl while many of the enterprises are located across the State. It is difficult for them to provide adequate and timely credit to the enterprises which are located in semi-urban and rural areas.

Sources of Initial Capital

Initial capital may be defined as the amount of capital required for the establishment of an enterprise initially. Sources of initial capital remain one of the major problems for micro and small entrepreneurs, more so for first generation entrepreneurs. It is attempted to identify the sample entrepreneurs' sources of initial capital to start enterprises. The entrepreneurs' major sources of initial capital are shown in Table 8.3. Over 47 per cent (194 out of 406) of the entrepreneurs cited have their own funds as a major source of initial capital contributed by them. On the other hand, 7.6 per cent (31 out of 406) of the entrepreneurs depended on borrowings from relatives and friends to start the enterprises. Only 6.7 per cent (27 out of 406) of the entrepreneurs started their entrepreneurial activity by availing bank loans.

5.7 per cent (23 out of 406) of the sample entrepreneurs availed government assistance as a major source of initial capital. Most of the entrepreneurs under this category utilized funds under the New Land Use Policy (NLUP) scheme of the Government of Mizoram. NLUP scheme was under operation during 1993-1998 under which the entrepreneurs were granted initial capital by the government to start business enterprises. However, 26.6 per cent (108 out of 406) of the respondents did not want to specify their initial source of capital.

Table 8.3: Major Sources of Initial Capital

Sl.No.	*Major Sources*	*No. of Units*	*%*
1.	Own funds	194	47.8
2.	Assistance from government agencies	23	5.7
3.	Loans from government agencies	11	2.7
4.	Loan from banks	27	6.7
5.	Borrowings from moneylenders	5	1.2
6.	Borrowings from friends/relatives	31	7.6
7.	Other sources (Please specify)*	7	1.7
8.	No. of entrepreneurs not responded	108	26.6
	Total	406	100.0

* Other sources include sale of land, saving from salary of spouse and retirement money of parents.

Source: Field survey.

Only small proportion of entrepreneurs could have access to bank loans because of the reluctance shown by banks to grant loans to micro-entrepreneurs. The problem of bank finance takes various forms of delays in sanctioning and disbursing of loans to outright rejection of loan proposals. The delays occur because of procedural formalities, shortage of persons capable of appraising loan proposals at bank branches, and to guide and counsel the entrepreneurs, unambiguous communication between the banks and entrepreneurs, delay in completing documentation formalities, and lack of extension motivation at banks (Mali, 2005). Lack of extension motivation is reflected in the expression of the feeling that there was heavy load of work in the bank branches, shifting of responsibility to higher authority whenever possible. Bankers are also afraid of creation of Non-Performing Assets (NPA) while taking decisions in favour of micro and small entrepreneurs. Most of these delays are avoidable delays and can be avoided with little efforts and proper mindset. If delays can be avoided or at least minimized, most of the problems of bank finance may be solved. At the same time, many entrepreneurs do not have fixed assets for collateral security without which banks cannot give loans. For all these reasons, some of the entrepreneurs depend on moneylenders and their relatives and friends to borrow funds at very high rate of interest. Hence, large proportion of entrepreneurs who cannot get loans from banks but at the same time, hesitate to borrow from private source at high rate of interest, find it difficult to start and run their enterprises due to paucity of funds. Mali (2005) suggested that in order to improve the situation, the decision making process in banks and financial institutions should be quick and time bound.

It is found that a small number of entrepreneurs under the present study started their entrepreneurial activities by utilizing loans under PMRY (Prime Minister Rozgar Yojana) scheme, in addition to their own funds. The scheme covers both rural and urban areas. The aim of the scheme is to assist the eligible youth in setting up self-employment ventures in different sectors. The scheme has been implemented by the Directorate of Industries in collaboration with banks. Banks have been providing finance to the beneficiaries of PMRY. Since, it is a sponsored programme, the PMRY beneficiaries could get finance from banks without any collateral security. However, in the field study, many sample micro-entrepreneurs expressed their displeasure over the favouritism shown in the selection of beneficiaries under the PMRY scheme.

Repayment of Loans

The entrepreneurs under the present study who had availed financial assistance from government agencies, loans from banks, borrowings from moneylenders, and borrowings from friends/relatives were asked whether they were repaying their loans. As indicated in Table 8.4, 37.8 per cent (28 out of 74) of the entrepreneurs have not repaid their loans, 32.4 per cent (24 out of 74) of the entrepreneurs were repaying their loans with interest on time, and the remaining 29.7 per cent (22 out of 74) of them were repaying only some portion of their loans.

Table 8.4: Are You Able to Repay the Loan?

Sl.No.	*Response*	*No. of Entrepreneurs*	*%*
1.	Yes	24	32.4
2.	No	28	37.8
3.	Only partially	22	29.7
	Total	74	100.0

Source: Field survey.

Reasons for Non-repayment of Loans

The entrepreneurs who could not repay their loans and those who could repay only partially were asked the reasons for their non-repayment or partial payment of their loans (Table 8.5).

Table 8.5: Reasons for Non-Repayment of Loans

Sl.No.	*Reasons*	*No. of Entrepreneurs*	*%*
1.	Lack of liquidity	7	14.0
2.	Due to business loss	21	42.0
3.	Due to high rate of interest	14	28.0
4.	The agency is not serious about repayment	2	4.0
5.	Any other reasons (Please specify)*	6	12.0
	Total	50	100.0

* Other reasons include tight repayment period, direction of loan for family needs, and want to repay later.

Source: Field survey.

The main reasons cited by the sample entrepreneurs for non-repayment of their loan are business loss (42%), high rate of interest (28%) and lack of liquidity (14%). In this context, instead of granting only loans by banks and providing only one time assistance to the entrepreneurs by the government in the form of subsidy, cheap finance, machinery, etc. they should also involve in monitoring and counselling activities so as to prevent the entrepreneurs from facing the problem of repayment.

Conclusion

The study reveals that a high rate of interest was the most serious financial problem, followed by meagre assistance from government agencies, red-tapism in banks and red-tapism in government agencies. In Mizoram, the loan recovery from micro and small enterprises sector is very less. On an average, only 23.38 per cent of banks' annual disbursement could be recovered from this sector. The poor loan recovery by financial institutions hampered the process of sanctioning fresh loans (Kabra, 2008). For obtaining required finance without lengthy formalities, the entrepreneurs seek funds from the unorganized sector like private moneylenders, relatives and friends, etc. However, the moneylenders are hesitant to provide finance in large amount at the stage of establishment of enterprises. Such lenders doubt as to whether the entrepreneurs would be successful or not and whether they would be able to repay the loan amount with interest as per time schedule. The interest rate is very high from non-formal sources which is a major problem faced by the entrepreneurs. The high rate of interest from unorganized sector and the problem of getting loans from banks due to poor recovery create problems in the development of entrepreneurship. There is an immediate need for intervention of the State government and commercial banks especially public sector banks to expand access to credit and banking facilities to the micro-entrepreneurs. The government and banks need to work hand-in-hand with better coordination on a continuous basis. Both bankers and the government functionaries have the responsibility to spread public awareness towards loan repayment. Collateral security should be dispensed away in the case of micro-enterprises provided they have reliable guarantors because most of the micro-entrepreneurs in Mizoram belong to lower middle income group. Many of them have hardly any property or other assets in their own name to be guaranteed as collateral security. Any delay in addressing the challenge of financial inclusion could adversely affect the survival and growth of micro-enterprises in the state.

REFERENCES

Chanambam, Nalini Shija (2006). *Women Entrepreneurship in North-Eastern Region of India*, Vista International Publishing House, New Delhi.

Deb, Ranabijoy (1993). *Small Scale Industries in India: A Case Study from Assam*, Mittal Publication, New Delhi.

Dhameja, S.K. (2004). *Women Entrepreneurs: Opportunities, Performance and Problems*, Deep & Deep Publication, New Delhi.

Economic Survey: Mizoram (2007-08). Department of Planning and Programme Implementation, Government of Mizoram, Aizawl.

Economic Survey: Mizoram (2009-10). Department of Planning and Programme Implementation, Government of Mizoram, Aizawl.

Economic Survey: Mizoram (2010-11). Department of Planning and Programme Implementation, Government of Mizoram, Aizawl.

Kabra, K.C. (2008). *Economic Growth of Mizoram: Role of Business and Industry*, Concept Publishing Company Pvt. Ltd., New Delhi.

Laskar, Baharul Islam (2010). *Industrialization in Mizoram: Problems and Prospects*, New Central Book Agency, Kolkata.

Lingaiah, K. (1998). *Industrialization in Tribal Areas*, RBSA Publishers, Jaipur.

Mali, D.D. (2005). *Promoting Entrepreneurship: Lessons from India's North-East*, Speed Publication, Guwahati.

Murthy, B.E.V.V. (1992). "Problems of Small Scale Industries: Case Study of Chittoor District in Andhra Pradesh", *Sedme Journal*, No. 2, June.

Murthy, D.G. (1998). "Institutional Finance for the Development of Small Scale Industries in Karnataka", *Finance India*, Vol. xii, No. 1, March.

Pathak, H.N. (1991). *Financial Management Issues in Small Scale Enterprises*, IGNOU, New Delhi.

Ramswamy, Rama (2012). "Financial Management Practices of Micro-Handloom Enterprises: A Case Study of Thenzawl Cluster in Mizoram", *The IUP Journal of Entrepreneurship Development*, Vol. IX, No. 1.

Rao, Gangadhara (1986). *Entrepreneurship and Growth of Enterprise in Industrial Estate*, Deep & Deep Publications, New Delhi.

Third Census of Small Scale Industries (2001-02). Ministry of Small Scale Industries, Government of India, New Delhi.

Vepa, R.K. (1988). *Modern Small Industry in India: Problems and Prospects*, Sage Publication, New Delhi.

9

FINANCIAL INCLUSION IN MIZORAM
Business Correspondent (BC) Model

Daniel Lalawmpuia and *Lalhriatpuii*

Introduction

The process of economic growth, especially when it is on high growth trajectory, must strive to encompass participation from all sections of society. Lack of access to finance for small and marginal farmers and weaker sections of the society has been recognized as a serious threat to economic progress especially in developing countries. Moreover, prolonged and persistent deprivation of banking services to a large segment of the population leads to a decline in investment and has the potential to fuel social tensions causing social exclusion.

The Twelfth Five Year Plan has explicitly stated *Faster, Sustainable and More Inclusive Growth* as its objective. Growth needs to be sufficiently inclusive if its benefits have to be shared among all or else the growth process itself shall be jeopardized and derailed. In order to achieve 'inclusive growth', both State based interventions and Market based instruments are required. However, an important limitation of 'market' as an institution is that it is 'not wealth neutral' and given this perspective, the concept of 'Financial Inclusion' fits in. Financial inclusion needs to be seen as an instrument that would move the wealth effect towards a neutral domain. Thus, as a concept financial inclusion has the potential to contribute substantially towards 'inclusive growth'.[1]

The objective of Financial Inclusion (FI) is to extend financial services to the large hitherto unserved population of the country to unlock its growth potential. In addition, it strives to achieve more inclusive growth by making financing available to the poor in particular. FI enables Banks to channelize the savings of the unserved population of the country and offers new business avenues for lending to this group. Prior to the recent sustained efforts on FI, the banks were barely scrapping the potential business, both on the deposit and lending side.[2]

Financial inclusion has the ability to generate positive externalities: it leads to increase in savings, investment and thereby, spurs the processes of economic growth. It also provides a platform for inculcating the habit of saving money, especially amongst the lower income category that has been living under the constant shadow of financial duress, mainly because of absence of savings, which makes them a vulnerable lot. Presence of banking services and products aims to provide a critical tool to inculcate the savings habit. It also creates avenues of formal credit to the unbanked population who are otherwise dependent on informal channels of credit like family, friends and moneylenders. Availability of timely, adequate and transparent credit from formal banking channels will allow the entrepreneurial spirit of the masses to increase outputs and prosperity in the countryside. It will open the doors of formal remittance facilities to the low income and unbanked populace who, presently, are forced to use all kinds of informal and costly ways of sending money from one place to another.[3]

As we all know, financial inclusion has now been viewed as a remedy to plug gaps and leaks in distribution of government benefits and subsidies through direct benefit transfers to beneficiaries' bank accounts rather than through subsidizing products and making cash payments. Thus, on the whole, financial inclusion has the potential to bring in the unbanked masses into the formal banking system, channelize their savings, stoke their entrepreneurial ambitions by making available credit and thus give a fillip to the economy.[4]

Concept of Financial Inclusion

Financial inclusion or inclusive financing is the delivery of financial services, at affordable costs, to sections of disadvantaged and low income segments of society, compared to financial exclusion, where they are not. Unrestrained access to public goods and services is the *sine qua non* of an open and efficient society. It is argued that as banking services are in the nature of public good; the availability of banking and payment services to the entire population without discrimination is the prime objective of this public policy. The term "financial inclusion" has gained importance since the early 2000s, and is a result of findings about financial exclusion and its direct correlation to poverty.[5]

A World Bank report states, "Financial inclusion, or broad access to financial services, is defined as an absence of price or non-price barriers in the use of financial services." It recognizes the fact that financial inclusion does not imply that all households and firms should be able to borrow unlimited amounts or transmit funds across the world for some fee. It makes the point that creditworthiness of the customer is critical in providing financial services.[6]

The United Nations (2006) elaborates on the scope of financial inclusion as follows: "A financial sector that provides access to credit for all bankable people and firms, to insurance for all insurable people and firms and, to savings and payment services for everyone. Inclusive finance does not require that everyone who is eligible should use each of the services, but they should be able to choose to use them if (they) desired." Thus, the scope was widened not only to cover the 'access to services', but also to the wider choice offered to people.[7]

Centre for Financial Inclusion (CFI) has also defined financial inclusion as "a state in which all people who can use them have access to a full suite of quality financial services, provided at affordable prices, in a convenient manner, and with dignity for the clients. Financial services are delivered by a range of providers, most of them private, and reach everyone who can use them, including disabled, poor, rural, and other excluded populations."

The Committee on Financial Inclusion (C. Rangarajan, 2008) has defined financial inclusion as "the process of ensuring access to financial services and timely and adequate credit where needed by vulnerable groups such as weaker sections and low income groups at an affordable cost". Meanwhile, according to Raghuram Rajan's Committee, "Financial inclusion refers to universal access to a wide range of financial services at a reasonable cost. These include not only banking products but also other financial services such as insurance and equity products." According to Dr. K.C. Chakrabarty, Deputy Governor, Reserve Bank of India, "Financial inclusion is the process of ensuring access to appropriate financial products and services needed by all sections of the society in general and vulnerable groups such as weaker sections and low income groups in particular at an affordable cost in a fair and transparent manner by mainstream institutional players."

The above definition gives importance to accessibility of credit at an affordable cost to the disadvantaged sections of the society. In brief, the broad area of financial inclusion not only provides an enabling environment to use financial services, but also removes both external and internal constraints that stand in the way of people becoming a part of the formal financial system.

Review of Literature

The study of financial inclusion is highly important for the society because the consequences of financial exclusion may be quite harmful. Financial exclusion may generate lower investment resulting from difficulties in getting access to credit or gaining credit from informal sector at very high interest rates. Particularly, without broad and easy access consequences may be grave for the small business sector and poor sections of the society (Beck *et al.*, 2004; Levine, 2005; Galor and Zeira, 1993; Honohan, 2004). A well-developed financial system is highly important for economic development. It is likely that through entry of new firms financial development will promote economic growth (Klapper *et al.*, 2004).

Mahendra Dev, S. (2006) writes that, financial inclusion is important for improving the living conditions of poor farmers, rural non-farm enterprises and other vulnerable groups. Financial exclusion, in terms of lack of access to credit from formal institutions, is high for small and marginal farmers and some social groups. Apart from formal banking institutions, which should look at inclusion both as a business opportunity and social responsibility, the role of the self-help group movement and micro-finance institutions is important to improve financial inclusion.[8] This requires new regulatory procedures and de-politicization of the financial system.

According to Kelkar, V. (2009), by financial inclusion, we mean the delivery of financial services, including banking services and credit, at an affordable cost to the vast sections of disadvantaged and low-income groups who tend to be excluded. The various financial services include access to savings, loans, insurance, payments and remittance facilities offered by the formal financial system. Among the key financial services that are of great relevance here are risk management or risk mitigation services *vis-à-vis* economic shocks. Such shocks may be an income shock due to adverse weather conditions or natural disasters, or an expenditure shock due to health emergencies or accidents, leading to a high level of unexpected expenditure. This aspect of financial inclusion is of vital importance in providing economic security to individuals and families.[9]

Oya Pinar Ardic *et al.* (2011) state that the strong relationship between financial development and economic growth is well documented in the literature. From their investigation using the financial access database by Consultative Group to Assist the Poor (CGAP) and the World Bank group, their findings indicate that there is yet much to be done in the financial inclusion arena. Fifty-six (56%) per cent of adults in the world do not have access to formal financial services. The situation is even worse in the developing world with 64 per cent of adults unbanked. Nevertheless, high income countries also have to worry because approximately one in every five adults is unbanked. On the contrary to conventional wisdom, poor people indeed need and use financial services, albeit in small amounts and usually from informal sources as it is costly for formal providers to provide services for such small amounts. Recent empirical evidence highlights that access to basic financial services can make a substantial positive difference in improving poor people's lives. Accordingly, financial sector reforms that promote financial inclusion are increasingly at the core of policymakers' agendas.

Rama and Rupayan (2012) in their paper entitled "*Income Related Inequality in Financial Inclusion and Role of Banks: Evidence on Financial Exclusion in India*" analyze income related inequality in financial inclusion in India using a representative household level survey data, linked to State-level factors. They find that (a) the extent of financial exclusion is quite severe among households across all income groups, (b) income related inequality in financial inclusion varies widely across sub-national regions in India, but it is quite high in most of the cases, and (c) income related inequality in financial inclusion cannot be considered as synonymous to income inequality. A notable result is that greater availability of banking services fosters financial inclusion, particularly among the poor.[10]

Chakrabarty, K.C. (2013) states that, the task of financial inclusion in a country like India with large population and geographical spread is, indeed, challenging. The recent data released by the Census of India indicate that only 58.7 per cent of households in India avail of banking services with the figure being 54.4 per cent for rural areas and 67.8 per cent for urban areas. While there is greater awareness among policy makers and financial sector participants about the importance of prioritizing the goal of universal financial access, there is a need to ensure that progress on the ground is in line with these expectations. The opening of bank accounts is only the first stage and the focus now is not just on improving access but also on better use of the financial infrastructure. In this regard, the collaborative approach combining financial inclusion with financial literacy, along with closer monitoring of progress in transactions, is expected to boost operations in FI accounts.[11]

Sharma and Kukreja (2013) write that for developing nations the era is of inclusive growth and the key for inclusive growth is financial inclusion. Their paper "*An Analytical Study: Relevance of Financial Inclusion for Developing Nations*" focuses on the role of financial inclusion and its strengthening the India's position in relation to other countries economy. They concluded that undoubtedly financial inclusion is playing a catalytic role for the economic and social development of society but still there is a long road ahead to achieve the desired outcomes.[12]

Objectives of the Study

1. To examine the present status of financial inclusion in Mizoram and issues involved in extending banking services to weaker sections of the society.
2. To find out the viability of Business Correspondent Model as part of financial inclusion plan in Mizoram.
3. To identify the problem faced by Business Correspondents and their clients and give remedial measures.

Present Status of Financial Inclusion in India

Efforts have been made to provide financial services, especially credit facilities, to the rural population since the eighteenth century. Taccavi loans were provided to the poor farmers in order to buy seeds and agricultural implements. The institutionalization of systems for financial inclusion in India began with the establishment of credit cooperatives following the enactment of the Cooperative Credit Societies Act in 1904. After Independence, these efforts were intensified, following the recommendations of the All India Rural Credit Survey Committee of 1954. The expansion of the traditional commercial banks to rural areas commenced with the nationalization of the Imperial Bank of India and its conversion to the State Bank of India in 1955.[13]

The nationalization of 14 major commercial banks in 1969 and another six commercial banks in 1980, along with the introduction of the Lead Bank Scheme in 1970, were steps that facilitated rapid expansion of the banking system into 'hitherto unbanked areas'. Regional Rural Banks (RRBs) were established under the RRBs Act, 1976, to overcome the difficulties faced by commercial banks, like cultural barriers in dealing with rural people and the high costs involved in the setting up of rural branches. The cooperatives, which had made sufficient inroads into rural India, suffered from inadequate resources and a lack of professional competence in banking.

RRBs were envisaged as hybrid banks, incorporating the technical competence and professionalism of the commercial banking system with the local field-level knowledge and low-cost structure of the cooperative banking system. The issues of outreach and credit were fundamental and integral to the concept of RRBs. There are 67 RRBs in India with a total network of 16,000 branches as on January 2013. The creation of the National Bank for Agriculture and Rural Development (NABARD) in 1982 was specifically intended to extend credit and financial services to farmers and the rural population. The appointment of the Committee on Banking Sector Reforms (R. Narasimhan) in 1998, the Committee on Financial Inclusion (C. Rangarajan) in 2008, and the agriculture debt waiver and debt relief scheme introduced by the Government of India in 2008 have further pushed the cause of financial inclusion. The introduction of a universal and targeted public distribution system (PDS), the provision for employment in rural areas through the National Rural Employment Guarantee Scheme (NREGS), the implementation of the project to bring the population under a unique identification number (AADHAR) and the Direct Benefit Transfer (DBT) scheme in 2013 are the most recent measures by the government to realize inclusive growth targets.[14]

The present status of financial inclusion in India has been highlighted below with the help of Table 9.1.

Table 9.1: India's Position Compared with Other Countries
(*Per 0.1 million Adults*)

(*As per cent of GDP*)

Sl.No.	*Country*	*Number of Branches*	*Number of ATMs*	*Bank Credit*	*Bank Deposit*
1.	India	10.91	5.44	43.62	60.11
2.	Australia	11.81	18.16	35.26	32.57
3.	Brazil	13.76	120.62	29.04	47.51
4.	France	43.11	110.07	56.03	39.15
5.	Mexico	15.22	47.28	16.19	20.91
6.	UK	25.51	64.58	467.97	427.49
7.	US	35.74	173.75	46.04	53.14
8.	Korea	18.63	250.29	84.17	74.51
9.	Philippines	7.69	14.88	27.57	53.02

Source: World Bank, *Financial Access Survey* (2010).

Table 9.1 reveals per 0.1 million adults coverage in nine countries (including in India). Maximum number of 43.11 branches in France, 250.29 number of ATMs in Korea, 467.97 bank credit in UK, 427.29 bank deposit in UK. India has 10.91 number of branches in seventh place, 5.44 number of ATMs in ninth place, 43.62 bank credit in fifth place, 60.11 bank deposit in third place compared with other nine countries. As a whole, India's position compared with other countries is in moderate level.[15]

Table 9.2 reveals the position of household availing banking service in the country. As shown in Table 9.2, 30.1 per cent of the rural households are availing baking service while 49.5 per cent of the urban household can avail banking services. In addition, only 35.5 per cent of the total population in the country was availing banking service in the country in 2001. According to 2011 Census, the position of household availing banking service in the country has been increased from 30.1 per cent to 54.4 per cent in rural area; similarly, it has increased from 49.5 per cent to 67.8 per cent in urban area. Meanwhile, 58.7 per cent of the total household in the country can avail banking service in the country.

Table 9.2: Position of Households Availing Banking Services

Households	*As per Census 2001*			*As per Census 2011*		
	Total Number of Households	*Number of Households Availing Banking Services*	*Per cent*	*Number of Households Availing Banking Services*	*Number*	*Per cent*
Rural	138,271,559	41,639,949	30.1	67,826,730	91,369,805	54.4
Urban	53,692,376	26,590,693	49.5	78,865,937	53,444,983	67.8
Total	191,963,935	68,230,642	35.5	246,692,667	144,814,788	58.7

Source: Ministry of Finance, Government of India.

Table 9.3 illustrates the number of Scheduled Commercial Bank Branches in the country as on 31st March, 2013 in rural, semi-urban, urban, metropolitan areas and the entire country. A total bank group-wise number of branches are: Public sector bank 70,421, Private sector bank 14,584, foreign bank 331 and regional rural bank (RRB) 17,007.

The number of functioning branches of Scheduled Commercial Banks during the last five years is shown in Table 9.4 since 31st March, 2009. It indicates that Scheduled Commercial Bank branches have been increased tremendously from 80,200 total branches in 2009 to 1,02,343 branches in 2013.

Table 9.3: Number of Branches of Scheduled Commercial Banks as on 31st March, 2013

Bank Group	*Rural*	*Semi-Urban*	*Urban*	*Metro-politan*	*Total*
Public Sector Bank	23,286	18,854	14,649	13,632	70,421
Private Sector Bank	1,937	5,128	3,722	3,797	14,584
Foreign Bank	8	9	65	249	331
Regional Rural Bank (RRB)	12,722	3,228	891	166	17,007
Total	37,958	27,219	19,327	17,844	1,02,343

Source: Ministry of Finance, Government of India.

Table 9.4: Number of Functioning Branches of Scheduled Commercial Banks during last Five Years

As on	*Rural*	*Semi-Urban*	*Urban*	*Metropolitan*	*Total*
March 31, 2009	31,476	19,126	15,273	14,325	80,200
March 31, 2010	32,493	20,855	16,686	15,446	85,480
March 31, 2011	33,905	23,114	17,599	16,419	91,037
March 31, 2012	36,356	25,797	18,781	17,396	98,330
March 31, 2013	37,953	27,219	19,327	17,844	1,02,343

Source: Ministry of Finance, Government of India.

Table 9.5 reveals the number of branches of Scheduled Commercial Banks opened during the last five years. Expansion of bank branches plays a crucial role in the country.

Table 9.5: Number of Branches of Scheduled Commercial Banks Opened during Five Years

Year	*Rural*	*Semi-Urban*	*Urban*	*Metropolitan*	*Total*
2008-09	706	1,290	1,046	953	3,995
2009-10	1,021	1,729	1,417	1,139	5,306
2010-11	1,422	2,258	919	981	5,580
2011-12	2,453	2,686	1,186	982	7,307
2012-13*	1,598	1,422	546	451	4,017

* Provisional.
Source: Ministry of Finance, Government of India.

Table 9.6 shows that the average population per bank branch (APBB) as on 31st March, 2013 in the country is 12,100.

Table 9.6: Number of Villages and Average Population per Branch (APPB)

Number of Villages in India as per the 2001 Census	600,000 (approx.)
Average Population per Bank Branch (APBB) as on 31-3-2013	12,100

Source: Ministry of Finance, Government of India.

Table 9.7 shows the number of Automated Teller Machine (ATM) in the country as on 31st March, 2013 of the different sector banks in rural, semi-urban and in the metropolitan.

Table 9.7: Number of ATMs in the Country as on 31st March, 2013

Bank Group	*Rural*	*Semi-Urban*	*Urban*	*Metro-politan*	*Total*
Public Sector Banks	8,552	18,445	22,518	20,137	69,652
Old Private Sector Banks	768	2,760	2,354	1,684	7,566
New Private Sector Banks	2,214	6,484	10,995	15,842	35,535
Foreign Banks	30	21	244	966	1,261
Total	11,564	27,710	36,111	38,629	1,14,014

Source: Ministry of Finance, Government of India.

Status of Financial Inclusion in Mizoram

There are 8 Districts in the State. The entire district was identified by the State Level Banker's Committee (SLBC), State Bank of India for achieving 100 per cent financial inclusion in the state. In Mizoram there were 14 villages with a population of over 2000, which do not have banking facilities in the State. Out of 14, 3 villages are allocated to SBI and remaining 11 villages are allocated to Mizoram Rural Bank for providing banking facilities by March 2012 either through branches, ATMs or BC. Banks have already covered all the villages having population of 5000 and above in the first phase of financial inclusion drive 2000 and above in the second phase. However, in the third phase only 17 out of 76 villages having population of 1,000 and above and up to 1999 have been covered at the end of September 2012. A road map has been prepared in the state for providing banking services in every village having population below 2000 and by the end of March 2013 all the unbanked villages with a population below 2000 will be covered by either brick and mortar branches or Business Correspondents.

"There are a total of 21 banks in the state comprising 18 commercial banks, 1 Regional Rural Bank (Mizoram Rural Bank), 1 State Cooperative Apex Bank (Mizoram Cooperative Apex Bank) and 1 Urban Cooperative Bank (Mizoram Urban Cooperative Bank) extending financial service to the state through their brick and mortar branch."[16] In addition to brick and mortar branches, State Bank of India and Mizoram Rural Bank are providing financial services to rural population through Business correspondent and business facilitator Models. As per the instructions contained in the Government of India's letter on financial inclusion, the SLBC, Mizoram has constituted a Sub-Committee under the

Chairmanship of GM, NABARD, Mizoram RO to prepare a comprehensive financial inclusion plan for implementation in the State.

A pilot project involving opening of 40,000 accounts in 4 blocks of 2 districts, *viz.* Aizawl and Kolasib through ICT based solution has been sanctioned by NABARD to MRB, ₹ 20.48 lakh was already released during 2012-13 towards startup expenses. Senrysa Private Technology Ltd. has been appointed as BC by MRB and the project is in its initial stage. Further, out of 11 unbanked villages allocated to MRB, 3 villages are covered under the above pilot project. MRB has opened a branch in Hnahlan village in Champhai district and appointed CSP in the remaining villages. There are 26 Blocks in the state. All the blocks are covered with bank branches and hence there is no unbanked Block in the State. According to State Level Bankers Committee (SLBC) Mizoram, they have already completed the task of providing banking services in villages having population of over 2,000 within 31 March, 2012.

Most of the branches of the Mizoram Rural Bank are participating in issuing of 'No Frills Account' in the entire State besides the SBI (Lead Bank) and other commercial banks. Mizoram Cooperative Apex Bank (MCAB) has also started opening of No frills Accounts, Issue of General Credit Card (GCC), Kisan Credit Card (KCC), and Self-Help Group (SHG) accounts. The total bank branches functioning as on 31 December, 2012 stood at 129 branches against 126 bank branches as on 31 December, 2011 which is an increase of 2.38 per cent.

Recently, Government of India has advised banks that villages having a population of over 1000 in hilly states like Mizoram may be covered by September 2012. The entire state is geographically in isolated location with the land characterized by difficult terrains sparsely populated by a small population of 10,91,014, according to 2011 Census. As understood there are many villages not having access to the banking facilities, it has been observed that to make growth more inclusive, financial inclusion is one of the most crucial issue to be addressed by policy makers. The efforts and initiatives made by Government of India, RBI, NABARD, Commercial Banks and Regional Rural Banks need to be strengthened. For this purpose, grassroots level institutions like local bodies, civil society groups and self-help groups need to be mobilized in the most effective manner and financial inclusion should be made a movement for empowerment and participatory initiatives.

Business Correspondent Model (BCM): An Empirical Analysis

Business Correspondent (BC)[17] model is one of the most convenient models which have been widely used by banks to reach remote areas across the country. The concept of BC has been started in 2006. BC agents are the representative of banks who provide banking services through use of Information and Communication Technology (ICT) based solutions in his/her own or nearby villages. Banks give remuneration or transaction based commission to him against his/her service. Mizoram Rural Bank (MRB) has been selected for the purpose of the study. i.e. MRB has the highest concentration of Customer Service Providers (CSP) in Mizoram in five districts, namely, Serchhip, Champhai, Kolasib, Mamit and Aizawl. At present, there are 10 villages having 2000 or above population in Mizoram which do not have banking facilities where MRB has appointed BC/CSP in each village. The study is based mainly on primary data and secondary data.

1. *Impact of BC Model on Account Holder*

Sixty customers those who have opened account through the CSPs have been selected for primary data, 10 clients from each village. Most of the clients (93.33%) served by CSP are married while 6.66 per cent of the clients are unmarried. The study shows that clients who have accounts are mature enough. They have responsibility of their family. It is also found that 100 per cent of the customers came to know about the facilities and service of the Business Correspondent model through CSPs itself. As mentioned earlier, most of the accounts that have been opened as part of financial inclusion are yet to be operating soon. From the survey, 85 per cent of customers are male and 15 per cent of the customers are female. This simply implies that the men are more aware about the facilities and service of BC than women. The average number of adult members in their family is 4, i.e. 2 men and 2 women.

Most of the villagers are not aware about the services provided by banks and CSP. Hence, the outcome of BC model is yet to be seen. Very few people are aware of BC model and FI. In Mizoram most of the clients (more than 90%) are not satisfied with BC model and services because no transactions have been done till date and smart card is still not activated. Actually financial inclusion in the State is in its initial stage. The problems are mainly related to smart card availability or inadequate infrastructure accessibility as well as the process is very slow. The CSPs are working well in their villages and are reliable, but the main stumbling block for the implementation of financial inclusion is ineffective BC. The technology service provider for Mizoram (Senrysa Private Technology) is from outside the State.

Suggestions from Account Holder

1. The study revealed that most of the clients want that the BC Model should be operating as soon as possible.
2. There is a high demand of financial service and they would like to make basic financial services like savings, deposits, loans, pension, etc.
3. More than 90 per cent of clients are satisfied with the CSPs but most of them have complaints with technology service provider, invalid Smart Card (Smart-card is the only way to access account which was opened by CSP), non-availability of deposits, etc.

2. *Impact of BC Model on CSP*

CSP is the grassroots channel of financial inclusion especially under BC model. Banks have selected CSPs who are well recognized by the villagers and responsible people. The selected CSPs are well aware of banking services. Banks have imparted training to CSPs after selection. In training they learn how to use POS device and how to solve basic device related problems. The study revealed that all the selected CSPs are serving in their own village only at present. They are available 24 hours in their village and provide services all 7 days of week. CSP opens account manually and send the detailed data to the Bank, and the bank (headoffice) forwards to Senrysa Pvt. Technology for issuing of smart card. After the process is over, smart card has been sent to the bank, and account holder gets their smart card through CSP.

Process of Account Opening

The CSPs are given a device (handheld machine) which has online connectivity through internet. As the device has webcam and fingerprint identifier for opening of account, CSP takes photo and fingerprint of client. This identity is used as the proof for opening of account. When account holder wants to access his account, fingerprint is required for identification. Unfortunately, in Mizoram the device is not working properly due to network connectivity and device problem.

CSPs are doing their work of service along with their main occupation. As shown in Table 9.8, we can see that 100 per cent of CSPs have taken up CSP business as subsidiary occupation, most of them are also engaged with other occupations. So, it is important to motivate them to get more interest in CSP occupation. Average number of accounts opened by CSP is 277, which ranges from 65 to 555. The customers (account holders) are much more in rural areas than in urban areas where the bank is far from their village. This indicates that BC model will give more benefit to the rural areas where there is a high demand for financial services.

Table 9.8: Details of Selected CSPs

Sl.No.	*Name of CSP*	*Name of the Village in which CSP is Working*	*Do You Used CSP as Main Occupation?*	*District*
1.	Lalrinawmi	Khawlailung	No	Serchhip
2.	Lalchhanchhuaha	Farkawn	No	Champhai
3.	C. Lalrawngbawla	Hortoki	No	Kolasib
4.	R. Lalrinfela	Thingdawl	No	Kolasib
5.	Laldinmawii	Kawrtethawveng	No	Mamit
6.	Lalfamkimi	Phuaibuang	No	Aizawl

Suggestions from CSPs

1. Hand-held device is not working properly due to technical and network connectivity problems,
2. Financial Awareness campaign should be organized from the bank especially the meaning and motive of financial inclusion to the villagers.
3. All the CSPs feel that BC Model is one of the best methods to reach the unbanked village if the mentioned hindrances can be solved to some extent.

3. *Impact of BC Model on Bank Branches*

All Bank branches have adopted KYC norms for persons who wanted to open account through CSP. They are asking photo identity card, family ration card and driving licences, etc. for residential proof. MRB head office (Aizawl) has taken the main initiative and the branches have not much participation for the implementation of BC Model in Mizoram. As shown in Table 9.4, each village has one CSP. The branch is already merged with Core Banking Solution (CBS). Actually in some branches the bank staffs are also not aware about the implementation of financial inclusion and Business Correspondents Model. In order to make the BC model more success, the branch should advise to take more initiatives.

Some Impediments Observed by the Bank in the Implementation of FIP

(i) *Road Communication:* Because of the difficult terrain, the road connectivity to the remote villages is a biggest problem in the State. In many places, a bank officer has to walk/climb for a long distances to reach the remote villages.

(ii) *Network Communication:* The Internet connectivity is good in district places and near the highways, however, in remote villages, Internet connectivity is a problem which may lead to in-efficient operations by the CSP.

(iii) BC (Senrysa Private Technology Ltd.) is from outside the State and not available when needed.

(iv) Absence of Supervision.

(v) Far distances of allotted villages from branches.

(vi) *Geographical Hindrances:* One of the main suggestions from bank is that the State Government should play a vital role in removing those hindrances faced by the branch in the implementation of FIP in Mizoram.

Major Findings

(i) All the accounts that have been opened as part of the financial inclusion are not working nor in operation (i.e. No deposit and withdrawal till date) due to invalid Smart Card and network connectivity problem. The BC Model in Mizoram has not yet started operating in the true sense.

(ii) The study clearly reveals that the main stumbling-block for the implementation of FI in Mizoram is that the Business Correspondent (Senrysa Private Technology) is not functioning effectively due to inherent problems of inoperable Smart Cards and complete lack of after sales service. In the absence of effective Business Correspondent, Financial Inclusion in true sense will only be a distant dream.

(iii) Issued device has not been working properly as it has many technical and network connectivity problems.

(iv) It takes two to three months for getting Smart Card after opening of Account.

(v) Most of the people (more than 90%) are not satisfied with BC model and services because the transactions have not taken place till date and Smart Card is still not activated.

(vi) The study revealed that all the CSPs selected are serving in their own villages only at present. They are available 24 hours in their respective villages and provide services all 7 days of the week.

(vii) 100 per cent of CSP have taken up their CSP service as subsidiary occupation; most of them are also engaged with other occupation.

(viii) All Bank branches have adopted KYC norms for persons who wanted to open account through CSP.

Suggestions

(i) From the opinion of rural people during the survey, it is observed that the BC model is one of the most viable methods for the delivery of financial services in Mizoram as a component of financial inclusion policy. However, it is imperative that functioning of present BC needs to be improved or another BC may be identified to undertake the activities under financial inclusion.

(ii) All the CSPs feel that BC Model is one of the best methods to reach the unbanked villages if the mentioned hindrances can be solved to some extent. It is also found that there is a high demand of financial service in rural area to deposit their idle income.

(iii) A good training should be given to CSPs for helping them to understand device easily.

(iv) Good network connectivity within the village should be ensured so that handheld machine can be effectively used.

(v) There is a need to organize awareness campaign about FI in the village with the help of NGOs and Village Councils.

(vi) Smart Cards should be issued to the clients as soon as possible after opening of accounts.

Conclusion

Every citizen of India should have an account in any bank which is the ultimate goal of Government of India. It is not economically viable for banks to open brick and mortar branches in every village of the country. Therefore, alternative model like ultra-small branches, mobile-van facility and business correspondent (BC) or business facilitator (BF) models are introduced to make financial services available in rural areas. The clients have opined that if the BC Model can be properly implemented, indeed the hitherto unbanked people will reap the benefits of FI in many ways. This will uplift the economic and social conditions of the rural people and increase the volume of savings and investment which is one of the most important goals of the Planners and policymakers from the beginning. To make Mizoram a self-sufficient and financially included State, more efforts should be made by creating awareness amongst the people about benefits of financial inclusion, sensitizing the bank staff about the operational modalities of financial inclusion and identifying a Business Correspondent Firm which is more relevant to the local conditions. Financial inclusion is the need of the hour to build uniform economic development and ushering in greater economic and social equity.

NOTES

1. NABARD (2009). *Financial Inclusion — An Overview*, Department of Economic Analysis and Research (DEAR), National Bank for Agriculture and Rural Development, Occasional Paper 48.
2. Ministry of Finance, Government of India (2012). "Banking, Insurance, Pension Theme: Financial Inclusion." A *Journal of the Department of Financial Services*, Issue 1, September, 2012.
3. Chakrabarty, K.C. (2013). *Financial Inclusion in India: Journey So Far and Way Forward*, Keynote address delivered by Dr. K.C. Chakrabarty, Deputy Governor, Reserve Bank of India at the Finance Inclusion Conclave organized by CNBC TV 18 at New Delhi on September 6, 2013, p. 4.
4. *Ibid.*
5. *Financial Inclusion from Wikipedia*, the free encyclopedia (www.wikipedia.org).
6. NABARD (2009). *Financial Inclusion — An Overview*, Department of Economic Analysis and Research (DEAR), National Bank for Agriculture and Rural Development, Occasional Paper 48.
7. Gounasegaran, C. *et al.* (2013). "Financial Inclusion: Progress So Far — Banking and Finance", *FACTS FOR YOU*, September 2013.
8. Mahendra Dev, S. (2006). *Financial Inclusion: Issues and Challenges.*
9. Kelkar, V. (2009). "Financial Inclusion for Inclusive Growth", *ASCI Journal of Management*, 39(1), September.
10. Pal, Rama and Rupayan Pal (2012). *Income Related Inequality in Financial Inclusion and Role of Banks: Evidence on Financial Exclusion in India*, Indira Gandhi Institute of Development Research (IGIDR).
11. Chakrabarty, K.C. (2013). *Reviving up the Growth Engine through Financial Inclusion*, p. 4.
12. Sharma, Anupama and Kukreja, Sumita (2013). "An Analytical Study: Relevance of Financial Inclusion for Developing Nations", Research Inventy: *International Journal of Engineering and Science*, ISNN: 2278-4721, Vol. 2, Issue 6 (March, 2013), pp. 15-20.
13. Gounasegaran, C. *et al.* (2013). "Financial Inclusion: Progress So Far — Banking and Finance", *FACTS FOR YOU*, September, 2013.
14. *Ibid.*
15. Paramasivan, C. and Ganeshkumar, V. (2013). "Overview of Financial Inclusion in India", *International Journal of Management and Development Studies*, Vol. No. 2 (2013), Issue No. 3 (March), ISSN (Online): 2320-0685.
16. NABARD (2013). *State Focus Paper for the XII Five Year Plan, 1012-17*, p. 13.

17. Business Correspondents (BC) in this study refers to Business Correspondent Agents (BCAs) appointed by MRB not the corporate BC. The village BCAs is sometimes called as BC or Customer Service Provider (CSP) interchangeably.

REFERENCES

Chakrabarty, K.C. (2013). *Financial Inclusion in India: Journey So Far And Way Forward*, Keynote address delivered by Dr. K.C. Chakrabarty, Deputy Governor, Reserve Bank of India at the Finance Inclusion Conclave organized by CNBC TV 18 at New Delhi on September 6, 2013.

Chakrabarty, K.C. (2013). *Reviving up the Growth Engine through Financial Inclusion*, Address by Dr. K.C. Chakrabarty, Deputy Governor of the Reserve Bank of India, at the 32nd Skoch Summit, Mumbai, 6 June, 2013.

Gounasegaran, C. *et al.* (2013). "Financial Inclusion: Progress So Far — Banking and Finance", *FACTS FOR YOU*, September 2013.

Government of Mizoram (2013). *Economic Survey*, Mizoram 2012-13, Planning and Programme Implementation Department.

Kelkar, V. (2009). "Financial Inclusion for Inclusive Growth", *ASCI Journal of Management*, 39(1), September.

Mahendra Dev, S. (2006). "Financial Inclusion: Issues and Challenges", *Economic and Political Weekly*, October 14, 2006.

Ministry of Finance, Government of India, (2012). "Banking, Insurance, Pension. Theme: Financial Inclusion", *A Journal of the Department of Financial Services*, Issue 1, September 2012.

NABARD (2009). *Financial Inclusion — An Overview*, Department of Economic Analysis and Research (DEAR), National Bank for Agriculture and Rural Development, Occasional Paper-48,

NABARD (2013). *State Focus Paper for the XII Five Year Plan 2012-1017* (with detailed suggestions for 2013-14), Mizoram Regional Office, Aizawl.

Pal, Rama and Rupayan Pal (2012). *Income Related Inequality in Financial Inclusion and Role of Banks: Evidence on Financial Exclusion in India*, Indira Gandhi Institute of Development Research (IGIDR).

Paramasivan, C., and Ganeshkumar, V. (2013). "Overview of Financial Inclusion in India", *International Journal of Management and Development Studies*, Vol. No. 2 (2013), ISSUE No. 3 (March) ISSN (Online): 2320-0685.

Sharma, Anupama and Kukreja, Sumita (2013). "An Analytical Study: Relevance of Financial Inclusion for Developing Nations", *Research Inventy: International Journal of Engineering and Science*, ISSN: 2278-4721, Vol. 2, Issue 6 (March, 2013), pp. 15-20.

WEBSITE

NABARD www.nabard.org
RBI www.rbi.org.in
Ministry of Finance, GoI, http://finmin.nic.in/
World Bank, www.worldbank.org

10

FINANCIAL INSTITUTIONS AND WOMEN OF MANIPUR

Mayanglambam Sarda Devi

"*Empowering people — particularly women — is a sure way to link growth and human development.*"

UNDP, Human Development Report 1995, 123

Introduction

In recent years, there has been considerable interest in the economic development of women in developing countries of the world like India. Regarding this, there is special need to provide credit to women as a way of strengthening their economic activities. Government of India has several governmental schemes like, anti-poverty programmes, subsidics, incentives for women's activities. International organizations like, UNIFEM, World Council of Credit Unions, Women's World Banking, The Trickle-Up Programme and others have also played a very active role in the field of providing credit to poor women. Yet, most of the poor women of our country cannot find basic financial assistance which is provided by the banking Institutions because of the lack of banking knowledge and also collateral security. Not only this, all the government schemes cannot reach the targeted poor women. In such conditions Micro-finance institutions and non-governmental organizations had been promoting micro-finance in Manipur. For the first time, micro-finance model were established in Bangladesh by Muhammad Yunous in 1976, then it spread out to Indonesia, Philippines, Sri Lanka and India. Bangladesh's micro-credit bank is known as Grameen Bank. Pakistan has set up a special women's Bank.

In Finance, credit is the provision of resources between individuals or groups which have agreement for deferred payment. It can be long-term and short-term loan or non-financial like service provided to consumers. In the economy, credit funds are available from various sources. Regarding this financial Institution may be analyzed in two ways, such as:

- Formal Institutions like Banks, National and International agencies, Government programmes.
- *Non-formal Institutions:* Informal financial system like, Person's own funds, Family funds, Friends and relatives, charitable institutions, Moneylenders, Saving groups and Credit societies and revolving loan funds.

The data (Figure 10.1) show that non-formal sources of finance in the North-Eastern Region dominate the financing activity than the formal institutions. As per the 59th round of National Sample Survey (NSS) data on indebtedness of farmer household in NES, 45 per cent of the finance availed of by the farmers was from the formal financial sector, while the remaining 55 per cent was from the non-formal sector.[1] Among the NESs, Assam has the highest formal financial institutions than Nagaland, Arunachal Pradesh and Mizoram. Meghalaya has the lowest formal financial institutions and highest non-formal institutions. Manipur follows Meghalaya and lies in the sixth rank among the North-Eastern States.

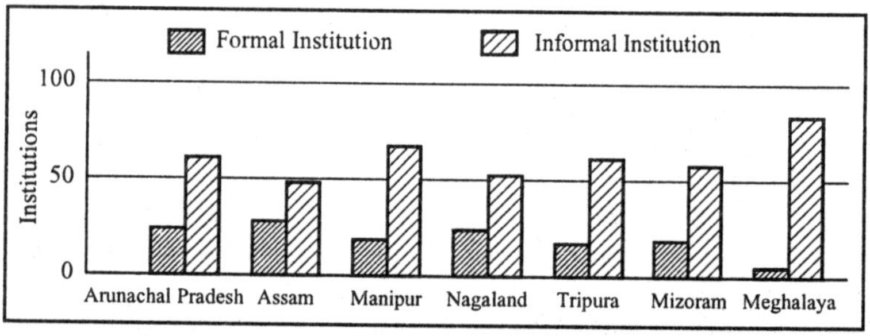

Source: Economic and Financial Developments in the North-Eastern States (Speech delivered by Shri Deepak Mohanty at Gauhati University on March 24, 2011).

Figure 10.1: Formal and Non-formal Financial Institutions in NER of India.

Formal Institutions

The formal financial system in India is dominated by banks. Proper functioning of financial system is the key to sustainable economic development of a country. Regarding this, Bank takes most important leading roles. Bank has been actively engaged in the development of the financial sector in the country for a long time. The Banking services of Manipur are provided by the State Bank, Commercial Bank, Bank of Baroda, Vijaya Bank, Regional Rural Bank, Cooperative Bank, etc. Now, other banks like ICCR, HDFC, Exim Bank, Syndicate Bank and Bank of India are coming recently and spread out in Manipur. Manipur, however, lags behind other parts of India in terms of development of banking. This is evident from the low banking penetration (having higher average population per branch) in Manipur as compared with all-India average. The credit-deposit (C-D) ratio in NES is much lower at 34 per cent at the end of March 2010 than that of 73 per cent at the all-India level (Table 10.1). Even as credit expanded at a faster pace than deposits in the last decade, the gap remained very wide.

Table 10.1: Banking Development Indicators in Manipur

State	*Population per Branch (as on June 2010)*	*C-D Ratio (per cent)*		*Average Growth (2000-01 to 2009-10)*	
		End-March 2001	*End-March 2010*	*Credit*	*Deposits*
Manipur	34,000	38.9	40.7	23.1	20.7
NES	20,000	27.8	33.5	22.5	19.8
India	14,000	59.2	73.2	21.9	18.9

(Speech delivered by Shri Deepak Mohanty at Gauhati University on March 24, 2011).
Source: Economic and Financial Developments in the North-Eastern States.

Table 10.2: CD Ratio and Investment Plus CD Ratio of Commercial Banks in Manipur

Year (ended 31st March)	*Credit Deposit Ratio*		*Investment Plus Credit Deposit Ratio*	
	APS	*PPU*	*APS*	*PPU*
2002	25.5	64.9	NA	NA
2007	55.1	55.6	76.8	77.4
2008	48.4	50.3	65.0	66.8
2009	38.7	NA	NA	NA

APS = As per sanctioned, PPU = As per utilization, NA = Not available
Source: NEC: Basic Statistics of NER-2006, Government of India.

Many questions had been raised that whether low credit penetration in Manipur was due to lack of absorptive capacity in the region. According to Statistical Abstract, Manipur 2009, bank lending to women entrepreneur of Manipur were 7,500 and amount was only ₹ 2,559 lakh as on 31-3-2004.[2] This data shows that women beneficiaries in the formal Banking institutions were very low. This reason may be because of the lack of banking knowledge and also collateral security. As a result, non-formal sources of finance like Moneylenders, Saving groups and Credit societies and revolving loan funds in the region dominate the financing activity in the rural sector.

Micro-Credit in Manipur

Large sections of people are covered by banks but most of the poor and illiterate women of our State cannot find basic financial assistance which is provided by the banking institutions because of the lack of banking knowledge and also collateral security. In such conditions Micro-finance institutions and non-governmental organizations had been promoting micro-finance in Manipur. "*Micro-finance is defined as the provision of thrift, credit and other financial services such as money transfer and micro-insurance products for the poor, to enable them to raise their income levels and improved living standard*" (Karmakar, 2008:36). Micro-finance is modern financial institution which provides credit to the poor people specially women to increase their income and build assets through various activities such as, savings, income generation activities, productive activities, etc. It has stepped up its efforts in recent years to enhance the penetration of the formal financial sector and promote financial inclusion with a view to improve the well-being of our society. In many remote areas of the Manipur, where formal banking institutions have not yet reached, traditional micro-finance systems are the only means for savings and credit.

Progress Under Micro-Finance

The way of expanding the successful operation of micro-finance institutions in the informal sector is through strengthened linkages with their formal sector counterparts. Informal sector micro-finance institutions have comparative advantage in terms of small transaction costs achieved through adaptability and flexibility of operations (Ghate, 1992). They are better equipped to deal with credit assessment of the urban poor and hence to absorb the transaction costs associated with loan processing. On the other hand, formal sector institutions have access to broader resource-base and high leverage through deposit mobilization (Christen, 1994). The progress of Micro-finance in the North-Eastern States is given in Table 10.3.

A large number of NGOs have adopted the SHG model to provide credit to poor people. In 2000, SHG was started in Manipur under the

Table 10.3: Savings of SHGs with Banks and Percentage as on 31st March, 2012

States	*Commercial Banks*		*Regional Rural Banks*		*Cooperative Banks*		*Total*	
	No. of SHGs (%)	*Saving Amount (%)*	*No. of SHGs (%)*	*Saving Amount (%)*	*No. of SHGs (%)*	*Saving Amount (%)*	*No. of SHGs (%)*	*Saving Amount (%)*
Assam	102764	5991.53	149291	3039.10	24510	815.35	276565	9845.98
	(68.75)	(85.15)	(83.82)	(45.79)	(62.65)	(51.66)	(75.42)	(64.56)
Arunachal Pradesh	6983	103.14	959	54.20	421	28.98	8363	186.32
	(4.67)	(1.47)	(0.54)	(0.82)	(1.08)	(1.84)	(2.28)	(1.22)
Manipur	5955	103.34	5784	106.06	972	9.98	12711	219.38
	(3.98)	(1.47)	(3.29)	(1.60)	(2.48)	(0.63)	(3.47)	(1.44)
Meghalaya	9057	231.30	2507	143.16	2527	40.28	14091	414.74
	(6.06)	(3.29)	(1.41)	(2.16)	(6.46)	(2.55)	(3.84)	(2.72)
Mizoram	2104	43.57	2202	507.04	670	22.30	4976	572.91
	(1.41)	(0.62)	(1.24)	(7.64)	(1.71)	(1.41)	(1.37)	(3.76)
Nagaland	6353	132.93	679	50.99	3679	190.56	10711	374.48
	(4.25)	(1.89)	(0.38)	(0.77)	(9.4)	(12.07)	(2.92)	(2.46)
Sikkim	4626	178.21	0.00	0.00	654	81.79	5280	260.00
	(3.09)	(2.53)			(1.67)	(5.18)	(1.44)	(1.70)
Tripura	11636	252.68	16696	2736.28	5689	388.99	34021	3377.95
	(7.78)	(3.59)	(9.37)	(41.23)	(14.54)	(24.65)	(9.28)	(22.15)
Total	149478	7036.69	178118	6636.83	39122	1578.23	366718	15251.75

Source: National Bank for Agriculture and Rural Development, *Status of Micro-finance* (2011-12).

Women Cooperative Education project by the Institute of Cooperative Management (ICM) in Imphal East District (Singh and Devi, 2004). In 2004, Manipur contributed 2.4 per cent of the total SHG that are credit linked in the North-Eastern Region (Singh, 2008). As on 31 March, 2012, Manipur has total number of 12,711 SHGs with saving performance of 219.38 lakhs against 3,66,718 SHGs with saving amount of ₹ 15,251.75 lakh in the NE region. Out of these, 5,955 SHGs are linked with the Commercial Bank; 5,784 SHGs are linked with the Regional Rural Banks and 972 SHGs with Cooperative Bank. While comparing other NE states, Assam (75.42%) stood in the highest rank and Manipur (3.47%) lies in the fourth position followed by Meghalaya (3.84%). Before two years, as on March 2010, the total number of SHGs of Manipur was only 10,831 with saving performance of 218.56 lakh.

Table 10.4 shows that total Loans Disbursed Amount of Manipur under micro-finance project is only 1.9 per cent compared to 41.54 per cent of Assam, 51.28 per cent of Tripura, 1.53 per cent of Mizoram, 1.38 per cent of Nagaland and 1.08 per cent of Meghalaya. Arunachal Pradesh (0.35%) has the lowest per cent among the NE States.

It can be said that micro-finance offers a promising institutional structure to provide access to credit to the poor women. Micro-credit plays an important role for the development of rural poor women and their families. It solves the unemployed problem of the poor rural women. It increases the assets and property of our country and also increases per capita income of the nation. It also makes women empowerment and gives financial freedom to the women. Some of the Micro-Credit institutions which operated in Manipur are given below:

Chanura Micro-Finance

Chanura Micro-finance was established in 2007. Presently, the organization renders its various services to more than 12 thousand families through 7 branches in 4 districts of Manipur. The borrowers are provided with different types of financial and non-financial services for investment in their Income Generating Activities (IGAs) and consumption purpose. 100 per cent clients of Chanura are women and the organization is playing a vital role in women empowerment through engaging these women in different IGAs. By maintaining 100 per cent recovery rate a substantial number of small loan borrowers are gradually migrated to bigger loan considering their capacity and successes of the previous loans. Micro-finance programme has steadily grown up with continued product innovation over the last four years. This growth was achieved mostly through vertical as well as horizontal expansion in terms of

Table 10.4: Progress under Micro-finance: Loans Disbursed during the Year

States	*Commercial Banks*		*Regional Rural Banks*		*Cooperative Banks*		*Total*	
	No. of SHGs	*Loans Disbursed Amount*	*No. of SHGs*	*Loans Disbursed Amount*	*No. of SHGs*	*Loans Disbursed Amount*	*No. of SHGs*	*Loans Disbursed Amount*
Assam	10072	8228.09	16279	8691.61	1661	1827.28	28012	18746.98 (41.54)
Arunachal Pradesh	48	94.12	15	24.50	67	39.34	130	157.96 (0.35)
Manipur	828	554.37	433	185.65	47	117.50	1308	857.52 (1.9)
Meghalaya	168	138 87	391	220.21	132	130.14	691	489.22 (1.08)
Mizoram	7	11 48	542	640.18	26	38.54	575	690.20 (1.53)
Nagaland	466	475 86	44	112.31	352	33.12	862	621.29 (1.38)
Sikkim	356	324 08	0	0.00	40	99.62	396	423.70 (0.94)
Tripura	1104	1729.29	16301	19469.51	1624	1943.07	19029	23141.87 (51.28)
Total	13049	11556.16	34005	29343.97	3949	4228.61	51003	45128.74

Source: National Bank for Agriculture and Rural Development, *Status of Micro-finance* (2011-12).

providing financial services in existing and new areas within the state of Manipur.

Loyalam Bank Project (LBP)

Rural Development Organization (RDO), Lamshang has introduced micro-finance programme under Loyalam Bank Project (LBP) with the model of Grameen Bank of Bangladesh for the first time in NER. Presently, it provides micro-finance to over 12,700 rural womenfolk through six branches of LBP in Imphal West, East, Thoubal and Bishnupur districts (*The Assam Tribune*, 2009).

Youth Voluntary Union (YVU) Microfin

YVU, Thoubal Wangmataba, Manipur is well recognized organization in North-East India (Table 10.5). YVU Microfin is also one of the leading micro-finance institutions in Manipur. The micro-finance activities of YVU are spread over in 6 Districts of Manipur, viz. (i) Thoubal District, (ii) Bishnupur, (iii) Imphal West, (iv) Imphal East, (v) Chandel, and (vi) Senapati District. Outside Manipur, its Micro-finance operation has been expanded in two states, i.e. Assam and Delhi. YVU started its micro-finance operation in October 1996 under the name of Women Credit and Thrift Project (WCTP). The activities of the micro-finance operation reach the underserved remote villages in Manipur, Assam and Delhi.

Table 10.5: Profiles of YVU as on August 31, 2013

Sl.No.	*Particulars*	*Total*
1.	No. of Members	32,307
2.	No. of Borrowers (Group loan)	1,404
3.	Total no. of active clients	3,844
4.	No. of village/ward covered	543
5.	Repayment rate	99.93

Micro-finance, both credit and savings, has also been proposed as a potential tool for empowering poor women in developing countries. It strengthens women's economic roles and making their lives more public and this programme may abolish men made gender norms and men's violence against women.

Informal Institution

Marup is one of the most popular traditional micro-finance systems in Manipur. The study of traditional micro-finance system has become necessary to find out what has made them more popular than banks. Marup is informal financial institution which is widespread in Manipur that provides financial needs to the people of Manipur. Basically, it means, 'Friendship' among the people and embodies coming together and helping each other. Every *leikai* or locality provides credit for mutual help at the time of death, marriage, birth and other financial needs. In the early days, Marup was popularly known as Singlup.[3] From the early days till date Marup is popular among people in Manipuri society and it is organized everywhere in Manipur. Over the years, these systems have evolved into efficient financial institutions. Around 90 per cent of the total population of Manipur has involved in Marup system. They organize Marup to get access to the credit needs. The size of the Marup depends on the financial conditions and common interest of the members.

Conclusion

To sum up, the formal banking network in Manipur is very low as compared to other NE states. Most of the poor women of our country cannot find basic financial assistance which is provided by the Banking Institutions because of the lack of banking knowledge and also collateral security. As a result, non-formal sources of finance like Moneylenders, Saving groups, Credit societies and revolving loan funds in the region dominate the financing activity in the rural sector. Women are forced to borrow from the local moneylenders at exorbitant interest rates and that makes women poorer. Lack of education, lack of access to credit, savings and insurance make it even harder for the poor to sustain their livelihood. So, to solve these problems, formal sector finance institutions could form a joint venture with informal sector institutions. Micro-finance will support the low income households and micro-entrepreneurs in developing and expanding their business and thereby augmenting their income which ultimately leads to improving their quality of life. It will reduce poverty by giving them the capital to start or expand small businesses. Women Entrepreneurs in Manipur have contributed in a large scale in the economic development of the region. Women of Manipur are naturally hardworking, courageous, and talented. Empowering women is an active process to realize the hidden identity and power of women in all aspects of life. Micro-finance, both credit and savings has also been proposed as a potential tool for empowering poor women in developing countries. Micro-finance programmes can reduce women's vulnerability to men's violence by strengthening their economic roles and making their lives more public.

Lastly, this chapter highlights the need and importance of empowerment of women for social, economic and financial development. Women's participation in economic activities through financial system will be appreciated in the context of Manipur because Manipuri women carry the burden of family responsibilities. Professor Amar said "Women are the real backbone of the Manipur economy" (Yumnam, 1999, p. 3). Micro-finance programmes would serve to bring a major change in the economic and social condition of Manipuri women and would also serve to reduce gender inequality.

NOTES

1. 59th Round of National Sample Survey (NSS).
2. *Source:* Lead District Managers' Office, UBI, Imphal.
3. Singlup is traditional name of Marup for helping deceased's family in organizing rituals. This Singlup system is now continuing in Rural areas in Manipur.

REFERENCES

Amar, Y. (1999). *Women in Manipur: A Real Backbone of the Economy*, Paper presented at the 3 days Seminar of Gender Equity, organized by Department of Adult and Continuing Education, Manipur University.

Atmadip, R. (2009). *North-East Banking Sector on Fast Track*, ET Bureau, October 15, 2.43 pm IST.

Banking in North-Eastern India East India vis-à-vis. An Overview. http://shodhganga.inflibnet.ac.in:8080/jspui/bitstream/10603/5308/10/10_chapter %203.pdf

Chriseten, R. Peck; Rhyne, Elisabeth and Vogel, Robert C. (1994). *Maximizing the Outreach of Micro-enterprise Finance: The Emerging Lessons of Successful Programmes*, September, IMCC, Arlington, Virginia.

Directorate of Economics and Statistics, Government of Manipur, *Statistical Abstract*, Manipur, 2009.

Economic and Financial Developments in the North-Eastern States (Speech delivered by Shri Deepak Mohanty at Gauhati University on March 24, 2011).

Ghate, P. (1992). *Informal Finance: Some Findings from Asia*, Oxford University Press, Hong Kong.

Karmakar, K.G. (2008). "Regulatory Framework for Micro-finance Institutions", in Karmakar, K.G. (ed.), *Micro-finance in India*, New Delhi, Sage Publication, p. 36.

Melody, K. (2008). "Micro-finance and Informal Credit in Manipur", *International Journal of Social and Economic Research*, Vol. 2, Issue 2, pp. 266-75, July-December.

National Bank for Agriculture and Rural Development, *Status of Micro-finance*, 2011-12.

Nair, T. (2010). "Institutionalizing Micro-finance in India", *Economic and Political Weekly*, Vol. 36, No. 4.

Singh, W.C. (2009). "Informal Financial Sector: A Case of State of Manipur", *International Review of Research Paper*, Vol. 5, No. 5.

11

DEMOGRAPHIC FACTORS OF POLICY-HOLDERS OF LIC IN MIZORAM

Laishram Gyanendra Singh and *N.V.R. Jyoti Kumar*

Introduction

The life insurance industry in India has registered an impressive growth since the beginning of twentyfirst century. The market has witnessed dynamic changes including entry of a good number of global players. Most of the private firms are joint ventures with well known foreign players. The new players not only succeeded in establishing themselves, but also captured a healthy market share. The Life Insurance Corporation of India (LIC) has been still the dominant market leader. With the opening of economy, 23 private companies entered into life insurance business which are challenging the supremacy of the market leader. For example, the market share of LIC in terms of the first year premium was declined to 65.08 per cent in 2009-10 from 98.65 per cent in 2001-02. With regard to renewal premium, LIC's market share was decreased from 99.99 in 2001-02 to 73.64 per cent in 2009-10. Share of LIC's total premium also decreased from 99.46 per cent in 2001-02 to 70.10 per cent in 2009-10. It is needless to highlight the gains made by the new private players in respect of market share during the period. The private players, though new in Indian market, entered into the arena with a rich and long experience of their partners from the developed nations. They have been offering different types of innovative products with aggressive promotional campaigns. As a result, it becomes imperative for LIC to improve its marketing performance. In other words, it has become more a compulsion to reengineer its marketing practices than an option in order to defend its market share.

Marketing a life insurance product is not comparable to the marketing of a product like toothpaste or a ball pen or a mobile set. Life insurance as a business has not only a commercial dimension but also has a social dimension. Unlike many other commercial products, life insurance goes a long way in providing financial as well as social security to the individuals and their families especially in underdeveloped regions such as India's North-East (NE) region where a significant proportion of population are underprivileged. Hence, there is a greater need to evolve a marketing strategy for the purpose of realizing the overall goal of inclusive development.

Life Insurance in Mizoram

Mizoram is a hilly, landlocked small tribal State in India's NE region. People in Mizoram had slowly started taking keen interest in life insurance in the early nineties with the initiatives taken by some influential agents and development officers of LIC. In Mizoram, a branch of LIC was opened in its capital city Aizawl, on 16th March, 1981 with only one Development Officer. The jurisdiction of the branch covers the entire state of Mizoram. As per records available in 1988-89, LIC Aizawl branch insured 1690 lives with a sum assurance of ₹ 10.66 crore and with a First Premium Income (FPI) of ₹ 1.96 crore. A total number of 3,784 and 3,579 lives were insured in 2008-09 and 2009-10 respectively. The FPI was ₹ 17.84 crore in 2008-09 and it was ₹ 15 crore in 2009-10 (LIC Aizawl Office records).

Since, the entry of private insurers in Mizoram, they have been trying to gain competitive advantage in the market by adopting different marketing policies to the customers. The public sector giant LIC with its single branch in the state is leading the market in terms of Number of Policies (NOPs), FPI and also in terms of productivity of agents, yet LIC has to adopt strategic marketing to retain and expand its market share. A vast potential still exists for life insurance players to explore in the state. The remaining seven districts do not have any office of life insurance, either of LIC or of private insurers.

The importance of customer profile in life insurance industry and various related issues have been discussed by several studies in literature (Ward and Zurbruegg, 2000; Rao, Ramakrishna, 2000; Padmavathy and Pandian, 2005; Sheela and Arti, 2007; and Shrivastava *et al.*).

Objectives and Methodology

This chapter intends to analyze the customer profile of the sample policyholders of LIC in Mizoram. In other words, the policyholders' demographic factors such as age, gender, income and occupation, and also the details of the life insurance products owned by them is the core of this article. For this purpose, a policyholder survey was conducted during 2009. The survey was limited to the policyholders of LIC. A person who purchased at least a single policy from LIC and who has a minimum five years of experience as a customer of LIC were the criteria used for drawing the purposive sample of policyholders.

The sample consisted of a total of 160 policyholders. The sample was drawn equally from eight districts of Mizoram, viz. Aizawl, Champhai, Kolasib, Lawngtlai, Lunglei, Mamit, Saiha and Serchhip. Thus, the sample consisted of 20 LIC policyholders of each of eight districts. The respondents were identified in consultation with the only branch office of LIC located in Aizawl and the agents.

Results and Discussion

The Socio-Economic Bases

The socio-economic background of a customer is an important factor influencing the purchase of insurance products. This article intends to identify the policyholders by age, number of dependents in the family, gender, occupation, educational qualification, rural-urban background and income level. Tables 11.1 to 11.8 show the socio-economic origins of the sample policyholders of LIC.

Age

Table 11.1 shows that 62.50 per cent of the respondents were in the age group of 35-50 years and 27.50 per cent of the respondents were in age group of 25-34 years and only 8.75 per cent of the respondents belonged

Table 11.1: Age-wise Classification of the Respondents

Age (in years)	*No. of Respondents*	*Per cent*
Up to 14	—	—
15–24	2	1.25
25–34	44	27.50
35–50	100	62.50
51–65	14	8.75
Total	160	100.00

n = 160 respondents.
Source: Field Survey.

to the age group 51-65 years. Only two of the total respondents (1.25%) were in the age group of 15-24 years. In other words, 90 per cent of the respondents in the present study were in the age group of 25-50 years of age.

Sheela and Arti (2007) in their study conducted in Visakhapatnam observed that 91 per cent of the respondents were in the age group of 31-60 years. In another study conducted by Shrivastava *et al.* (2007), in Bhillai (Chhattisgarh), it was found that 58 per cent of the respondents were in age group of 21-40 years and 34 per cent in 41-60 years of age group. There are a few plans such as Endowment Assurance for which the minimum age of entry is 12 years. The minimum age for most of the endowment policies is 12 years and maximum age is 65 years. Minimum age at entry varies from one plan to another. In case of children's plans, minimum age at entry is below one year. The parents or guardians normally purchase children's policies in the name of their children.

Number of Dependents in the Family

Table 11.2 highlights the number of dependent family members of the sample policyholders. The quantum of savings of the policyholders depends upon the size of the family. Table 11.2 shows that 45 respondents (28.13%) have only three dependent family members, 39 respondents (24.38%) have two dependent members and 31 respondents (19.38%) have four dependent members. It is to be observed that more than one-fifth of the respondents have five or more number of dependents in their family.

Table 11.2: Classification of the Respondents on the Basis of Number of Dependents in the Family

No. of Dependents	*No. of Respondents*	*Per cent*
0	4	2.5
1	7	4.38
2	39	24.38
3	45	28.13
4	31	19.38
5	21	13.13
6	7	4.38
7	2	1.25
8	3	1.88
9 and above	1	0.63
Total	160	100.00

n = 160 respondents.
Source: Field Survey.

Gender

Table 11.3 shows the gender of the policyholders. Out of the total sample of 160 policyholders of LIC, two-third (66.25%) were males and one-third (33.75%) of the policyholders were females.

Table 11.3: Classification of the Respondents on the Basis of Gender

Sex	*No. of Respondents*	*Per cent*
Males	106	66.25
Females	54	33.75
Total	160	100.00

n = 160 respondents.
Source: Field Survey.

Women respondents in the survey were mostly employees having a source of income. It may be quoted that the Mizo women as a whole are very hardworking, many of them are having unemployed husbands, they are financially supporting their families, looking after the children and also sharing the family burden. The Mizos being patriarchal, property is inherited by men rather than women.

Christianity ushered in changes in the entire mode of living and mindset of the Mizos, not only to the institutions relating to women. One such circumstance was that to improve the status of women to modernize and codify customary laws which gradually became the important aim and objective of the 'Mizo Union', a political party formed on April 11, 1946. Since 1950, the Mizo women's literacy rate has been on the rise and a number of women began to excel men in many professions. Christianity and education indeed opened new doors for women to enter the public domain, in many ways in spite of the above indications of progressive changes; the new social structure is yet far short from driving home a status of equality for women. Despite the increasing number of educated women only few women hold important positions in government jobs and also in politics. The political economy is still controlled by men.

The Mizo women play quite an important role in the society. The hidden hand of a Mizo wife can be seen in any deal a Mizo husband enters into. However, the customs and the laws of the land keep her behind the scene (Verghese and Thanzawna, 1997). The sex ratio has improved to 1000:971 in the 2011 Census from 1000:964 in the 2001 Census (*Newslink*, 2nd July 2011).

Normally in family decision making wives play a dominant role in the purchase of products such as cleaning products, kitchenware, children's clothes, and food. Husbands dominate in such decisions as life insurance, savings, and purchase of cars and garden tools (Davis and Benny, 1974). Katja Meier *et al.* (1999) found that spouses play a relatively dominant role in decisions concerning different forms of investment. As determinants of spouse's dominance, partnership characteristics, such as partnership role, attitudes, marital satisfaction and individual expertise in relation to different investments were considered. They conducted survey on 142 Austrian couples. Spouses with higher expertise than their partners exerted more dominance in decision-making processes.

From the view point of life insurance business, the female lives are categorized into Category-I, II and III. Category I includes women with earned income, professionals, working women; Category II includes women with unearned income attracting income tax or with sizeable personal properties and investment yielding income attracting income tax; Category-III includes single women, married women, self-employed women, major unmarried women and widows. Literate females aged below 35 years and Sum Assured (SA) up to four lakh are insured without medical test; aged between 36 and 45 years with SA up to two lakh and aged between 46 and 50 years with SA up to one lakh having own income are exempted from medical test at the time of purchase of LIC policies. But all these exemptions are allowed under certain plans and only with a standard age proof (Wings Ready Reckoner, 2004).

Medical examination is necessary for illiterate female lives, pregnant ladies and housewives without income; physically handicapped lives; NRI cases; persons employed in hazardous occupations due to dust, radiation, fumes, etc., X-ray operators, sweepers; weight beyond non-medical range; persons (other than doctors) attending leprosy/TB patients; class IV employees working in hospitals, nursing homes, etc. like *Ayahs, Dhobis*; risk plan on minor lives; persons having adverse health history like surgeries, accidents, pre-existing diseases, etc. and where the latest policy is accepted with health extra (Wings Ready Reckoner, 2004). In the present study, 50 women respondents out of 54 (92.59%) belonged to Category-I.

Occupation

The nature of occupation also influences consumption patterns. Product choice is greatly affected by economic circumstances: spendable income, savings and assets, debts, borrowing power, and attitudes towards spending and savings.

Table 11.4 depicts the occupation of the sample policyholders. It is found that 83.75 per cent of the policyholders were in government service, followed by 8.13 per cent in private service and 6.25 per cent in business sector. It is also observed that white-collared employees are more interested in buying insurance policies. It is found that among the respondents all the business persons have more than three life insurance policies.

Table 11.4: Classification of the Respondents on the Basis of Occupation

Occupation	*No. of Respondents*	*Per cent*
Government Service	134	83.75
Private service	13	8.13
Housewives	2	1.25
Students	1	0.63
Business	10	6.25
Total	160	100.00

n = 160 respondents.
Source: Field Survey.

Under Clause 26 of Section 10 of the Income Tax Act, 1961, any income which accrues or arises to any member of a Scheduled Tribe (ST) residing in the State of Nagaland, Manipur, Tripura, Arunachal Pradesh, Ladakh and Mizoram are fully exempted from income tax. Thus, here is a fair chance of cross selling of life insurance products among the non-Mizo tax-payers in the State.

Educational Qualification

As shown in Table 11.5, 80 per cent of the respondents were either graduates or post-graduates or professionals holding degrees such as engineering and management. The post-graduates (46.25%) far outnumbered the graduates (21.88%).

Table 11.5: Educational Qualification of the Respondents

Educational Qualification	*No. of Respondents*	*Per cent*
Class X	18	11.25
Class XII	14	8.75
Graduate	35	21.88
Post-graduate	74	46.25
Professionals	19	11.88
Total	160	100.00

n = 160 respondents.
Source: Field Survey.

As noted earlier, the literacy rate was very high in Mizoram with 91.58 per cent. All the respondents covered under this study are literates. Education plays an important role in life insurance business too. A proper investment in LIC products requires a reasonable degree of understanding of clauses involving life insurance, their implications, etc. which can clearly be seen from a larger proportion of respondents having higher educational attainments (graduates and post-graduates). In their study, Sheela and Arti (2007) found 95.93 per cent of the respondents in Visakhapatnam were either graduates or post-graduates. In another study conducted by Padmavathy and Pandian (2005) in Villupuram (Tamil Nadu), it was found that 55 per cent of the respondents were studied up to class 10th. All the respondents in their study were literates and have a monthly source of income to afford life insurance.

Urban/Rural and Ethnic Background

Table 11.6 shows the composition of respondents on the basis whether they reside in rural or urban areas. Almost three-fourth of the respondents resides in urban areas while the rest of the respondents live in rural areas. LIC has to capture the unexplored rural market in Mizoram by devising special promotional programme and by expanding branches and appointing more number of agents in rural areas.

Table 11.6: Classification on the Basis of Rural and Urban Background

Location	*No. of Respondents*	*Per cent*
1. Rural	42	26.25
2. Urban	118	73.75
Total	160	100.00

n = 160 respondents.
Source: Field Survey.

From Table 11.7 it can be observed that 130 respondents were Mizos (all Christians) and 30 were non-Mizo respondents. In other words, Christians constitute 81.25 per cent, Hindus 12.5 per cent and Muslims 1.88 per cent.

Income

As shown in Table 11.8, only 18.13 per cent of respondents' annual income was ₹ 1 lakh or below. 31.25 per cent of the respondents earn ₹ 1 lakh to ₹ 2 lakh. The same per cent of respondents (31.25%) earn ₹ 2 lakh to ₹ 5 lakh. Nearly 20 per cent of the respondents earn above

₹ 5 lakh. In a similar study in Visakhapatnam, Sheela and Arti (2007) observed that out of 1206 respondents, 895 were within the income group of ₹ 3,00,000-5,00,000 representing 74 per cent of total respondents.

Table 11.7: Classification on the Basis of Religion

Religion	*No. of Respondents*	*Per cent*
Hindu	20	12.50
Mizo Christian	130	81.25
Muslim	3	1.88
Others	7	4.38
Total	160	100.00

n = 160 respondents.
Note: Others include Buddhists, and Apokpa (a small religious sect from Manipur).
Source: Field Survey.

Table 11.8: Classification of the Respondents on the Basis of Income Level

	Annual Income (₹)	*No. of Respondents*	*Per cent*
1.	Up to 50,000	9	5.63
2.	50,001 to 1,00,000	20	12.50
3.	1,00,001 to 2,00,000	50	31.25
4.	2,00,001 to 5,00,000	50	31.25
5.	5,00,001 and above	31	19.38
	Total	160	100.00

n = 160 respondents.
Source: Field Survey.

The respondents were asked (Table 11.9) whether their spouse was working or not. Over one-third of the respondents have a working spouse. All the working spouses have at least one LIC policy each. Apart from life insurance they have other forms of investments such as post office savings, and fixed deposits. 53.75 per cent of the respondents were single income families. 19 respondents (11.88%) did not respond.

Table 11.9: Whether Spouse is Working or Not?

Response	*No. of Respondents*	*Per cent*
Working	55	34.38
Not working	86	53.75
No response	19	11.88
Total	160	100.00

n = 160 respondents.
Note: No response includes those respondents, who were not married, widowed and divorcees.
Source: Field Survey.

A statistical survey has shown that 44.1 per cent of rural women in Mizoram were employed during 2004-05, against the national average of 32.7 per cent. The urban women employment rate in the state was 28.1 per cent, compared to India's 16.6 per cent. On the whole, it is found that age, education, occupation, income and rural-urban background are closely interrelated, having a chain relationship among them. Better education leads to better employment opportunities, higher income and urban living, ultimately resulting in more purchase of insurance products (Kumar, Jyoti NVR, 2003).

Working couples and their earnings are a significant contribution to total family income and as such double income families are an important target market. But in a study conducted by Rubin *et al.* (1990), the researchers found that there was no difference in expenditure pattern of single and dual earner households within the same income bracket. The study concluded that income, not single *versus* dual earning capacity, is the best predictor of spending patterns.

Because of the growing number of double income single kid families, now they can afford to spend more for things hitherto they were hesitant to buy. The economic and demographic landscape of India has changed over the last decade. Economic growth has resulted in greater disposable income. At the same time, advances in healthcare have significantly improved life expectancy. Today, an Indian lives at least a decade beyond the retirement age [The results of a Max New York Life-NCAER (National Council of Applied Economic Research)]. India Financial Protection Survey revealed that 69 per cent of Indian households save for their old age, the third most important reason for savings after emergencies and children's education (Bennett, 2007).

As found in the present study, people earning a reasonable income and one who can afford to pay future premiums found maximum interest in life insurance. The major part of the LIC business has remained largely confined to those having a regular income and savings potential, namely affluent group of people and salaried classes. The LIC has failed generally to extend its business to the class which does not have a regular income and even to the large sections of rural people devoid of savings potential.

No. of Policies Held by a Family

Table 11.10 exhibits that the total number of LIC policies owned by 160 respondents' families was 443. 11.88 per cent of the respondents' families have six or more number of insurance policies. One-tenth of the families have five policies. In other words, 65 per cent of the families have two or more number of life insurance policies, over one-third (35%) of the families has a single life insurance policy. On an average, each of 160 respondent families has 2.76 policies.

Table 11.10: Number of Policies Held by the Respondent's Family

No. of Policies	*No. of Families*	*No. of Policies Owned*
1	56 (35.00)	56 (12.64)
2	29 (18.13)	58 (13.09)
3	25 (15.63)	75 (16.93)
4	15 (9.38)	60 (13.54)
5	16 (10.00)	80 (18.06)
6 and above	19 (11.88)	114 (25.73)
Total	160	443 (100.00)

n = 160 respondents.
Note: Figures in the parenthesis indicate percentages.
Source: Field Survey.

Table 11.11 shows the number of policies owned by the individual respondents. The respondents having only one policy constitute 48.75 per cent of the total. 23.13 per cent of the respondents have two policies, 10.63 per cent of the respondents have three policies, and 5.63 per cent of policyholders have four policies. 11.88 per cent of them have five or more number of policies. In other words, more than 50 per cent of the individual respondents have at least two or more life insurance policies. In all, 160 respondents possessed a total of 334 life policies. On an average, each of 160 respondents owned 2.09 policies.

Table 11.11: Number of Policies Owned by the Individual Respondents

No. of Policies	*No. of Respondents*	*Total No. of Policies*
1	78 (48.75)	78 (23.35)
2	37 (23.13)	74 (22.16)
3	17 (10.63)	51 (15.27)
4	9 (5.63)	36 (10.78)
5	19 (11.88)	95 (28.44)
Total	160 (100)	334 (100.00)

n = 160 respondents.
Note: Figures in parenthesis indicate percentages.
Source: Field Survey.

Term of Policies

Table 11.12 shows the classification of the respondents' policies on the basis of the policy term. It is observed that 42.21 per cent of insurance policies cover a moderate policy term of 11-15 years; 31.44 per cent of the policies are for a term of 16-20 years. Only 13.77 per cent of the policies cover a short term of up to 10 years. Similarly, 12.58 per cent of the policies cover a long term of 21 years and above.

Table 11.12: Classification of the Respondents on the Basis of Policy Term

Policy Term	*No. of Policies*	*Per cent*
Up to 10 years	46	13.77
11–15 years	141	42.22
16–20 years	105	31.44
21–25 years	36	10.78
26 years above	6	1.80
Total	334	100.00

n = 160 respondents.
Source: Field Survey.

Sum Assurance

From Table 11.13, it can be observed that 30 per cent of the policies have a Sum Assurance (SA) of ₹ 50,000 to ₹ 1 lakh. 24.38 per cent of the policies have a sum assurance of ₹ 1 lakh to ₹ 2 lakh. About one-fifth of the respondents have a SA of ₹ 2 lakh to ₹ 5 lakh. Only 10.63 per cent of the total policies have a sum assurance of ₹ 5 lakh and above.

Table 11.13: Classification of Respondents on the Basis of Sum Assured

Sum Assured (₹)	*No. of Respondents*	*Per cent*
Below 50,000	23	14.38
50,001 to 1 lakh	48	30.00
1,00,001 to 2 lakh	39	24.38
2,00,001 to 5 lakh	33	20.63
5,00,001 lakh and above	17	10.63
Total	160	100.00

n = 160 respondents.
Source: Field Survey.

SA is the amount of money to be paid by the insurer to the insured in case of death or maturity of the policy. Interestingly, some of the respondents did not have a clear cut idea of the concept sum assurance; they had to verify from their policy documents at the time of field survey.

How Often Did You Buy the LIC Policy?

The frequency of purchase of LIC policy by the customers is a good indicator of trust prevailed upon the LIC. Table 11.14 shows that 36.88 per cent of the respondents purchased life insurance policy once in a life time. 31.25 per cent of the respondents buy LIC policies as and when there is surplus money. Only 11.25 per cent of respondents buy life insurance policy once in a year. 10.62 per cent of the respondents preferred to buy life insurance policy once in three years.

Table 11.14: How Often Did You Buy the LIC Policy?

Frequency	*No. of Respondents*	*Per cent*
Once in a year	18	11.25
Once in 3 years	17	10.63
Once in 5 years	10	6.25
As and when there is surplus money	50	31.25
Once in life time	59	36.88
No response	6	3.75
Total	160	100.00

n = 160 respondents.
Source: Field Survey.

It can be inferred that nearly 22 per cent of the respondents were in the habit of buying a policy of LIC once in a year or three years. It shows their loyalty towards LIC as a company and the trust they have about LIC. Though such customers displaying a strong loyalty towards the firm constituted over 20 per cent of the respondents, their repeat purchase behaviour could provide a great opportunity to generate more sales and profits. The LIC should try to retain such strong loyal customers.

At the same time, LIC should evolve suitable marketing strategies in order to convert one time buyers (which constituted 36.88 per cent of the respondents) into frequent buyers.

Preferred Mode of Premium Payment

People from different market segments require different ways of premium payment facility to suit their convenience. In a contract of insurance, the insurer promises to pay to the policyholder a specified sum of money in the event of a specified happening. The policyholder has to pay a specified amount called 'premium' to the insurer, in consideration of this promise.

The respondents were asked to assign five ranks in order of preference as regards the mode of payment of insurance premium. The most preferred mode of payment carried five points, the second four points, the third three points, the fourth two points and the fifth one point. Overall ranking is given on the basis of weighted scores and rating per cent as shown in Table 11.15.

Table 11.15: Mode of Payment of Insurance Premium

Mode of Payment	*No. of Respondents*					*Weighted Score*	*Rating per cent*	*Rank*
	Policyholders' Ranking Number							
	One	*Two*	*Three*	*Four*	*Five*			
SSS	58	79	19	—	—	663	31.72	1
Through the agent	48	60	51	1	—	635	30.38	2
By Self	49	20	84	6	—	589	28.18	3
By post*	2	1	2	45	12	122	5.84	4
Through Internet	3	—	1	16	31	81	3.88	5
No response	—	—	3	92	117	—	—	
Total	160	160	160	160	160	2090	100.00	

n = 160 respondents. * A cheque sending by post.
Note: Other modes included payment through family members, friends, etc.
Source: Field Survey.

On the question of mode of payment of premium by the respondents, 156 out of 160 respondents indicated SSS as one of the three most preferred modes of payment. The Salary Saving Scheme (SSS) policies, often known as 'payroll insurance', are intended to cater to the needs of the salaried class. The insurer arranges with the employer to deduct the premium from the salary of the employee-policyholder and remit the same to the insurer's office every month. The scheme benefits the policyholder, because the premium is deducted, making premium payment easy and without a default. At the same time, it would also help LIC to get a prompt and regular remittance of premium from the policyholders.

It is not surprising to find that all the respondents except four preferred premium payment through SSS because 92 per cent of the respondents in the present study were employees either in government sector or in private sector.

Payment through the agent is the second ranking mode of the respondents. All the respondents preferred this mode of payment as one of the four preferred choices. It may be inferred that the agents still play an important role in life insurance business in Mizoram despite the occurrence of a few instances where some dishonest agents indulged in misappropriation of premium amount collected.

Payment of premium by self is the third ranking mode of the respondents with 28.18 per cent rating. Making of payment by sending a cheque by post and payment through the Internet were least preferred modes of payment in that order.

Type of Policies Owned and Periodicity of Payment

Table 11.16 shows the number of policies owned by the respondents and the type of policies. Further, the table exhibits the periodicity of premium payment, viz. SSS, Monthly, Quarterly, Half yearly, Annually and Single payment.

Table 11.16: Number and Type of Policies Owned and Periodicity of Premium Payment

Type of Plan	*NOPs*	*Mode of Payment*				
		SSS	*Quarterly*	*Half Yearly*	*Yearly*	*Single*
Term assurance plan	6 (1.8)	3 (2.73)	1 (2.27)	—	2 (2.08)	—
Whole life plan	9 (2.7)	3 (2.73)	—	3 (4.76)	3 (3.13)	—
Endowment plan	107 (32.0)	39 (35.45)	16 (36.36)	26 (41.27)	26 (27.08)	—
Money back plan	105 (31.44)	43 (39.09)	18 (40.90)	21 (33.33)	23 (23.96)	—
Joint life plan	13 (3.9)	4 (3.64)	2 (4.55)	2 (3.17)	5 (5.21)	—
Children's plan	33 (9.9)	8 (7.27)	2 (4.55)	7 (11.11)	16 (16.67)	—
Pension plan	12 (3.6)	2 (1.82)	1 (2.27)	1 (1.59)	8 (8.33)	—
Single premium plan	14 (4.2)	—	—	—	—	14 (66.67)
ULIP	26 (7.8)	2 (1.82)	4 (9.09)	2 (3.17)	11 (11.46)	7 (33.33)
Composite plan	9 (2.7)	6 (5.45)	—	1 (1.59)	2 (2.08)	—
Total	334	110	44	63	96	21

Note: Figures in the parentheseis indicate percentages.
Source: Field Survey.

As noted earlier (refer Table 11.11), 160 respondents owned 334 policies at the time of conducting field survey. In other words, each of the respondents owned two policies on an average. Of 334 policies, 107 policies (32%) were endowment plans; 105 policies (31.44%) were money back plans. Nearly 10 per cent of the policies were children's plans; and 7.8 per cent of policies were ULIP. In other words, approximately two-third of the policies owned by the respondents were either endowment plans or money back plans which clearly shows popularity of these two types of plans.

The LIC has to evolve a marketing strategy exclusively for certain plans like pension plans, health plans, single premium plans, etc. to make them quite attractive to the market. In the present study, it is found that a few customers owned these plans.

The policyholders have many options with regard to the periodicity of premium payment, viz. Single premium, Annual payment, Half yearly payment, Quarterly payment, Monthly payment. Normally, all insurance organizations keep this aspect of consumer choices into consideration and design their insurance policies which permit premium payment as per customer's convenience. Product flexibility (surrendering of policy, getting loan, revival of lapsed policy, etc.) is yet another prerequisite, which facilitates selection of life insurance products.

Conclusion

It is high time for LIC to evolve a strategy for the purpose of identifying and rewarding high value customers, may be in the form of premium discounts. The LIC should track the behaviour of such high value customers in terms of the type of products they buy and how much premium they pay. In the long run, the success of any organization depends on its measures to incentivise the best customers to remain them loyal, rather than allowing them to spread their patronage among other competitors.

In the present era of information technology, it is suggested to harness a new segmentation variable that reflects customers' willingness and ability to use the new technology. As observed from the study, most of the policyholders in Mizoram had not in the habit of using IT. This may not be the case of only Mizoram; LIC may be having this kind of customers across the country in large number. In such situations, the market leader should take responsibility for educating the less experienced customers. Customers' education need to be given an important role in promotion strategy for life insurance players. Lack of knowledge about premium payment through the Internet, method of lodging a complaint, etc. can lead to frustration with the process and even put the customer at risk. Customers depend on employees for advice and support and are frustrated if they get unsatisfactory results. Therefore, LIC has to play a proactive role to educate and train customers so that they have the required knowledge and technical skill to handle different situations. As pointed out by Das (1999), deploying IT strategically to improve and expand services is going to be the principal determinant for dominating the future. The capacity to do this effectively will not only add value to customers' benefit but will also reduce the effective cost of producing the services leading to higher profitability. IT will enable the service firm to create and manage the data base on customer transactions and also help employees to provide more targeted service offerings of higher quality, productivity, and at lower costs. It will also progressively help in reducing dependency on intermediaries such as branches and agents in the long run.

REFERENCES

Bennett, Gary (2007). "Insure your Retirement", *Money Today*, October 18, p. 49.

Das, Ranjan (1999). *Strategic Management of Services*, Oxford University Press, New Delhi.

Davis, Harry L. and Benny P. Rigaux (1974). "Perception of Marital Roles in Decision Process", *Journal of Consumer Research*, Vol. 1, p. 57.

Katja Meier, Kirchler Erich and Angela Christian Hubert (1999). "Savings and Investment Decisions within Private Households: Spouses' Dominance in Decisions on Various Forms of Investment", *Journal of Economic Psychology*, 20, pp. 499-519.

Kumar, Jyoti N.V.R. (2003). *Newspaper Marketing in India*, Anmol Publications, New Delhi, p. 221.

Newslink (2011). "Mizoram has High Rate of Women Employment", 2nd July, p. 1.

Padmavathy, S. and Pandian, Ronnammal K. (2005). "Social Security Insurance for the Underprivileged Gender," in Nalini Prava Tripathy, Prabir Pal (eds.), *Insurance Theory and Practice*, Prentice Hall of India, New Delhi, p. 171.

Rao, Rama Krishna T.S. (2000). "The Indian Insurance Industry: The Road Ahead," *Journal of Insurance Chronicle*, Vol. III, Issue 1, January, p. 31.

Rubin, Rose M.; Bobye J. Riney, and David J. Molina (1990). "Expenditure Pattern Difference between One-Earner and Duel-Earner Households: 1972-73 and 1984", *Journal of Consumer Research*, Vol. 16, pp. 43-52.

Sheela, P. and G. Arti (2007). "A Study on the Awareness of Life Insurance Policies in Visakhapatnam", *Insurance Chronicle*, September, pp. 6-65.

Shrivastava Amit, Bhuwan Shrivastava and Ravikant Agarwal (2007). *Effects of Demographical Factors in Consumer Buying Behaviour: A Study with Specific Reference to Indian Life Insurance Industry*, Shivalik Institute of Management Education and Research, Durg, Chhattisgarh.

Verghese, C.G. and R.L. Thanzawna (1997). *A History of Mizo*, Vol. 1, Vikas Publishing House, p. 17.

Ward, Damian, and Ralf Zurbruegg (2000). "Does Insurance Promote Economic Growth: Evidence from OECD Countries", *Journal of Risk and Insurance*, Vol. 67, No. 4, pp. 489-506.

Wings Ready Reckoner for LIC Premiums (2004), Wings Publications, Bangalore, p. 59.

Wings Ready Reckoner for LIC Premiums, 24th edition, Bangalore.

12

IMPACT OF MARUP CREDIT SYSTEM TO THE MEITEI WOMEN OF MANIPUR

Arambam Sophia

Introduction

The meaning of the term 'credit' varies in different contexts. In finance, credit is the provision of resources by individuals or groups to one another with agreement for deferred payment. Credit delivery methodologies include all the practices which provide credit access to people such as through formal institutions like banking and micro-finance, and through informal institutions like moneylending practices in villages, savings and loan scheme practices and traditional practices (Kshetrimayum, 2012:266).

Women, especially in developing countries often lack access to land, assets, credit, training and extension facilities and other services. Women's access to formal sources of finance is constrained in the form of legal barriers, cumbersome application procedures, relatively high opportunity and transaction costs, socio-cultural constraints or lack of secure title to property and other forms of collateral, even if they play a major role in production and marketing in the agricultural sector. They are, therefore, forced to depend mainly on informal sources of finance to meet their credit needs.

Objectives and Methodology

This chapter highlights the various sources of credit of Meitei women of Manipur, particularly the Marup system which meets credit needs for all purposes. It seeks to find out what is the main reason for dependence on this informal source of finance. The chapter is limited to some primary data (from my Ph.D. thesis on "Women and Development in Manipur—A Case Study of Meitei Women of the Valley") to highlight the sources of credit of women of Manipur. The study is both descriptive and analytical. A sample of 400 respondents was taken from the four valley districts of Manipur — Imphal West, Imphal East, Bishnupur and Thoubal districts. Stratified random sampling method was used; strata were the four valley districts. Measures of central tendency and frequency distributions were used to generate information on women's access to credit among the Meitei women of Manipur.

Review of Literature

Gender differences in access to resources occur because men are more likely to be perceived as workers needing these inputs and because laws sometimes bar women from ownership of property and other goods needed for production or for collateral purposes. The right to land in law is never implemented. In India too, women were seen only as members of families or groups, as daughters, wives and mothers and not as individuals with an identity or right of their own (Kantor, 2002:287).

Women have fewer opportunities than men to get access to credit for various reasons cited above including formal institutions' refusal to accept household assets as collateral for loans, high transaction costs and negative perceptions of women desirous of loans by such institutions as not being creditworthy, etc. Women also may lack information on how to go about securing a loan. Facing restricted access to formal credit, women have relied heavily on informal finance, not only in the face of emergencies, but also for routine consumption needs. "Informal finance is perhaps most intuitively defined relative to what it is not. It is not to do with banks or micro-finance institutions (MFIs), credit unions, cooperatives, insurance companies, etc." (Aliber, 2002:2)

Borrowing from these informal sources often involves exploitative rates of interest and results in strengthening of systems of oppression (Ranadive, 2002:1). Yet the poor and women who use individual and household savings for most investments such as micro-enterprises, other business ventures in the informal sector, or for personal uses such as consumption and children's education, when such resources are insufficient, rely on informal credit sources because formal institutions require collateral, do not recognize the importance of household savings and may require literacy and credit history. Another important source of informal savings and credit are rotating savings and credit associations

(ROSCAs) which is an "association formed upon a core of participants who agree to make regular contributions to a fund which is given, in whole or in part, to each contributor in rotation" (Ardener, 1964:201). In its simplest form the frequency of contribution is linked to income flows and the order of rotation is determined by lot (Mayada, Bahloul and Adams, 1993). It is a means to 'save and borrow' at the same time. ROSCAs through various incentives, monitoring and sanctioning mechanisms can minimize the costs of screening new borrowers by capitalizing on local information about individuals' past behaviour. Reputations and the self-selection of members help these institutions reduce adverse selection and moral hazard problems as shown by Fadiga and Fadiga-Stewart (2004) in their study in Senegal. High rates of interaction, proximity and effective mechanisms such as first, second, and third-party enforcement make it easier for mutual monitoring among members to occur and helps ensure that the benefits of cooperating minimize the temptation to default. Social capital such as shared norms, networks of relationships, and trust are important factors that explain how these institutions have been able to remain sustainable (Fadiga and Fadiga-Stewart, 2004:7-8).

A ROSCA known as upato is also found in Tanzania. These associations are found throughout the world, not only in the Third World, but also in the US, especially, within newer immigrant communities and in countries like Italy, England and Canada (Ali Mari Tripp, 2006). In Egypt also such ROSCAs called gam'iyas are common (Mayada *et al.*, 1993:5). Chit funds are the Indian equivalent to the ROSCA (Rao, 2007).

Marup System in Manipur

Marup literally means 'friendship' in Manipuri. Marups are indigenous unorganized rotating savings groups/schemes where women take turns monthly to receive the joint pool, thus enabling each woman to meet urgent expenditures or effect personal savings. The institution lies outside the formal banking system, but the women adapt to traditions of mutual trust and cooperation to put into effect this financial flow. Even the committee set up by the Ministry of Rural Development under the Swarnjayanti Gram Swarozgar Yojana (SGSY) was impressed with the functioning of the marup system (Dasgupta, 2009:21).

In a monthly share taking marup, for example, 20 people join a marup of ₹ 5,000 each and take turns to receive money from the pool monthly. There are various ways of deciding the list of members. A lottery each month will decide who gets the money that month, or, a lottery is called in the beginning and a list of the members is drawn up, the first member on the list will get the first share. The list may also be decided on the collective decision of the members and the agent. People in dire need of credit (borrowers) will opt for placement in the beginning months, while those who are interested in earning interest (savers) will opt for placement in the ending months. The first share is usually taken by the agent. The agent's gain is that each time a member collects, he/she may get a share, that is, in each turn she receives ₹ 5,000 for herself, which show how much she is gaining, implying high cost of marup. The high participation of Meitei Manipuri women in marup despite its high cost displays their faith in the institution.

Tender money is another form of marup. For instance 64 people join and contribute 1000 per month to the fund. Each month there is a type of auction. Any number of people can bid for the money, but money is given to the lowest bidder. A person who has got the bid, however, low it may be cannot get any further money. "The marup system of Manipur is an important and effective socio-economic organization which provides security to every individual at every stage of his or her life" (Nixon, 2011:11). "The marup system is an expression of the faith of the Meitei people in the collective spirit and the women, being in the forefront of the traditional economic set-up, benefit as much or even more from it as the men" (Chaki-Sircar, 1984:47-50).

Marup is believed to have started in the seventeenth century during the reign of King Khagemba as singlup where each household in a particular area needed to contribute firewood for the cremation of the death. The concept of cooperative savings and loan system evolved around 1960 when money marup developed out of people's need to cope with credit. It is a means to overcome poverty without having to undergo the long process of availing facilities provided by formal banks (Kshetrimayum, 2012:273-274). Policies and programmes that improve women's access to formal credit would lead to more efficient allocation of resources and increased production (Fletschner, 2008:682).

Women of Manipur's Access to Credit

Table 12.1 shows how few women (36%) had savings in banks. Hence, many women still either were unable to save other than living a hand to mouth existence, or did not have access to or are unaware of the advantages of entrusting their savings to formal institutions like banks, etc. But most of the respondents are engaged in marup and had also borrowed from moneylenders, etc.

Table 12.1: Access to Credit and Control Over Income

(Percentage)

Category	*Primary*	*Secondary*	*Tertiary*	*Unemployed*	*Total*
Respondents with bank accounts/savings	3.3	12.1	51.6	18.2	36.0
Respondents who borrowed money from private individuals like moneylenders, friends, etc.	76.7	57.6	50.8	27.3	54.5
Respondents engaged in marup	76.7	78.8	88.9	72.7	84.5
Respondents who had taken bank loans	3.3	6.1	26.2	0	18.0
Respondents who tried to obtain a loan and had failed	0	12.1	1.6	18.2	4.0

Source: Personal Survey.

Just a few respondents (18%) had taken loans from banks in their own names. They were 3.3 per cent of primary sector respondents, 6.1 per cent of secondary respondents, and 26.2 per cent of tertiary sector respondents. Some (4%) of the total respondents; 12.1 per cent in the secondary sector, 1.6 per cent in the tertiary sector, and 18.2 per cent in the unemployed group, had tried to obtain a loan and had failed.

The interest paid per month was around 1-5 per cent per month for 65.1 per cent of the respondents who had borrowed money from private moneylenders (Table 12.2). It was around 6-10 per cent per month for 31.2 per cent of these respondents. Hence, we see that, not having any easy access to credit, women had to resort to borrowing from friends and private moneylenders, who charged exorbitant rates of interests.

Table 12.2: Interest Paid per Month for those Who Took Loan from Private Money-lenders, etc.

(Percentage)

Sl.No.	*Interest per Month*	*Primary*	*Secondary*	*Tertiary*	*Unemployed*	*Total*
1.	1–5%	60.9	52.6	70.3	66.7	65.1
2.	6–10%	34.8	47.4	25	33.3	31.2
3.	More than 10%	4.3	0	4.7	0	3.7
Total	100	100	100	100	100	100

Source: Personal Survey.

Of the total respondents, 20 per cent considered that the most important problem connected with the process of taking a loan from formal sources was that it was time consuming, 18.5 per cent considered lack of connections/influence as the most important problem, 15 per cent did not even know how to secure bank loan, 4.5 per cent found insistence on collateral to be a problem and 30.5 per cent had no idea about anything to do with bank loans.

Table 12.3: Marup Activity

(Percentage)

Categories	*Primary*	*Secondary*	*Tertiary*	*Unemployed*	*Total*
Engaged in Marup Activity	76.7	78.8	88.9	72.7	84.5
Percentage who contributed all their income to household needs	73.3	60.6	34.1	9.1	43.0
Reasons for Joining Marup					
To help in own expenses	17.4	7.7	15.2	0	13.6
To save for unforeseen contingencies/future	43.5	50.0	35.7	25.0	38.5
To maintain household expenses	8.7	11.5	9.8	37.5	11.2
To save for future education of children	13.0	26.9	31.2	37.5	28.4
To save for children's marriage	17.4	0	2.7	0	4.1
Others	0	3.8	5.4	0	4.1

Source: Personal Survey.

Though the women found access to institutional sources of credit difficult, most (84.5%) of the respondents were engaged in the marup system, mainly because of its easy accessibility. Of those who joined marups, reasons for joining were, to save for unforeseen contingencies/ future (38.5%), to save for future education of children (28.4%), to help in own expenses (13.6%), to maintain household expenses (11.2%), to save for children's marriage (4.1%), and other reasons (4.1%). Of all respondents engaged in marup activity, to save for unforeseen contingencies/future was the major reason in primary sector (43.5%), secondary sector (50%), and tertiary sector (35.7%). A high percentage of women in each sector contributed all their income to household needs.

With the income from marup, women indulge in activities which are beneficial to the household. Hence, a larger share of entitlements accruing to females would result in greater household investment, which is desirable from a human development perspective as it increases the avenues available to children and increase household well-being.

Further, my study found that 87 per cent of the respondents do not have title to property. Of the primary sector (96.7%), secondary sector 90.9 per cent and tertiary sector 83.3 per cent had no land in their name. Of total respondents 70.5 per cent believed that they will not demand share even if necessity arises. Of this, 33.3 per cent gave "it is not the custom for women to demand share" as the main reason for their not wanting to demand share, even if necessity arises.

Hence, we see that women still do not have access to property and women have been socialized to believe that it is the norm that brothers/ men should inherit familial property, and that it is not right or good for the sisters/women to demand their share of familial property. This is an impediment when women try to obtain credit from formal institutions. The excessive dependence on the marup system implies constraints in accessing credit from formal sources.

The main drawbacks of informal credit institutions are that they are not dependable, often have a high cost, and offer limited capital. Participation in these institutions does not link women to the mainstream financial system, perpetuating the marginalization of women's economic activities (ILO, 2000:4).

In such instance, the coming up of self-help groups and micro-financing options is a good phenomenon. But the savings of SHGs with banks in Manipur as on 31.3.2012 is just 1.4 per cent of that of the total savings of the North-East SHGs with banks. Assam's share was 64.6 per cent (NABARD, 2012).

Conclusion

Women, particularly Meitei women of Manipur mainly rely on informal sources of credit like moneylenders, relatives, friends, etc., but such sources charge exorbitant rates of interest. They thus depend actively on the marup system which is based on mutual trust and cooperation and is extremely popular. Their high participation displays their faith in the system, but this dependence on marup despite its high cost signifies that women usually have difficulty in obtaining credit from formal financial institutions and that there are constraints in their access to formal sources of credit. Some of them do not even know how to obtain credit from formal sources. This suggests that women face financial exclusion in the form of lack of access to formal credit for consumption and investment purposes. One reason for such exclusion may be their lack of collateral to offer, for most women do not have property in their names, and hence they cannot give land documents as security for the loan, which are often required.

Emerging area of micro-finance which is useful for productive purposes has still low outreach in Manipur as compared to other states of the North-East. Its outreach should be expanded. It is essential to empower women so that they may utilize major shares of institutional financing. Policies and programmes that improve women's access to credit would in turn lead to more efficient allocation of resources and increased production. Further, a larger share of entitlements accruing to women would result in greater household investment, which is desirable from a human development perspective as it increases the avenues available to children and increases household well-being.

Financial inclusion of women which would imply delivery of banking services at an affordable cost to the vast sections of disadvantaged and low-income women should be facilitated.

REFERENCES

Aliber, Michael (2002). "Informal Finance in the Informal Economy: Promoting Decent Work among the Working Poor", Working Paper on the *Informal Economy, Employment Sector 2002/14*, International Labour Office, Geneva.

Ardener, S. (1964). "The Comparative Study of Rotating Credit Associations", *Journal of the Royal Anthropological Institute*, Vol. XCIV, No. 2, pp. 201-29.

Baydas M. Mayada, Zakaria Bahloul and Dale W. Adams. (1993). "Informal Finance and Women in Egypt: 'Banks' within Banks", *Economics and Sociology*, Occasional Paper No. 2078, Accessed 4/10/2013,
Available at www.sme-egypt.org/Documents/Finance/INFORMAL % 20 FINANCE%20AND%20WOMEN%20IN%20EGYPT.pdf

Chaki-Sircar, Manjusri (1984). *Feminism in Traditional Society — Women of the Manipur Valley*, Shakti Books, Vikas Publishing House, New Delhi.

Dasgupta, Rajaram (2009). "SGSY: Need for a Paradigm Shift", *Economic and Political Weekly*, Vol. 44, No. 43, pp. 21-23.

Fadiga, Mahamadou L. and Leslie A. Fadiga-Stewart (2004). *Collective Action and Informal Financial Institutions: An Empirical Analysis of Rotating and Savings Credit Associations (ROSCAs) in Senegal*, Paper prepared for presentation at the American Institute of Agricultural Economic Association Annual Meeting, Denver, Colorado, August 1-4.

Fletschner, Diana (2008). "Women's Access to Credit: Does It Matter for Household Efficiency?" *American Journal of Agricultural Economics*, Vol. 90, No. 3, pp. 669-83.

ILO (International Labour Office) (2000). *Modular Package on Gender Poverty and Employment*, International Labour Office, Geneva.

Kantor, Paula (2002). "A Sectoral Approach to the Study of Gender Constraints on Economic Opportunities in the Informal Sector in India", *Gender and Society*, June, Vol. 16, No. 3, pp. 285-302.

Kshetrimayum, Melody (2012). "Micro-finance and Informal Credit in Manipur", *International Journal of Social and Economic Research*, Vol. 2, No. 2, pp. 266-75.

NABARD (National Bank for Agriculture and Rural Development). (2012). *Status of Micro-finance in India 2011-12*, Mumbai.

Nixon, Elangbam (2011). "Rural Savings and Its Investment in Manipur: A Case Study of Formal Finance *vis-à-vis* Marups", *Management Convergence*, Vol. 2, No. 2, pp. 10-30.

Ranadive, Joy Deshmukh (2002). "Database Issues: Women's Access to Credit and Rural Micro-Finance in India", *Accessed* 17/4/2009, Available at http://www.un.org.in/unnew/iawg/gndrdev/DB.pdf

Rao, Preethi (2007). "Chit Funds — A Boon to the Small Enterprises", Working Paper Series, Institute for Financial Management and Research, Small Enterprise Finance Centre, Chennai.

Tripp, Aili Mari (2006). "Deindustrialization and the Growth of Women's Economic Associations and Networks in Urban Tanzania" in Nalini Viswanathan, Lynn Duggan, Laurie Nisonoff and Nan Wiegersmi (2006) (ed), *The Women, Gender and Development Reader*, Zed Books Ltd., London and New Jersey, First published in 1997.

13

ROLE OF MIZORAM RURAL BANK IN FINANCIAL INCLUSION

C. Vanlalkulhpuia and *Elangbam Nixon Singh*

Introduction

The period of economic reform has witnessed the key catalytic role played by banks in the achievement of high growth in the Indian economy. While the benefits of growth due to reforms have concentrated in the hands of those already served by the formal financial system, a large section of the rural poor still does not have access to the formal banking channel. Further, the backward regions of the country, too, lack basic financial infrastructure (Debesh Roy, 2011). An essential prerequisite for inclusive and sustainable growth is capital formation through credit and financial services. Therefore, access to a well-functioning financial system, by creating equal opportunities, enables economically and socially excluded people to integrate better into the economy, so as to actively contribute to development and protect themselves against economic shocks (RBI, 2008). The Reserve Bank of India (RBI) has, therefore, formulated the policy of financial inclusion with a view to provide banking services at an affordable cost to the disadvantaged and low-income groups.

Besides the volume of credit required, spatial diversities and social complexities of rural life calls for a multi-agency approach to rural credit and the need for a third financial agency in rural areas was keenly felt. Given the rising demand for rural credit and the need to replace moneylenders with institutional agencies, there existed scope for another agency. This agency would combine the advantages of both the cooperatives and the commercial banks leaving out the disadvantages of both. This then was the background in which the Working Group on

Rural Banks headed by Narasimham recommended the setting up of RRBs in 1975 (Velayudham and Sankaranarayanan, 1990).

Financial Inclusion

Financial inclusion is the delivery of financial services at an affordable cost to the vast sections of disadvantaged and low income group of people who have been excluded from it. Financial inclusion is emerging as a priority for policymakers and regulators in financial sector development, with an increasing number of countries introducing comprehensive measures to improve access to and usage of tailored financial services, informed by a fast-growing body of experience and knowledge. More than 60 countries have initiated financial inclusion reforms in recent years. The growing priority placed on financial inclusion is illustrated by the commitments made by financial regulators from more than 20 developing countries to financial inclusion under the Maya Declaration (The World Bank, 2012).

Financial inclusion is one of the topmost policy priorities of the Government of India. Taking cue from the state proclivity towards inclusive growth agenda, the Reserve Bank of India (RBI) has taken a proactive role in ushering the enabling environment for expediting financial inclusion across the length and breadth of the country through bank led model (Siva Kumar Tadepalli and Hema Divya K., 2012).

Today, inclusive growth is a national as well as global focus. The Financial Stability and Development Council (FSDC) headed by the Finance Minister is mandated to focus on financial inclusion and financial literacy. All financial sector regulators including the Reserve Bank of India are committed to the mission. And, very publicly, so are banks and other financial sector entities. If we are advocating any kind of stability whether financial, economic, political or social and inclusive growth with stability, it is not possible to attain these goals without achieving financial inclusion.

Financial inclusion promotes thrift and develops culture of saving, improves access to credit both entrepreneurial and emergency and also enables efficient payment mechanism, thus strengthening the resource base of the financial institution which benefits the economy as resources become available for efficient payment mechanism and allocation. Empirical evidence shows that countries with large proportion of population excluded from the formal financial system also show higher poverty ratios and higher inequality. Thus, financial inclusion is no longer a policy choice today but a policy compulsion. And, banking is a key driver for financial inclusion/inclusive growth (Chakrabarty, 2010). The main objectives of financial inclusion are to extend formal banking system among excluded people who have less privilege in urban and rural India, and wean them away from unorganized money markets and moneylenders. Also supply them with the items needed for a particular purpose and make them confident to make informed financial decisions.

Role of Banks in Financial Inclusion: An Overview

The banking industry has shown tremendous growth in volume and complexity during the last few decades. Despite making significant improvements in all the areas relating to financial viability, profitability and competitiveness, there are concerns that banks have not been able to include vast segment of the population, especially the underprivileged sections of the society, into the fold of basic banking services. Internationally, also efforts are being made to study the causes of financial exclusion and designing strategies to ensure financial inclusion of the poor and disadvantaged (V. Leeladhar).

There are supply side and demand side factors driving financial inclusion or inclusive growth. Banks and other financial service players are largely expected to make less severe the supply side processes that prevent poor and disadvantaged social groups from gaining access to the financial system. Access to financial products is constrained by several factors which include lack of awareness about the financial products, unaffordable products, high transaction costs and products which are inconvenient, inflexible, not customized and of low quality.

However, we must bear in mind that apart from the supply side factors, demand side factors such as lower income and/or asset holdings also have a significant bearing on inclusive growth. Owing to difficulties in accessing formal sources of credit, poor individuals and small and micro-enterprises usually rely on their personal savings and internal sources or take recourse to informal sources to invest in health, education, housing and entrepreneurial activities to make use of growth opportunities. The mainstream financial institutions like banks have an important role to play in overcoming this constraint, not as a social obligation, but as pure business proposition (Chakrabarty, 2009).

Borman and Chanu (2013) in their study of role of RRBs in financial inclusion in tribal areas a case study of Langpi Dehangi rural bank in Assam hills, they found that even though there is a strong initiative from the Government of India and RBI for financial inclusion and financial reach to vast section of the especially weaker sections of the society, the performance of bank not appeared to be satisfactory and suggested that, the Government should take strong initiatives for financial inclusion by formulating pro-poor people policy and programmes.

Mizoram Rural Bank: An Overview

The nationalization of 14 major commercial banks in 1969 was an important landmark in the history of financial inclusion. It was felt that the nationalized banks can make a big push into the rural areas. At present, nearly seventy per cent of people in India live in villages. High level of rural indebtedness is identified as the root cause of rural poverty. Village moneylender was the focal point on which rural credit system mostly depended. The majority of people living in rural area remain excluded from the purview of the financial institutions, even after 58 years of independence.

Regional Rural Banks (RRBs) are actively involved in promoting financial inclusion by opening 'No-Frill Accounts', issuing Kisan Credit Cards (KCC) and General Credit Cards (GCC) and dispensing micro-credit under the SHG-Bank Linkage Programme. Considering the strategic importance of RRBs in the acceleration of financial inclusion RBI has directed sponsor banks to implement CBS in all RRBs by September 30, 2011. Fifteen RRBs were identified from 14 States for R&D project on Financial Inclusion with ICT-based solutions, through use of smart cards, Point of Sale (PoS) devices and mobile technology, in different regions and client groups in the country.

Modern banking activity was ushered in Mizoram with the establishment of its first branch of MRB at Aizawl on 27th September, 1983. This chapter attempts to analyze the performance of Mizoram Rural Bank (MRB) on financial inclusion in the state of Mizoram. It also comes up with some of the problems faced by MRB and give suggestion for further policy measures.

Since its inception, the Bank is striving hard to achieve its set objectives by serving throughout the entire State of Mizoram covering all the 8 (eight) districts and 25 Rural Development Blocks. The Bank has now extended its coverage to 11 urban and 11 semi-urban centres. The Bank has a network of 61 branches covering all the eight districts of the State of Mizoram. The number of rural branches is much higher than the other commercial banks in MRB that is why MRB plays an important role in financial inclusion to the rural poor.

MRB and Financial Inclusion

Mizoram Rural Bank may be perhaps the only RRB in the country having its spread out in all the districts as well blocks in a state. Despite this, the Bank has taken upon itself the task of reaching out to remote and unbanked villages by way of BC model banking. Under the Financial Inclusion Technology Fund, NABARD has sanctioned ₹ 42 lakh for engaging BCs to cover 5 blocks with a target of opening 40,000 accounts under the Financial Inclusion Programme.

MRB surpassed its target in all the three key areas of performance such as deposits, advances and profit. Its performance under Government sponsored schemes such as KCC, SGSY, GCC and opening of No-frills accounts under the NREGS has been good accounting for more than 50 per cent of the aggregate figures of all banks operating in the state (MRB, 2011). The Bank has also wiped out its accumulated loss for the first time in its history of 27 years following significant improvement in its assets blocks and improved management of assets and liability. It has now joined the elite group of the "Sustainable Viable" RRBs.

Credit is a critical input for the development of rural economy. Many of the farmers and rural households do not have access to institutional credit, thereby depriving them an opportunity to take up economic activities. Reaching out to the hitherto unreached segment of population and providing basic financial services, is the need of the hour. Accordingly, the RBI in consultation with Government of India (GoI), has brought in the concept of financial inclusion. As at end-March 2008, 1,57,88,919 no-frills accounts have been opened in the country. The initiative could have a significant bearing on a very large portion of the population since, if executed properly, it has the capability to bring them into the banking net by offering variety of financial services such as savings, credit and insurance at affordable costs (RBI, 2007-08).

With a view to achieving the objectives of greater Financial Inclusion as per the Reserve Bank of India's directives, MRB has introduced the following basic banking schemes (MRB, 2009-10):

(i) **No-Frills Account** — A huge number of rural customers have been brought under the scheme. The bank has introduced Basic Banking with "No-frills account" either with "NIL" or with very low minimum balance Savings Bank Account in all our Branches. In this account, depositors are allowed overdraft facility up to a limit of ₹ 500.

(ii) **GCC** — To strengthen the credit delivery system at affordable cost the GCC scheme has been introduced in the bank as per RBI guideline. Credit limit has been fixed at ₹ 25,000. The scheme, however, is yet to get momentum in rural areas.

(iii) **O.T.S.** — A one-time settlement scheme has also been introduced in the bank with a limit fixed at ₹ 25,000 to reduce the burden of rural borrowers (non-intentional defaulters) and also to make them eligible for fresh credit. This will also help reduce our non-performing assets.

Literature Review

Various studies have been conducted in the area of financial inclusion and regional rural banks in India like problems and prospects of regional rural banks, commercial viability, earning capacity, cost efficiency, branch expansion, lending pattern and determinant of profit and profitability. Amol Agrawal (2008), in his study on the topic of 'The need for Financial Inclusion with an Indian Perspective' and finds that mechanism has been used to increase savings in many organizations. A similar mechanism could be deployed to increase usage of bank accounts in India. He also suggested that instead of giving cash transfers to the public, government should instead credit the bank accounts of the poor electronically. This will make people use their bank accounts. In 1995, Leyshon and Thrift in their paper defined financial exclusion as "those processes that prevent poor and disadvantaged social groups from gaining access to the financial system. It has important implications for uneven development because it amplifies geographical differences in levels of income and economic development."

Pal and Sura (2006) concluded that the overall position of RRBs in India is not quite encouraging. The poor credit-deposit ratio is still making dent on the desired functioning of RRBs. Since the RRB is supposed to be a bank for poor people, government should spread the branches of RRBs at grassroots level to provide such banking service to the really needy rural people and to take corrective measures to raise the credit deposit ratio of the bank that would make RRBs relevant in the rural India. Kumar Raj (1993) carried out a study on the topic "Growth and Performance of RRBs in Haryana". On the basis of the study of RRBs of Haryana, it is found that there was an enormous increase in deposits and outstanding advances. The researcher felt the need to increase the share capital and to ensure efficiency of distribution channels of finance to beneficiaries.

Siva Kumar Tadepalli and Hema Divya (2012) study on financial inclusion offering banking services for the poor concluded that the financial system in India has grown rapidly in the last three decades and more. The functional and geographical coverage of the system is truly impressive. There is an imperative need to modify the credit and financial services delivery system to achieve greater inclusion. While banks and other financial institutions can also take some efforts on their own to improve the absorptive capacity of the clients, it is equally important for Government at various levels to initiate actions to enhance the earnings capacity of the poorer sections of the society with special reference to daily wage earners where there is more need to create awareness and educate them on these lines.

From this literature we can infer that, there is no study relating to role played by Mizoram Rural Bank in financial inclusion, so, the present study concentrate and analyze the performance of MRB in financial inclusion in rural Mizoram.

Objectives, Methodology and Research Design

The present study was conducted with the following major objectives: (i) To analyze the role and performance of MRB on financial inclusion with regard to loan disbursed to priority sectors; and (ii) To highlight and analyze the amount of loan taken by the gender-wise beneficiaries of MRB. The present study is based on primary and secondary data. The secondary data have been collected mainly through the data bases of various reports published by Mizoram Rural Banks. Primary data collected through questionnaires among sample 390 MRB beneficiaries who are engaged in agricultural sector, the study covers all the MRB rural branches, i.e. 39 rural branches as per 2010 annual reports.

Hypotheses

The following hypotheses shall be tested for this present study to make conclusion on performance of MRB on financial inclusion in rural Mizoram:

(i) H_0: There is no significant difference in loan and advances given to priority sectors during the study period.

(ii) H_0: Rural people do not face problems in taking loans from MRB for agricultural purpose.

Findings of the Study

Loans and Advances Disbursed by MRB

RRBs occupy an important position in the rural credit market. Loans provided to the needy people have been categorized into two. One is priority sector and the other one is non-priority sector. Priority sector bank lending is an active instrument of Indian financial policy with an aim to restore sectored balance within credit disbursement and to channel credit to the weaker sections of the society. Priority Sector is a sector which is given priority in offering financial services by the banks. The concept of priority sector was first brought into the financial system in 1968, when the government imposed social control over the banks. Banks were directed to lend some percentage of loans to the sectors listed in the priority sector. In 1968 there were 3 sectors — agriculture, small industry and exports. Gradually, the list of segments under priority sector increased (Ibrahim, 2012).

Table 13.1 shows that total the loans and advances disbursed by MRB to different sectors like agriculture are up to ₹ 10,34,061 thousand, industries up to ₹ 4,46,130 thousand and services up to ₹ 14,82,858 thousand in last ten years (2000-2010). The increase in loans and advances from 2008-09 in agricultural sector and services are ₹ 4,336 thousand and ₹ 1,30,590 thousand respectively. Further, total loans and advances issued by the MRB gradually increases year-by-year. But, agricultural sector in the State has not been given much priority as compared to service sector.

Table 13.1: Total Loans and Advances Distribution to Priority Sectors

(*₹ in thousand*)

No. of Years	*Agriculture*	*Industries*	*Services*
2000-01	7174	4537	35722
2001-02	9364	5419	70659
2002-03	7617	4081	53049
2003-04	12249	8128	153314
2004-05	86989	20683	191283
2005-06	135680	39856	25526
2006-07	120830	96961	107545
2007-08	186178	163862	59190
2008-09	231822	42459	327990
2009-10	236158	60144	458580
Total	1034061	446130	1482858

Source: Mizoram Rural Bank Annual Reports (2000-2010).

It is important to observe from Table 13.2 that the loans issued to priority sectors shows an increasing trend. ANOVA single factor was performed to determine whether the disbursement of priority sector loans like agriculture, industry and service sectors significantly differs from each other.

Table 13.2: ANOVA Single Factor

Source of Variation	*SS*	*Df*	*MS*	*F*	*P-value*	*F-critical*
Between Groups	54062885132	2	2.7031E+10	2.56113	0.09584	3.35413
Within Groups	2.84972E+11	27	1.0555E+10			
Total	3.39035E+11	29				

Notes: *SS* — Sum of square
df — Degrees of freedom
MS — Mean Square.

From this ANOVA table it can be observed that *F*-value (2.6) is less than *F*-critical (3.4), i.e. (*F* < *F*-critical). The year-wise performance of MRB on loan and advances distributed to priority sectors like agriculture, industries and services compared to other year performance is not very different and as such it can be concluded that there is no statistically significant difference in loan and advances given to priority sectors during the study period. This had prompted to accept the null hypothesis (H_0) that there is no significant difference in loan and advances given to priority sectors during the study period.

Amount of Loan Taken by the Selected Respondents

It can be observed from Table 13.3 that out of the total sample population of 390 rural MRB beneficiaries, 269 males, i.e. 68.97 per cent respondents had taken loans from MRB while that of only 121, i.e. 31.02 per cent respondents are females. The respondents who have taken loans from MRB lesser than ₹ 3,000 is very less, i.e. only 7 male respondents and 8 female respondents. The respondents, who have taken ₹ 3,000 to ₹ 5,000 loan from MRB, are very high, that means 170 males and 61 females had taken loans from MRB. Further it can be observed that MRB disbursed more loans to customers ranging between ₹ 3,000 to ₹ 5,000 in the selected rural areas of Mizoram.

Analysis of Table 13.3 shows a simple conclusion that MRB gives priority to male customers as compared to female customers as regards to loan disbursement.

Table 13.3: Amount of Loan taken from MRB: Gender-wise

Loan Amount	*Gender of the Respondents*		*Total*
	Male	*Female*	
Less than 3000	7	8	15
3000 to 5000	170	61	231
5000 to 7000	63	31	94
7000 to 9000	10	14	24
9000 and above	19	7	26
Total	269	121	390

Source: Sample Survey.

Problems on Taking Loan from MRB for Agricultural Development

Table 13.4 highlights the problem faced by the sample respondents of MRB in loans taken from the bank in the State. Since, the sample respondents are selected from only rural State, most of them are poor. So, from the following table it can be observed that, 223 respondents faced problem on taking loan from MRB due to lack of mortgage. The other problem faced by sample respondents is not favoured by bank staff. Out of 390 respondents, 167 respondents faced problem in this situation. Out of five questions only two questions are answered by the respondents. So, it can be said that, lack of mortgage and not being favoured by MRB staff are the main problems faced by the sample respondents in taking loans from bank in the rural Mizoram.

Table 13.4 reveals that the opinion of the sample respondents. 197 respondents disagreed that rural people faced problem in taking loan from MRB, while 129 respondents stand at neutral and 33 and 32 respondents said agreed and highly agreed.

Table 13.4: Districtswise Problems Faced by Respondents in Taking Loans from MRB

Districts	*Lack of Mortgage*	*Not Being Favoured by Staff*	*Not having Valuable Things*	*Others*	*Total*
Aizawl	63	47	—	—	110
Lunglei	32	18	—	—	50
Champhai	45	25	—	—	70
Kolasib	20	20	—	—	40
Mamit	23	27	—	—	50
Serchhip	23	17	—	—	40
Saiha	5	5	—	—	10
Lawngtlai	12	8	—	—	20
Total	223	167	—	—	390

Source: Sample Survey.

To set the conclusion and testing hypothesis in this present study, ANOVA single factor was used as under Table 13.5.

Table 13.5: Observations from Respondents

Districts	*Rural Beneficiaries Faced Problem in taking Loan from MRB*				*Total*
	Agreed	*Highly Agreed*	*Neutral*	*Disagreed*	
Aizawl	14	9	48	39	110
Lunglei	4	3	18	25	50
Champhai	7	3	17	43	70
Kolasib	1	3	8	28	40
Mamit	1	7	17	25	50
Serchhip	3	3	10	24	40
Saiha	0	1	2	7	10
Lawngtlai	3	2	9	6	20
Total	33	31	129	197	390

Source: Sample Survey.

From this ANOVA Table 13.6 we can observe that *F*-value (8.16) is more than *F*-critical value (2.94668527), i.e. ($F > F$-critical). As such, it can be concluded that rural people do not face much difficulty in taking loan from MRB thereby accepting the null hypothesis (H_0).

Table 13.6: ANOVA Single Factor

Source of Variation	*SS*	*Df*	*MS*	*F*	*P-value*	*F-critical*
Between Groups	2434.375	3	811.4583333	8.1597534	0.000464946	2.94668527
Within Groups	2784.5	28	99.44642857			
Total	5218.875	31				

Conclusion and Suggestions

Every nation for her economic development need role of financial institution which is the backbone and very significant, without the proper functioning of the banking sector there is a problem to set the development target. So, banking performance and development go hand in hand. Today, banks are already offering services over mobile to communities that have been historically unbanked (Devi, 2013). In rural areas of Mizoram, where accessibility to bank is a big problem, but MRB extended their branches to cover all the districts and plays a very important role to introduce financial inclusion in the state as compared with other commercial banks.

From above study we can conclude that, MRB plays an important role to rural areas by providing loan to rural people and gives a good service to the rural customers. But, MRB have a still mile to go for uplifting and disbursed more loan to the rural women. As compared to rural men respondent's loan disbursed by MRB to women is very low. Also, bank should organize more awareness campaign programmes to motivate the rural people to come under the purview of financial inclusion and the procedure for opening bank account and the granting loan and advances should be simplified because, most of the rural customers are illiterate/uneducated.

REFERENCES

Annual Report of Mizoram Rural Bank published in the year 2009-10 & 2011.

Arputhamani, J. and Prasannakumari, K. (2011). "Financial Inclusion through Micro-Finance: The Way to Rural Development — A Case Study of Rajapalayam Block in Virudhunagar District". *KKIMRC IJRFA*, Vol. 01, No. 01.

Borman, Ratan and Chanu, Ibemcha, Ayekpam (2013). "Role of RRBs in Financial Inclusion in Tribal Areas: A case study of Langpi Dehangi Rural Bank in Assam Hills", *Financial Inclusion for Inclusive Growth*, edited by, Singha, Rajmani, A., Concept Publishing Company Pvt. Ltd., New Delhi, pp. 325 & 329.

Chakrabarty, K.C. (2009). *Banking: Key Driver for Inclusive Growth*, Address at the Mint's 'Clarity Through Debate' series on August 10th, at Chennai.

Chakrabarty, K.C. (2010). *Inclusive Growth — Role of Financial Sector*, Address at the National Finance Conclave 2010, KIIT University, Bhubaneswar on November 27.

Devi, Chanambam Nalini (2013). "Banking Service and Financial Inclusion in Mizoram: With Special Reference to NABARD Activity", *Financial Inclusion for Inclusive Growth*, edited by Singha, Rajmani, A., Concept Publishing Company Pvt. Ltd., New Delhi, p. 349.

Ibrahim, Syed M. (2012). "Role of Indian Regional Rural Banks (RRBs) in the Priority Sector Lending — An Analysis", *International Management Journal*, Vol. 1, No. 1-2, p. 28.

Roy, Debesh (2011). "Financial Inclusion in India Emerging Profitable Models", *Compendium*, 11: Layout, p. 129.

Siva Kumar Tadepalli and Hema Divya K. (2012). "Financial Inclusion: Offering Banking Services for the Poor", *THAVAN IJREB*, Vol. 1, No. 2.

Velayudham, T.K. and Sankaranarayanan, V. (1990). "Regional Rural Banks and Rural Credit: Some Issues", *Economic and Political Weekly*, Vol. 25, No. 38, September 22, pp. 2157-2159.

World Bank (2012). *Financial Inclusion Strategies — Reference Framework*, The G20 Mexico Presidency, www.worldbank.org/financialinclusion.

14

FINANCIAL SERVICES FOR URBAN INFORMAL WORKERS

Angshuman Sarma

Introduction

Earlier theories of development hypothesized that in the early stages of development rise in inequality is inevitable. Thus, that focused on expanding financial services to tap saving and then channel the fund to a wide variety of activities. Modern development theory perceives lack of access to financial services as a factor responsible for income inequality and slower growth as well. Financial service providers have traditionally focused more on supply side financial inclusion, i.e. they often tend to measure total number of branches, total customers, etc. rather than attempts to get into the messy business of poor and deserving customers live business and need. But just because somebody is excluded may not mean they demand financial services the most.

No doubt the world is going to be more urban than rural and India too would not be an exception. As per estimation 40 per cent of Indians would be living in urban areas by 2030. Nearly half of Indian population do not have access to formal financial services. In the urban settings, the working poor contribute immensely to city economies. They provide cheap and affordable services to people and help city grow in a socially cohesive manner but their own growth remains badly impacted in terms of secured life of their businesses, enhanced income generation, and overall decent financial condition. Most of the working population in urban areas work under utterly deplorable conditions in unorganized sector with a very few livelihood options. The deprivation of urban poor is further accentuated as more than 40 per cent of adult Indian urban population has no access to a bank account (this figure would be more if multiple accounts held by individuals are factored), and, thereby depriving them of savings, credit, remittance and other financial facilities from the formal financial system. In 2006, India conducted its first urban poverty census by Ministry of Housing and Poverty Alleviation, which reveals that 90 million people out of 300 million, living roughly in India's 45 cities and over 500 towns, are poor. In urban India only 49.52 per cent of households have access to banking services and 34 per cent of the India's urban population with annual income less than 50,000 have access to banking services. The latest National Sample Survey Organization survey reports that there are over 80 million poor people living in the cities and towns of India and they lack access to the most basic banking services such as savings accounts, credit, remittances and payment services, financial advisory services, etc.

Objectives

The study has the following objectives:

(i) To assess the extent of barriers for urban informal workers in accessing financial services; and
(ii) To compare how much holding of saving or insurance account is dependent on monthly average income.

Hypothesis

(i) Financial services positively affects livelihood of informal workers.
(ii) Financial services channelized through social protection scheme for informal workers is a better way of financial inclusion

Causes of Financial Exclusion of Urban Informal Workers

Voluntary Default

A loan may be taken for an ostensibly productive reason, but may be used for other needs that cannot be easily transformed into monetary repayment. Among the informal workers the risk of voluntary default is high. This is because of higher frequency of *consumption credit*, either because of a sudden downturn in their employment or a sudden increase in their consumption needs caused by illness, death, or festivities such as wedding. But this also underlines the demand for insurance. The possibility of sudden illness or unemployment can give rise to group of individuals who band together in some form of reciprocal relationship. Certainly that reciprocity can only be sustained over time by the recurrent possibility that each participant can someday be in the same unfortunate position.

Access to formal banking system is affected by several barriers such as culture, financial literacy, gender, income and assets, proof of identity, remoteness of residence, and so on. There are number of factors affecting access to financial services by weaker section of society in India. The lack of awareness, low incomes and assets, social exclusion, illiteracy are the barriers from demand side. The distance from bank branch, branch timings, cumbersome banking procedure and requirements of documents for opening bank accounts, unsuitable banking products or schemes, language, high transaction costs and attitudes of bank officials are the barriers from supply side.

Informal workers offer collateral in forms that are unacceptable to formal lenders. However, informal moneylenders may accept such collateral. For example, an employer or contractor may accept labour as collateral, in case the labourer-borrower fails to repay. Such *problem of collateral* pulls out them from ambit of formal financial institutions.

Higher Need of Financial Services for Migrant Workers

A quick study of the workers, who are migrants, reveals that they have very limited options for remittance, such as, postal money order, bank drafts, sending cash through returning friends/relatives. As compared to the option of sending money through postal money order at a charge of 5 per cent, money sent through bank drafts is though a cheaper option; most recipients do not have access to banks for encashment. The third option of sending money through friends/relatives would mean waiting for their visits to villages, and besides, there is a risk of theft.

Despite their low wages and low savings, they have to send back money, however, little, to their families through not-so-safe and costly money transfer services. On the other hand when their dependents in the village are faced with an emergency their only recourse is the money-lender, leading to more indebtedness thus, perpetuating them in a vortex of financial exclusion. So, the migrant workers are not only excluded they need those services more.

Financial Services and Livelihood of Urban Informal Workers

Through an improved access to high quality financial services, they will be able to quickly find their own way out of the "poverty trap" in which they find themselves. Access to safe, easy and affordable credit and other financial services by the poor and vulnerable groups, and lagging sectors is recognized as a pre-condition for accelerating growth and reducing income disparities and poverty. Theories of development advocate that financial development creates enabling conditions for growth through either a "supply-leading" (financial development spurs growth) or a "demand-following" (growth generates demand for financial products) channel. Moreover "empirical evidence indicates that up to a threshold level of economic development financial sector growth contribute to poverty reduction through the growth enhancing effect" (Kirkpetrick, 2005). Access to a well-functioning financial system, by creating equal opportunities, enables economically excluded people to integrate better into the economy and actively contribute to development and protect themselves against economic shocks.

Through the means of such improved access, if they have even a small measure of economic independence, even their ability to exert pressure on providers of public services could improve significantly. Access to finance also has links to improvement in individual productivity by permitting individuals to move to higher levels of consumption for basic items, investment in education and skill building that determines future earning potential, specialization in a few activities instead of over-diversifiction and an improvement in risk taking ability. Financial security during "frictional unemployment", which is very frequent for a informal worker, saves him from unnecessary diversification. With some financial security he can wait for a job opportunity which matches his already acquired skills. Finally, access may also have positive effects on the local economy through a general increase in wage labour opportunities and better utilization of surplus labour.

Methodology

A survey for the study was conducted from March 2013 to May 2013. Mixed methods, with the quantitative method as the dominant method, were used to draw a sample from the population and to analyze the data. The sample was drawn with the help of the quantitative method while some of the individual cases were developed based on in-depth interviews and observations using a qualitative paradigm. The unit of analysis of the present study is construction workers in Guwahati city.

Data Collection Tools

Personal interviews and group interviews were conducted. A total of 52 workers from all segments of work — mason, carpentry, electrical and petty unskilled workers — were covered for this study. A fair representation was tried best to be given to all segments of construction workers. One group session was conducted with 10-15 workers in each study area. In-depth interviews were conducted with 10 individual workers in order to understand and explore the current situation of construction industry. Three stages were used in sampling method to draw sample. The size of the sample was 52.

When a population is scattered over a region and complete list of the total population are not available, "clustering" is of assistance in sampling. The workers were covered from four spatial locations of the city —Maligaon area towards Adabari, Lokhra, GAMMON construction site at Jalukbari and IIT Guwahati campus. The central points of the city were not covered considering the fact that construction activities are now mostly shifted to the expanding areas of the city.

A fair representation was tried best to be given to all three segments of construction workers: (1) Construction workers in organized sector. (2) Workers working under a contractor. (3) Self-employed workers working mainly in private households. In our study there were 10 workers presently in a registered construction enterprise, 14 workers work under contractor and 28 are self-employed. Each of these categories face different kind of financial exclusion.

A semi-structured questionnaire, based on the objectives of the study, was used. Both closed and open-ended questions were included in the questionnaire. Since the study was exploratory in nature, open-ended questions were used to assist in exploring the current situation. A structured questionnaire was followed only in the case of construction workers to collect primary data. The interactions with the workers were made mostly at their residence during non-working hours except the workers under GAMMON interacted during their working hours with official permission from company authority.

Statistical Model

To look into the differences in the mean average monthly income of saving account holders and non-account holders we used Analysis of Variance Model (ANOVA). In order to determine the statistical significance of the differences of the average monthly income of workers between insurance holders and non-insurance holders, we can use the ANOVA model. The regression model is fitted as:

$$Y_i = \alpha_0 + \alpha_1 D_i + U_i$$

Y_i is the monthly income of the workers, *D* is dummy variable such that, $D = 1$ for insurance holders and $D = 0$ for non-insurance holders, *i* is a number of households, i.e. 1, 2, 3, ..., 52 and U_i is well behaved error term. Likewise in order to determine the statistical significance of the differences of the average monthly income of workers between saving account holders and non-account holders, we can use the ANOVA model. The model is fitted as:

$$Y_j = \beta_0 + \beta_1 D_j + U_j$$

Y_j is the monthly income of the workers, *D* is dummy variable such that, $D = 1$ for saving account holders and $D = 0$ for non-account holders, *j* is a number of households, i.e. 1, 2, 3, ..., 52 and U_j is well behaved error term.

Primary Data Analysis

There are mainly three kinds of employment relation prevailing among construction workers in the city of Guwahati: (1) Construction workers in organized sector, (2) Workers working under a contractor, and (3) Self-employed workers works mainly in private households. Out of total sample (N = 53), in our study there were 10 workers presently in a registered construction enterprise (organized sector), 14 workers work under contractor and 28 works in private household as they are self-employed.

Insurance and Saving

When 40 per cent of workers in organized sector have insurance policy (all of these are "life insurance" actually) and 43 per cent workers under contractor have insurance. That higher access to insurance by the later section is due to the implementation of BOCW (RE and CS). At the same time when 28.5 per cent of self-employed and workers under contractor have some kind of saving, that figure is 20 per cent for those who are in organized sector.

From Table 14.1, we can point out the average income of the workers who are insurance holders higher by ₹ 3,526.66 at 5 per cent level of significance. Similarly, the average incomes of the workers who had saving account higher by ₹ 2,917.97 at 5 per cent level of significance. So, the obvious conclusion is that households with higher income have higher probability to be financially included in the ambit of formal financial mechanism. So, mere branch expansion, more rural banking, financial literacy may not work well enough. Money income have to be raised or in other words we can add another factor of financial exclusion —low money wage. But increase of money wage among them ia a difficult task in present scenario. So, we may think of to find some other innovative ways to grasp them in financial services.

Table 14.1: ANOVA Results

Items	*Dummy coefficients*	*Sig.*
For Insurance holders and Non-Insurance holders	3526.667	0.001
For Saving account holders and non-account holders	2917.970	0.017

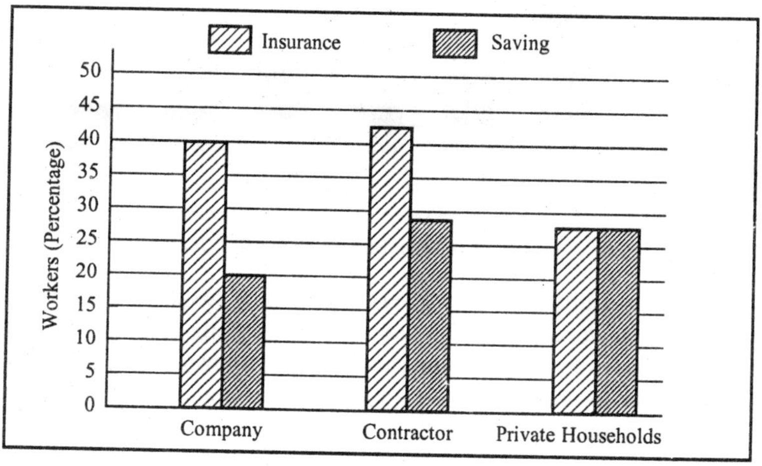

Figure 14.1: Insurance and Saving.

Migration

The survey revealed that construction workers are basically a migrant labour force. Information of place of origin reflects that about half of the workers in our sample are inter-district migrant workers and 14 per cent workers are intra-state migrants. Of course, the inter-state migrants have less informal option to send back money to place of origin. 81 per cent of workers send a portion of their earning back to their home.

Financial Sources of the Workers

Source of the finance plays an important role for their financial accessibility. The most frequent financial urgency in the life-cycle of a construction worker is health hazard, mainly of two kinds — accident and work related illness. Six types of financial sources, in case of sudden need, have been identified such as: (i) Savings, (ii) Friends, (iii) Family, (iv) Advance Wage (taking wage of next one or two months in advance), (v) Employer (extra payment), and (vi) Selling assets.

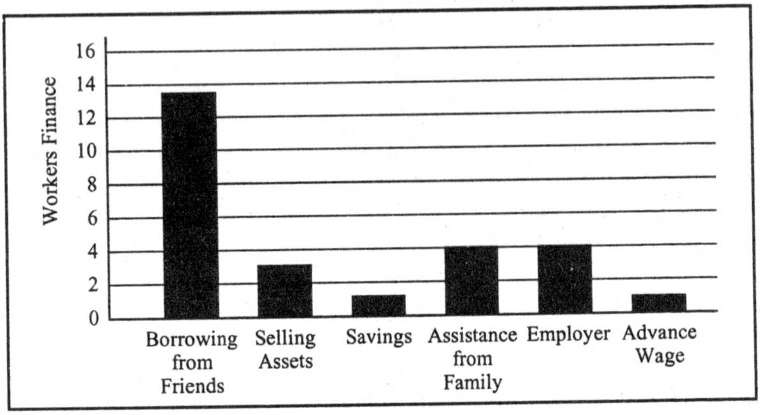

Figure 14.2: Financial Sources.

Twenty eight per cent workers faced health related hazard during construction work in the last 3 years of their working life. In most cases they have to resort to loan from close friend or known well to do person around him, for that plunge in their livelihood. But not a single case was found of getting help from any insurance policy or from any such concern scheme.

Workers Who have Financial Services Live Better Life

In our sample 26.41 per cent (14 workers) respondents have some sort of saving, mostly in bank. Out of them there is only 1 case of school dropout (i.e. 7%) of their children. Those who don't have any saving, that means out of 39 workers there are 6 cases (13%) of school dropout of their children. This is because with saving they can smoothen their fluctuating income and find a way out whenever there is higher need of money, say, enrollment of their children in higher standards.

Again those workers who have some sort of insurance (mostly LIC, 17 out of 19) have higher intention to own a house. As per estimation 42 per cent of the workers who have insurance live in their own house. In contrast 34 workers, i.e. 36 per cent workers among those who do not have insurance have their own house in city. Once they think for future life they also think for future accommodation also. In this way it can be said financial inclusion of informal workers also facilitates urbanization.

It is well known that financial inclusion reduces poverty. But, if we push that among informal workers that may give additional advantages in long run, because workers-*cum*-new customers of financial institutions now with higher social condition create new demands for financial services. For example, a construction worker once he had a bank account, may become a beneficiary of a scheme, now he may take payment in cheque from an employer. These demand creation will be much faster among them, since they are working in an urban area where the employment relations are constantly changing. New generation of those families will also be financially literate much earlier than others.

Business Option for Banks

The urban expansion in India is happening at a speed quite unlike anything that India has ever seen before. Within 20-25 years another 300 million people will get added to Indian towns. It took nearly forty years to raise India's urban population by 230 millions. But it could take only half the time to add next 250 million. The lion's share of that increase in city dwellers is as urban "informal workers" since formal employment is negative and becoming more negative. As the urban population and income rise (however pace of raise in income is sluggish) demand for every key services such as water, transportation, financial services will increase. Hence, banks can take up providing financial services to informal workers not only as Corporate Social responsibility but also as vibrant business model. The Union Bank of India has set an example in Mumbai how to feed this new demand (see below). As it is mentioned earlier we have to look for some innovative ways to grasp urban poor (most of them are informal workers). Here are some ideas and some successful examples created by some NGOs.

Formal Credit to Informal Moneylender

We can think of forging "vertical" links between the informal and formal credit systems, rather than the more traditional policy of "horizontally" displacing one system by another. Informal moneylenders are in better position to put up collateral which may not be acceptable for formal bank. They also have better informational base about borrower. The expansion of formal credit to these agents generates competition among them and this hopefully improves the borrowing terms faced by individuals who fall out of the ambit of formal credit system. Loan may be made to cooperative groups who are better placed to lend the funds because of social ties among members or potential borrowers.

Financial Inclusion Drive for Hawkers in Mumbai

Hawkers find it difficult to visit bank branches during regular work hours for the fear of loss of business. But they have the intention to save. To provide banking services at their doorstep, Union Bank of India (UBI) has given smart cards to hawkers and opened no-frills accounts for them with the help of the Hawker's Association of Mumbai and its partnership with the FINO Fintech Foundation. The Business Correspondents appointed by the latter go to these hawkers with 'point of transaction' (POT) terminals. By swiping the card on these handheld devices, hawkers can deposit their savings or withdraw money. The data from the cards, stored on the terminals get transferred to the bank's servers. To cover one lakh: hawkers in its drive, UBI has to place 200-250 terminals. This initiative will not only encourage the hawkers to save but also provide them credit through general credit card. As hawkers increase transactions, UBI would provide an insurance cover to them through a group policy from the Life Insurance Corporation of India. In the next stage of inclusion, UBI would provide loans for their children's education.

The Gujarat-based Self-Employed Womens' Association (SEWA) plan for social security is widely regarded as one of the more successful ones in this field. SEWA has established a bank for self-employed workers. These are women who work between 14 and 16 hours a day, and cannot, therefore, find time to travel to the local bank and make deposits. SEWA Bank initially guaranteed a nominal return of 12 per cent, and upon maturity, the money was returned as either a lump-sum or in an annuity format to the beneficiary. Since 2002, SEWA initiated a new plan offering only 7 per cent return with lower minimum contributions. Already SEWA Bank has over 5,000 accounts managing almost ₹ 7.5 million. The SEWA Bank scheme serves as an example worth emulation for many Self-Help Groups (SHGs) across India.

SEWA also offers a risk cover to its members in an integrated manner. For a premium of ₹ 60, an individual member is covered for illness, accident and disability, natural death, and loss of assets due to fire or flood, and also receives a maternity benefit. The accidental insurance for members and their spouses is carried out in collaboration with New India Assurance (NIA), while insurance for natural death and accident is still done by LIC. For an additional payment of ₹ 15 per annum, the husband of the member is also covered under the life insurance component of the LIC scheme. SEWA has designed another method to enable members to pay the premium. For the Lifelong Insurance Scheme or Fixed Deposit Scheme, the members pay a fixed deposit of ₹ 500 to the SEWA Bank and the premium is paid from the interest rate, which amounts to exactly ₹ 65. If the husband is to be covered under the life insurance scheme, the fixed deposit has to be ₹ 700. The Fixed Deposit customers get the maternity benefit as a bonus.

The women members of Annapurna Mahila Mandal in Maharashtra mobilize their small savings and once the amount reaches ₹ 5,000, it is invested in an LIC pension scheme. The savings amounts, invested by LIC in sound securities, double every six years and after 20 years, the amount becomes ₹ 50,000. On this principal amount, a fixed amount of ₹ 500 per month is paid to the woman beneficiary as old age pension. The principal can be paid to her nominee at the time of her death but the nominee is not eligible for the amount if the beneficiary's death is not natural.

Conclusion

The concept of financial inclusion also includes education and other support services that help people to make sound financial decision. Even if financial services are available they may not be affordable, or may not be available within reasonable physical proximity. Workers may have access to a bank account, yet that does not mean they can access full range of financial services that suit their needs. At various stages in a worker's life-cycle he/she may require specific financial services: for example to cover expenses related to education, housing, health, productive investment, marriage, or death of family member. The needs and circumstances of a petty worker/city dweller may be slightly different than others.

NOTES

1. The methodology in that Urban Poverty Survey was that: poor was identified through three specific vulnerabilities: (i) Residential, (ii) Occupational, and (iii) Social categories. Those who are houseless, live in temporary houses,

where usage of dwelling space is suspectible to insecurity of tenure and are effected by lack of access to basic services were considered as residentially vulnerable. Houses with people unemployed for significant proportion of time or with irregular employment or whose work is subject to unsanitary or hazardous condition or have no stability of payment for services regarded occupationally vulnerable. Households headed by women or minor or where the elderly are dependent on head of household or where the level of literacy is very low or members are disabled or chronically ill considered socially vulnerable. So all the informal workers come under that cluster of POOR.

Informal Worker: A person working in an unorganized enterprise, defined as those enterprises employing 10 or less than 10 workers and investing less than ₹ 5 lakh as capital, plus those workers who are working in organized sector but employed informally (casual labour, contractual labour, labours under contractors, etc.).

2. *BOCW (RE and CS) Act:* "Building and Other Construction Workers (Regulation of Employment and Condition of Services Act), 1996". In Assam, "Assam Building and Other Construction Workers Welfare Board" constituted as per the Act adopted two central insurance schemes, namely Rastriya Svasthya Bima Yojana (RSBY) — a popular flagship health scheme and Janashree Bima Yojana. RSBY is a health insurance scheme under National Rural Health Mission (NRHM). Assam Building and Other Construction Workers Welfare Board have planned to pay the required registration payment on behalf of registered workers. After which NRHM authority will find the workers in site and will issue Smart Card for them. Workers with Smart Card will get free treatment in hospitals prescribed by NRHM.

   Janashree Bima Yojana is a group insurance scheme by LIC. Any group of 25 people can get a group policy. Later on this brought under Other Construction Workers Welfare Board. Board now do group policy taking all registered workers as a group. This is yearly scheme. Board pays ₹ 100 premium each year on behalf of each registered worker. Any worker caused death or accident can get benefit. Recently a Siksha Bima Yojana has been subsidiary added to this. Under which children of construction workers from class IX to XII can get ₹ 100 per month, if he does not fail in examination.

REFERENCES

Francesco Obino (2013). "Housing Finance for Poor Working Women: Innovations of the Self-Employed Women's Association in India", *WIEGO Policy Briefs*, No. 14, March-May.

Kirkpetrick, H. (2005). *Journal of Development Studies*, Volume 41, Issue 4.

Masroor Ahmad Beg (2012). *Financial Inclusion: Gateway for Poverty and Unemployment*, Tata Institute of Social Sciences, Mumbai.

Nidhiya Menon, Yana Van der Meulen Rodgers (2009). "Self-Employment in Household Enterprises and Access to Credit: Gender Differences during India's Rural Banking Reform", *IPC Working Paper Series Number 86*, International Policy Center Gerald R. Ford School of Public Policy, University of Michigan, June.

Santosh Mehrotra (2008). "Social Insurance System for India's Unorganized Sector Workers: The Case and the Cost", *The Indian Journal of Labour Economics*, Vol. 51, No. 2.

Srinivasan, N. (2007). "Policy Issues and Role of Banking System in Financial Inclusion", *Economic and Political Weekly*, Vol. 42, No. 30 (July 28-Aug. 3), pp. 3091-3093+3095; Stable URL: http://www.jstor.org/stable/4419836. Accessed: 02/09/2013 05.

Yu-wei Hu and Fiona Stewart (2009). *Pension Coverage and Informal Sector Workers: International Experience*, OECD Working Paper on Insurance and Private Pension No. 31, January. www.oecd.org/daf/fin/wp.

—— (2013). "India Does First Urban Poverty Survey", *Deccan Herald*, October 17.

INDEX